Road Biking Florida

Help Us Keep This Guide Up to Date

Every effort has been made by the author and editors to make this guide as accurate and useful as possible. However, many things can change after a guide is published—roads are detoured, phone numbers change, facilities come under new management, etc.

We would love to hear from you concerning your experiences with this guide and how you feel it could be improved and kept up to date. While we may not be able to respond to all comments and suggestions, we'll take them to heart, and we'll also make certain to share them with the author. Please send your comments and suggestions to the following address:

The Globe Pequot Press
Reader Response/Editorial Department
P.O. Box 480
Guilford, CT 06437

Or you may e-mail us at:

editorial@GlobePequot.com

Thanks for your input, and happy riding!

Road Biking™ Series

Road Biking
Florida

A Guide to the Greatest Bike Rides in Florida

Rick Sapp

FALCONGUIDES ®

GUILFORD, CONNECTICUT
HELENA, MONTANA

AN IMPRINT OF THE GLOBE PEQUOT PRESS

FALCONGUIDES®

Copyright © 2008 Morris Book Publishing, LLC

Photos by Rick Sapp unless otherwise indicated
Maps by Tim Kissel © Morris Book Publishing, LLC

Library of Congress Cataloging-in-Publication Data
Sapp, Rick.
  Road biking Florida: a guide to the greatest bike rides in Florida/Rick Sapp.
    p. cm. — (Falcon guides)
  ISBN 978-0-7627-4448-0
1. Bicycle touring–Florida–Guidebooks. 2. Cycling–Florida–Guidebooks. 3. Florida–Guidebooks. I. Title
  GV1045.5.F6S37 2008
  796.6'409759–dc22
                          20080181577

Printed in the United States of America
10 9 8 7 6 5 4 3 2 1

Contents

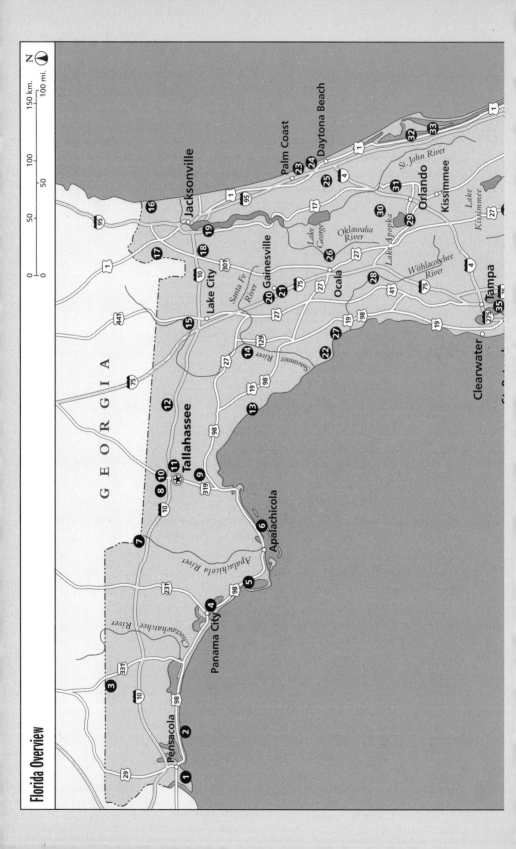

Florida Overview

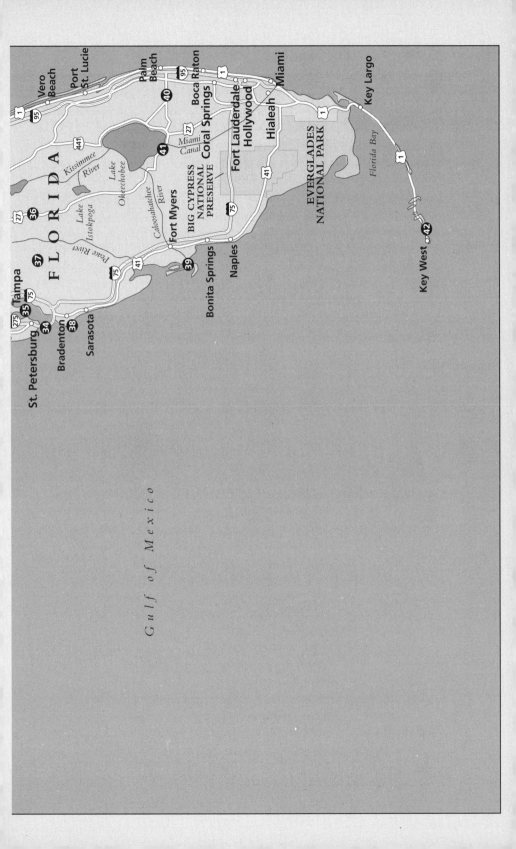

Preface

Biking, like swimming, is one of those amazing cardio exercises that benefit every part of your body. When your nose has been broken so many times that the mere thought of returning to the octagon brings out a cold sweat; when running across the street causes a sandpaper-like grinding in your knees; when just borrowing the neighbor's electric hedge clippers makes you want to find shade and get recumbent: It's time to get on your bike, strap on your helmet, and roll out into the bike lane. Put on a few serious miles. The only pain you'll have will be the hard seat bouncing against your undercarriage, and you'll soon get used to that.

I bought my Peugeot, too small and too old now, but too familiar to change—it is the devil that I know—at a bike shop in Minneapolis in 1986 or so. My wife suggested that we could ride around the lakes together—Harriet, Calhoun, Lake of the Isles. That proved worse for our conjugal relations than wallpapering the bathroom.

Somewhere in this book I write about losing myself while on a bicycle. I don't mean actually getting lost as in losing my way, although that has happened; rather it is a real sense of leaving my physical body. It is a point when pedaling—and remember that Florida is flat, because pumping up Colorado's Front Range would certainly be different—a point when muscular coordination becomes automatic and the brain enters a no-pain zone and stops tracking the miles. A point where I don't think about balancing and pedaling and turning. A point where the scenery is practically immaterial. It helps perhaps if the ride is "relative," the road relatively straight and the traffic relatively light. But every now and then I fall into it, "the zone," and it is like a deep draft of meditation. I never want it to end, never want to arrive at the end of the ride.

I have felt that sense of losing myself at other times and places, when engaged in other activities. I recall an evening of training for my first marathon when putting one foot in front of the other became effortless: I could have run to Los Angeles or Hong Kong. While boxing in college, I had an out-of-body experience once when I realized that I was lying face down on the canvas and could not recall how I got there—saw nothing, felt nothing, and did not remember being clobbered. . . .

Twenty years from now, for the next generation of cyclists, road biking in Florida will either be much too dangerous or we cyclists will have convinced the "decision-makers" to finally give us the room we need. There is evidence that, perhaps spurred on and aided by the threat of global warming, bike enthusiasts are becoming more successful in their lobbying for bike lanes and multipurpose trails.

All the more reason to bike Florida now—right now—while its delicate beauty and environmental diversity are still abundant. The rails-to-trails phenomenon is wonderful and expanding, and the public consciousness of bicycles as a genuine alternative to petroleum is also expanding, albeit slowly. I am guardedly optimistic that my 14-year-old daughter will eventually be able to bike to work, lead her children on a ride, and see some of the wonders of this remarkable state from the seat of a bike as I have.

I want to thank Houston and Marjorie for buying my first dime-store tricycle and, ultimately, a J. C. Higgins one-speed bicycle when I was . . . well, small. We lived on the highest point on Amelia Island, a surprisingly steep ridge on that otherwise flat barrier to inroads by wind and wave. Flying down either side of that steep hill was sheer ecstasy, even when my friend Jeff Rouse's shaggy brown dog did not race out to nip at my feet and legs.

In the middle of the past century, a bicycle was the ideal way for a kid to explore a small-town environment. Indeed, I was free to ride to the old wooden docks to watch fishermen. To the old fort to explore the beach and the deep woods around it. To grandma's house. A bicycle meant freedom. And it still does.

Florida is a magnificent place. Its radiant beaches of "sugar sand" look exactly like they do in the tourist brochures, only better in person. The thrill—I would say the "majesty," but you might think I was romanticizing it—of voyaging through space is very real, very present at the space center, even to a non-engineer, non-scientist like myself. The attractions, from the mega-events around Orlando to the most insignificant monkey-and-gator operations, are extraordinarily entertaining. The swamps and wetlands, beginning with the Okefenokee in the north and extending to the Everglades in the south, are precisely as advertised . . . even more so!

Thus, I also thank the editors who gave me the opportunity to ride Florida systematically and were then patient with my manuscript revisions. I've visited practically every corner, every niche of my state, and I'm grateful. For just as the iron-taloned osprey seizes its fish or a cool wind suddenly drafts at your back, cycling forces you to live in the moment. Forces you to concentrate. Observe. Like an anthropologist, only better, because you take part because you wish to do so, not because you are paid to do so. On a bicycle, one becomes a part while remaining apart, and that is a rare gift, indeed.

Introduction

Florida. Watch the advertising. Beaches. Sunshine. Orange juice. Greyhound racing. Indian casinos. Sunsets. Resorts. Youth. Warm and glorious.

Public messages about Florida have always had something of a glossy exterior. Early Spanish conquistadores used the myths of a "Fountain of Youth" and cities that paved their streets with gold to wring money from parsimonious monarchs. Nineteenth-century American politicians frothed about the menace of wild Indians and sent armies to make the land safe for settlers and their slaves. Developers waxed euphoric about the pristine conditions, about a land ripe for settlement, and soils so rich that simply sticking a fencepost into the ground yielded a bountiful harvest, that residents could simply raise a hand from their hammock and fruit would appear.

It has never been easy to bring the truth about Florida into coincident focus with the establishment images. Primarily plunderers rather than settlers, the Spanish found wide-spreading oak trees rather than precious metals. The few thousand remaining Creek Indians and runaway slaves who sought refuge in Florida fought several American armies, men dressed in thick woolens and equipped with slow-firing flintlocks, to a complete standstill.

Even the settlers who discovered that their purchase was actually above water were faced with a land of contradictions. The land was fertile, but in all directions vast bogs—the Okefenokee and the Everglades, Tate's Hell and the Green Swamp—bred disease-carrying (malaria and yellow fever) mosquitoes. Soils in the north and down the central spine were so precariously infertile that scrub or "cracker" cattle yielded a better income than long-staple cotton. Soils in the south were rich and dark with nutrients but subject to annual floods and violent hurricanes.

Florida in the twenty-first century is no less a contradiction than it has been at any time during its history . . . or its prehistory. The state is growing very rapidly and we, the citizens, are not keeping apace of the hard decisions we need to make to preserve the beauty and wonder of what was once a true subtropical paradise. By 2008 twenty million people will be shoehorned into the Sunshine State. Even today, you cannot take a single one of these rides without seeing scores of FOR SALE signs and bulldozers moving mounds of earth.

And yet, riding opportunities for cyclists both on- and off-road in the Sunshine State are still superb. Indeed, the diversity of rides is magnificent, although that certainly depends upon your definition of "magnificent." Few rides in Florida boast serious hills. Practically everything here is flat, one-third of the possible dimensions (long, wide, and high) having been spared by Mother Nature. Your most serious gear-shifting obstacle may be the high-rise center span of a bridge over the Intracoastal Waterway.

In this volume you will find rides of every sort—rambles that are merely warm-ups for experienced cyclists and true classics that will challenge any rider's

endurance. Several pedals are scenic from the moment you mount up to the moment you return the bike to the rack—while a couple are designed to show a side of Florida that may be a bit unsettling. Several rides travel through country so lonely that farmers and ranchers will look up from their work as you wheel past, children dizzy on tire swings will stare, and families shelling butter beans in the porch swing will smile and wave. A few rides are so uptown that your eyes may blur at the endless series of stops and turns.

Half of the rides have been modeled after active bike club routes, and those clubs are recognized. The nature of volunteer activities, however, is that clubs only maintain momentum while being driven forward by the effort of a few energetic leaders. As these leaders cycle through their involvement, however, as life moves them onward, clubs evolve.

Thus, if you try to access a Web site and it is unresponsive, recognize that the information was correct at one time—and, of course, the same can be said for motels, inns, and certainly for restaurants. One constant fact is that although there is turnover in the ranks of service providers in a popular tourist destination, two new enterprises will replace one that succumbs. And so, listing a few inns and eateries on most (but not all) road trails in Florida is simply cherry-picking the couple that look or seem or sound good among dozens and sometimes hundreds of deserving establishments.

As you know, anything can happen on the road, and sometimes it does. So for each ride, I have listed a sheriff's department contact, but understand that simply by dialing 9-1-1 you should be able to access—from any point you have telephone service—a vast network of highly qualified emergency responders.

Traffic and Hazards

Florida has traffic. It is a growing, crowded, urbanizing state and the traffic situation is not going to get better anytime soon.

Even though Florida is packed with people and vehicles, and even though more cyclists are killed in this state each year than in any other (sad, but true), the awareness of cycling and the benefits of bike riding are indeed growing.

When a careless driver killed a cyclist last year in my hometown of Gainesville— an unrepentant driver who went unpunished, I might add—I took part in a ride to commemorate the deceased cyclist's life and commitment to the bicycle. A motley crew of two dozen cyclists—hippies with children in tow, others on antique one-speeds, and a few fully equipped with helmets and lights—rode a dozen miles in heavy traffic, slowly and silently, bunched together to take up an entire lane. A few taunts were flung from passing pickup trucks by men who were obviously slightly delayed in some life-critical mission like buying more beer, but no bottles were

◀ *Packs and panniers in place, Julie Keen pedals north on Highway A1A just south of St. Augustine.*

Bearing down on an evening ride along a beach south of Clearwater, this biker will burn 750 to 1,000 calories per hour.

thrown and no shots taken. The police did not interfere (or help,) and most of the temporarily inconvenienced drivers took our demonstration in stride. Still, I was relieved when the ride ended and the group dispersed safely.

Each year Florida widens more roads for bike lanes, extends its paved trail system, and sells more vehicular license plates to support biking. With one hundred or so specialty plates available, Florida's SHARE THE ROAD license plate currently (as of September 2007) ranks fortieth overall in sales (see www.dmv.org/fl-florida/license-plates.php). That statistic is a testimony to the power of two-wheeling.

Defensive riding will pull you through years of biking without incident. This kind of riding begins with awareness of your situation and watchfulness. It would be nice to assume that we are all great riders and, by and large, we are, but we know that we have "those days" when, for whatever reason, we just can't seem to stay in the bike lane. Whether it is sand on the pavement from an intersecting dirt road, debris blown out of a truck bed, or trash thrown out the window by inconsiderate motorists, veering out of the bike lane happens. I believe that it is possible to eliminate most of our own carelessness on the road and avoid most road hazards by simply slowing down and looking.

Our riding safety in part depends on a continuing effort to educate one another and the general public. By setting a good example, we promote bicycle safety. All boring, perhaps, but all necessary, even vital.

Ride on!

Equipment, Clothing, and the Law

Specialized gear for Florida begins with requirements for water and visibility, to see and be seen. Think of it as a challenge, like sudoku.

If you often ride in warm to hot weather, consider investing in a hydration pack. Keep these remarkable devices clean and you will never regret the purchase. Hydrate and leave the camouflage pants in the boutique. Do whatever it takes to be visible on the road.

Awareness of what is happening around you is ultra-important because Florida traffic is as hot as the weather. I recommend using a helmet-mounted (even a handlebar-mounted) rearview mirror. It takes a little getting used to but is excellent in traffic or a fast peloton.

And if you think you can ride evenings in Florida without lights and bug spray . . . well, forget it. Our mosquitoes can fly faster than you can pedal and they will assault you. In addition, we have several varieties of biting flies and no-see-ums and Africanized honeybees (the so-called "killer bees"); thank goodness pterodactyls are extinct and alligators don't fly.

Here are a few special clauses in the Florida law as it pertains to bicycles:

1. A bicycle is a vehicle (like an automobile).

2. A bike rider is a driver, and as a driver you must obey rules developed specially for bicycles, but you also have all of the rights to the roadway applicable to any driver.

3. Between sunset and sunrise, a bicycle must be equipped with a light on the front with a white light visible to 500 feet, and both a red reflector and a lamp on the rear with a red light visible to 600 feet.

4. Cyclists may not wear headsets, headphones, or listening devices other than hearing aids while riding.

5. Riders under 16 must wear helmets.

6. Riders must obey all applicable signals and signs.

7. According to the *Florida Driver's Handbook,* motorists passing cyclists "should maintain" at least 3 feet of clearance.

8. On a public roadway, cyclists may not ride more than two abreast.

9. Cyclists must signal intent to turn.

10. When riding on a sidewalk, a cyclist has the rights and duties of a pedestrian, must give an audible warning before passing, and must yield the right of way to pedestrians.

How to Use This Guide

This series of road-cycling guides has been developed with a standardized set of ride categories that are only slightly modified for riding in Florida, which is hot and humid but 99 percent flat. These categories are artificial groupings, and you probably will find that they do not entirely apply or are not especially meaningful for you or your situation. I will not be offended.

Many things affect a ride: the weather; your bicycle's performance; your attitude, health, and age; what you had for dinner the night before; your partner's chutzpah; and whether you are riding alone or with a partner or in a group. I have given base data that I found to be accurate—or my best guess or assessment—at the time that I was compiling and writing about these rides.

- **Rambles** are mild rides that take a few hours to complete. Novices can easily finish a ramble in a half day and experienced riders will breeze through them without breaking a sweat. Distances typically are 25 miles or less.

- **Cruises** are rides from 25 to 50 miles long that can be completed by excellent riders in a half day, but if you are new to biking or perhaps just pedaling occasionally, you may want to budget a full day for a cruise—with the evening spent in an easy chair with a Scotch-on-the-rocks, and an early bedtime.

- **Challenges** are rides that require a small step up in length, but a significant step up in endurance—a challenge presents a biking puzzle. A ride of 50 to 70 miles or so will test your heart's ability to pump oxygen and perhaps your will, especially if there is a headwind or the day is especially hot and humid. To avoid the kind of fatigue that lasts for days after strenuous and extended exercise, novice riders may want to break this ride into two days.

- **Classics** are long rides, more than 75 miles, with significant stretches between shelters. Novices should ride the classics, but always with a buddy and after some planning is done for road assistance in case there is a spill and a bent rim. If the scenery is spectacular, even experts may want to take this ride in multiple-day stages.

Giving precise mileage figures over a complex ride is a problem, and you will find slippages (hopefully only minor) in what you experience and what I reported. Odometers or bike computers are not all calibrated exactly in the same manner—and sometimes they are calibrated incorrectly. As I gathered the data for this book, I often retraced portions of a ride: evaluating the scenery or taking a photograph, detouring around construction, buying a snack, or even rechecking the mileage.

The reported mileage will slip a little here and there for a dozen and one other reasons. Florida is a dynamic state. People move out of the snow zones. Highways are expanded and rerouted. New towns appear where the old map says there were

Florida is home to thousands upon thousands of committed cyclists, and they are making an impact developing rails-to-trails and adding bike lanes throughout the state.

orange groves. So use the maps carefully, be alert to changes in the topography, and then be tolerant when, not if, you find differences in what you experience and what I have written. I have truly made every effort to ensure the accuracy of the information in this book.

Ride well. Ride safely. But ride. . . .

Florida Road Rides at a Glance

(Listed in order of distance)

Rambles (14)

9.0 miles	Inverness–Lake Henderson Ramble, ride 28
9.8 miles	Navarre Beach Ramble, ride 2
11.4 miles	Highest Ride Ramble, ride 3
15.6 miles	Kennedy Space Center Ramble, ride 33
20.2 miles	Panama City Ramble, ride 4
22.4 miles	Bridges of Apalachicola Ramble, ride 6
22.7 miles	Tampa Interbay Ramble, ride 35
23.1 miles	DeSoto Best Ride Ramble, ride 34
27.9 miles	Hatch Bend Ramble, ride 14
29.0 miles	Atlantic Beach Ramble, ride 24
29.0 miles	Astatula Hills Ramble, ride 30
30.6 miles	Wacahoota Ramble, ride 21
32.3 miles	Suwannee River Ramble, ride 15
38.2 miles	Lake Mary Ramble, ride 31

Cruises (17)

34.7 miles	Cape Canaveral Seashore Cruise, ride 32
35.4 miles	Pensacola Bay Cruise, ride 1
35.4 miles	Sanibel Island Cruise, ride 39
36.5 miles	Amelia Island Cruise, ride 16
36.5 miles	Maclay Gardens Cruise, ride 10
37.0 miles	Quincy Cruise, ride 8
37.0 miles	The Great Florida Ranch Cruise, ride 25
38.1 miles	Chaires Shady Lane Cruise, ride 11
40.0 miles	Lake Wales Cruise, ride 36
42.2 miles	Phosphate Cruise, ride 37
42.9 miles	Wellington Cruise, ride 40
44.0 miles	Atlantic Beach Cruise, ride 23
44.4 miles	Lake Rousseau Cruise, ride 27
44.7 miles	Two Egg Cruise, ride 7
44.8 miles	Macclenny Cruise, ride 18
51.8 miles	St. Joseph Bay Cruise, ride 5
52.0 miles	Cedar Key Cruise, ride 22

Challenges (6)

54.5 miles	Sweet Potato Challenge, ride 19
55.7 miles	Poe Springs Challenge, ride 20
58.1 miles	Bakery Heart-of-Florida Challenge, ride 29
59.4 miles	On-the-Gulf Challenge, ride 13
63.4 miles	Bradenton Country Challenge, ride 38
65.3 miles	Ray Charles Challenge, ride 12

Classics (5)

73.9 miles	Florida Flatwoods Classic, ride 9
74.0 miles	Ocala National Forest Classic, ride 26
103.1 miles	Edge of the Okefenokee Classic, ride 17
105.0 miles	Florida Keys Over-the-Ocean Classic, ride 42
116.6 miles	Lake Okeechobee Classic, ride 41

Map Legend

━━1━95━━	Limited Access Freeway
━━1━ / ━━━	U.S. Highway/ Featured U.S. Highway
━(62)━ / ━━━	State Highway/ Featured State Highway
━━━ / ━━━	Local Road/ Featured Local Road
---------- / ----------	Trail/ Featured Trail
◉	City
○	Town
🄫	Starting Point
↙ 10.0	Mileage Marker
→	Directional Arrow
✛	Airport
■	Building or Structure
❑	Point of Interest
▲	Small Park or Forest
▲	Peak
⬬	Reservoir or Lake
～～～	River or Creek
·–·–·–·–	Large Park or Forest
New Hampshire —·—·— Massachusetts	State Boundary

The Panhandle Region

1 Pensacola Bay Cruise

Hang on to your hat because this ride swings you like a rag doll through the Pensacola of yesterday and today. It is industrial and railroad tracks; it is flying over high bridges; it is beach and wind and sun. All of Florida is packed into this one cruise.

Start: The parking lot of Bikes Plus at 3682 Barrancas Avenue/County Road 292.
Length: A 35.4-mile loop.
Terrain: Flat.
Traffic and hazards: Depending on the time and the day of your ride, traffic can be heavy and some of the roads, notably Barrancas and Main, are rough—especially the older, brick sections. Exercise caution on the bridges over Pensacola Bay and Santa Rosa Sound, as drivers tend to sightsee. U.S. Highway 98 through Gulf Breeze is always congested.

Getting there: From Interstate 10, which runs east-west through north Florida, take exit 12 south on Interstate 110. Use exit 1C west for US 98/West Garden Street. Barrancas Avenue quarters to the left (southwest) in about a mile. Take it to Bikes Plus at 3682 Barrancas Avenue/CR 292. The store and parking lot will be on your right on the north side of the road.

Here's a hang-loose but pay-attention ride. When I visited Bikes Plus near rush hour on a weekday afternoon, a group of riders took off immediately along Barrancas. Traffic was heavy with buses and trucks. I certainly recommend this ride—as you will see everything from residential to commercial to historic to industrial to tourist—but I recommend it for an early morning jaunt on Saturday or Sunday when traffic is light.

The Pensacola Bay Cruise begins at a small but nicely appointed bike shop on the southwest side of the city. Beginning there, the paving over the first half-dozen miles is inconsistent. It can be rough with railroad tracks and the remnants of old brick streets showing through ragged potholes. This portion is industrial and hard-working; the city proper lies to the left (north), and there are warehouses, docks, and ships on the right (south). The roadway to this point is occasionally four-lane, sometimes with a bike lane, and occasionally a tight two-lane.

When the road opens and becomes Bayfront Parkway, however, the industrial sector is left far behind, and not only do the green lawns of parks spread out on both sides, but the expansive view of Pensacola Bay will take your breath away. It is sensational, especially after the couple miles of warehouses and old road. Plus, there is often a breeze that both cools you and makes you pump a little harder. But that's good, right?

Pedal around the bend to the right and onto the causeway leading to the Pensacola Bay Bridge, which deposits you in Gulf Breeze and eventually onto the beach. The next 3 miles take you over the high central span of this bridge. It is precarious, but there is room to ride inside the 6-foot turnoff lane. It is customarily littered with miscellaneous detritus, however, so be careful.

Florida's scenic zones include views of ocean and dunes, high-rise condominiums, and road repairs following hurricanes.

The view from this bridge is spectacular, though. You can see in all directions: toward the Gulf of Mexico to the south, back across the city of Pensacola, and sweeping views of Pensacola Bay. Expect sailboats, oceangoing merchant ships, and perhaps the Navy's Blue Angels flying team practicing overhead. (They are based at Pensacola's Naval Air Station.) This view alone is worth the ride.

It may be difficult to curb your enthusiasm as you bike the downhill side of this bridge, but you must, because the road narrows for several miles in Gulf Breeze. The area is congested and commercial, with schools on either side of the road. Hang on and be vigilant, because it is not far to the causeway to Santa Rosa Island.

Santa Rosa is called a "barrier island," long and thin, as if it were a bulwark flung out to protect the bay from the continual pounding of wind and water. It is similar in appearance and function to the Outer Banks of North Carolina or Cape Cod in Massachusetts. While Mother Nature's intended function may be to protect her estuaries, we humans have adapted these islands for recreation and habitation, although erecting homes and stores here can be somewhat precarious.

As you ride over the Bob Sikes Toll Bridge from Gulf Breeze to Pensacola Beach—cyclists don't have to stop or pay tolls—you once again look over a wide

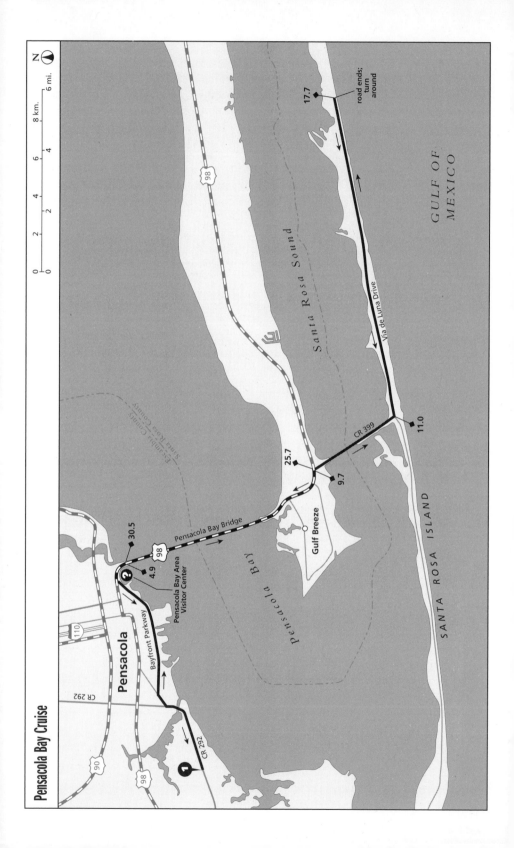

Pensacola Bay Cruise

Pensacola

CR 292

CR 292

Bayfront Parkway

Pensacola Bay Area Visitor Center

4.9

30.5

98

Pensacola Bay Bridge

98

Pensacola Bay

Gulf Breeze

25.7

9.7

CR 399

11.0

Via de Luna Drive

17.7

road ends; turn around

Santa Rosa Sound

Santa Rosa Island

SANTA ROSA ISLAND

GULF OF MEXICO

Escambia County / Santa Rosa County

N

0 2 4 6 mi.

0 2 4 6 8 km.

expanse of salt water. These are ideal waters for sailing and fishing, with places for snorkeling and scuba diving, but the rough surf has made the beaches here somewhat hazardous for swimming. The drop-off comes quickly, and the surf, too small and too quickly breaking to support a surfboard, can be harsh if it is propelled forward by a southerly wind.

Exposure to the elements wreaks havoc on the white-beach attraction of Fort Pickens State Park and Aquatic Preserve, which are open to the public as weather permits, but are certainly a must-visit for the historical-minded. (At this writing, the road is not repaired from the 2004–05 storm seasons and many of the dunes have still not reconstituted from the 1995 hurricanes.)

The 34,000-acre fort-and-water-playground surrounds the western end of Santa Rosa Island and the eastern end of Perdido Key, both of which are excellent examples of undeveloped barrier islands. The submerged lands along the northern sides of these islands are characterized by shallow water, continuous and patchy sea-grass beds, and salt marshes. According to Shelly Alexander in the Northwest Florida Aquatic Preserves office in Milton, Florida, "These communities provide habitat for wildlife and birds such as nesting sea turtles and shorebirds. Several species are listed as endangered or threatened."

Due to its proximity to the Gulf Intracoastal Waterway and the Pensacola Ship Channel, the preserve experiences some of the heaviest boat traffic (industrial, military, and recreational) in the Gulf region. Take heart, though, because there is an underwater archaeological park within the preserve. The sunken World War I battleship USS *Massachusetts* provides great diving and fishing opportunities, and the World War II aircraft carrier USS *Oriskany* is now an artificial reef just 22 miles offshore . . . but not until you have finished your ride!

Miles and Directions

0.0 Begin by turning left (east) out of the parking lot of Bikes Plus at 3682 Barrancas Avenue/CR 292. Stay on 292 as it bends to the left and crosses the bridge over Bayou Chico. Another Barrancas (!) is a smaller street that continues straight. (Should you miss this, as I did, it is less than a mile to the end of the road and this small peninsula. Simply turn around and turn right onto CR 292 when it once again intersects with Barrancas.)

2.0 Turn right on West Main Street immediately after crossing the railroad tracks.

3.6 Cross another set of railroad tracks. Main Street becomes Bayfront Parkway as the road emerges from the downtown industrial area onto Pensacola Bay. Bayfront Parkway bends, first north and then south, to cross the bay.

4.9 This is a marker point where Bayfront merges with US 98. Here, as you sweep south on Bayfront Parkway, you enter the causeway to Pensacola Bay Bridge. Across the road to your left is the Pensacola Bay Area Visitor Center.

8.2 At about this point, you have ridden over the high bridge and are proceeding southeast on Gulf Breeze Parkway (US 98).

9.7 Swing right (south-southeast) at the large sign of the leaping billfish to Pensacola Beach on County Road 399. Cross the Bob Sikes Bridge, which is Pensacola Beach Boulevard, over Santa Rosa Sound, and emerge on Via de Luna Drive.

11.0 Pass this toll booth and wave at the attendant. There is no toll for bicycles. Stay on Via de Luna as it swings roughly east away from Fort Pickens and toward Gulf Islands National Seashore.

17.7 The road ends. Turn around in the parking lot here and return on Via de Luna. **Option:** On the return ride, you have a choice of remaining on Via de Luna or turning off to the south (Avenida 23 to Maldonado or Ariola) or the north (Avenida 22 to Panferio) and riding parallel to Via de Luna for a few miles.

25.7 Recrossing the bridge over Santa Rosa Sound, swing left onto Gulf Breeze Parkway. Cross the Pensacola Bay Bridge.

30.5 Turn left (west) onto Bayfront Parkway at the traffic lights in front of the visitor center and park.

33.4 Turn left (southwest) onto Barrancas Avenue and cross the bridge over Bayou Chico.

35.4 Swing into the parking lot of Bikes Plus. This is the end of the ride.

Local Information

Escambia County Sheriff's Department, 1700 West Leonard Street, Pensacola; (850) 436-9664; www.escambiaso.com.

Tourism Division of the Pensacola Bay Area Chamber of Commerce, 1401 East Gregory Street, Pensacola; (800) 874-1234; www.visitpensacola.com.

Local Events/Attractions

National Museum of Naval Aviation, 1750 Radford Boulevard, Naval Air Station, Pensacola; (850) 453-2389 or (800) 327-5002; www.navalaviationmuseum.org. For history buffs or people interested in what Dad did in World War II, this is the place. Admission is free. Museum (9:00 a.m. to 5:00 p.m.) and IMAX theater.

Pensacola Greyhound Track, 951 Dog Track Road, Pensacola; (850) 455-8595 or (800) 345-3997; www.pensacolagreyhoundpark.com. You can bet on these dogs.

Pensacola Opera, 75 South Tarragona Street, Pensacola; (850) 433-6737; www.pensacolaopera.com/index.html.

Restaurants

Aegean Breeze, 913 Gulf Breeze Parkway, Gulf Breeze; (850) 916-0430. Gets good reviews online.

The Fish House and Atlas Oyster House, 600 South Barracks Street, Pensacola; (850) 470-0694; www.goodgrits.com. Downtown on the water. Fish of the day $19.

McGuire's Irish Pub & Brewery, 600 East Gregory Street, Pensacola; (850) 433-6789; www.mcguiresirishpub.com. Location, location, location. Martinis are $6.25. You'll pass this restaurant on both legs of the ride.

Skopelos on the Bay, 670 Scenic Highway, Pensacola; (850) 432-6565; http://myskopelos.com. Lunch Friday, dinners Tuesday through Saturday, Sunday brunch. Not casual. Reservations are recommended.

Accommodations

Big Lagoon State Park, 12301 Gulf Beach Highway, Pensacola; (850) 492-1595; www.floridastateparks.org/biglagoon. This 712-acre park has seventy-five campsites with electric and water hookups available through ReserveAmerica.com.

New World Landing, 600 South Palafox Street, Pensacola; (850) 432-4111; www.newworldlanding.com.

Paradise Inn, 21 Via De Luna, Pensacola Beach; (850) 932-2319 or (800) 301-5925; www.paradiseinn-pb.com. On the beach. One of a kind!

Pensacola Victorian Bed & Breakfast, 203 West Gregory Street, Pensacola; (850) 434-2818 or (800) 370-8354; www.pensacola victorian.com. Downtown and reasonably priced.

Bike Shops

Bikes Plus, 3682 Barrancas Avenue, Pensacola; (850) 455-4369; www.bikesplus.com. The beginning and end of your ride.

Cycle Sports, 2125 North Palafox Street, Pensacola; (850) 434-8100; www.cyclesports bicycles.com.

Restrooms

Mile 0.0: Bikes Plus, the beginning and end of the ride.

Mile 4.9: The visitor center on the north end, on the east side of the Pensacola Bay Bridge.

Mile 11.7: The visitor information center and at various beach parking areas.

Mile 17.7: Next to the parking lot that serves as the turnaround on this ride on Santa Rosa Island.

Maps

DeLorme: Florida Atlas & Gazetteer: Pages 42 A3 to B3, 43 B 1.

2 Navarre Beach Ramble

This is a marvelous ride because, thanks to the unfortunate power of several 2004–05 hurricanes, everything is new. Because the beach road was cut in numerous places by tidal surge, there is still very little traffic—except construction vehicles bringing workers and materials to rebuild.

Start: Navarre Beach parking facilities on Santa Rosa Island, near the intersection of the Navarre Beach Causeway and Gulf Boulevard.
Length: A 9.8-mile loop.
Terrain: Flat.

Traffic and hazards: Until the roads are repaired and opened along this coastal island, there will not be a great deal of vehicular traffic on this ride.

Getting there: From Pensacola, take U.S. Highway 98 south over the Pensacola Bay Bridge and then proceed east on US 98/Gulf Breeze Parkway to Navarre. Turn right in Navarre and drive over the Navarre Beach Causeway to the parking areas at the beach on Santa Rosa Island.

There are less than 10 miles to this ride, so just about the time you are set to turn on the power, it's over. So why not turn around and do it again or take the Navarre Beach Causeway to the mainland for some suds and then pedal back?

Like the computer phrase WYSIWYG—what you see is what you get—this ride will be sufficient in itself, but there is more here than meets the eye. First, what you will see . . . Everything is new and beautiful. Lovely pastel buildings. There is nothing old or dark or shabby on this beach. White sugar sand, so called because of its fine texture and white-on-white appearance. With early sun climbing over the water, the light can be blinding.

And "blinding" may be the correct term because everything you see in these 4 miles—as J. R. R. Tolkien wrote, "there and back again"—has recently replaced an older community. Old gives way to new, elder to younger. The older neighborhood was the usual old-Florida beachfront community, so shabby-chic you expected Jimmy Buffet to saunter around the corner with a beer in hand, a big smile, and a barbecue apron: "Ribs are ready. Come and get it!"

This shiny new community with no rot and no peeling paint is just waiting to be turned into comfortable shabby-chic. The blowing sand and salty air are hard to resist, but those gentle and customary forces of nature are not what shaped this beach, nor what brought people back to build newer, primarily pastel-colored two- and three-story homes on the margins of the road. But it was not the tax appraiser or even the military who came to build. (The military owns plenty of land hereabouts and, in fact, if you take Gulf Boulevard east until it ends, military land extends well beyond.) No, it was not the daily baking of sun and sand and salt that forced the most recent reconstruction of this sliver of island: It was the relentless hammering of hurricanes in 2004 and 2005. After all, Ivan came ashore not far away in 2004 and Katrina a little farther off in 2005, but the storm surge from those and other storms obliterated much of Santa Rosa Island. Hence, new homes rise amid the rubble of the old survivors.

Hurricanes are odd Pacifico-African creatures. They form in response to irregular cycles of heating and cooling over the Pacific Ocean and the Sahara Desert, and the northern hemisphere of our turning world simply spins them in our direction. But a hurricane is not a "meteorological phenomenon." It is a miserable beast.

Unless you have experienced a huge storm, been inside a hurricane when the eye passes overhead (or near the path of a tornado), it is almost impossible to imagine the raw power of earth's primeval forces. Having lived through a couple near misses with hurricanes and several blizzards in the upper Midwest (surviving one of them in the chilly interior of a marooned four-door Ford Fairlane in South Dakota), I can personally attest that when disaster-management officials suggest that you evacuate, they mean it.

And yet hurricanes also refill the parched Southeastern aquifer, frequently dropping more than a foot of water. Unfortunately, such a heavy splash is difficult for the land to absorb at one time and disastrous flooding occurs inland. Here on the beach, though, it is storm surge, a massive tonnage of ocean water heaving forward, pushed by hurricane winds, that does the damage. It was storm surge that overwhelmed Santa Rosa Island and wiped out the roads, the power grid, homes and businesses, and a few indomitable knuckleheads who remained behind for a "hurricane party."

Don't think of storm surge as a tidal wave, a tsunami, the wall of water that has sunk the passenger liner *Poseidon* twice in film and the fishing boat *Andrea Gail* once

◄ *It is important to stay hydrated on all rides—especially in Florida, where the sun, heat, and wind exert a strong but steady drain on your body's reserves of energy.*

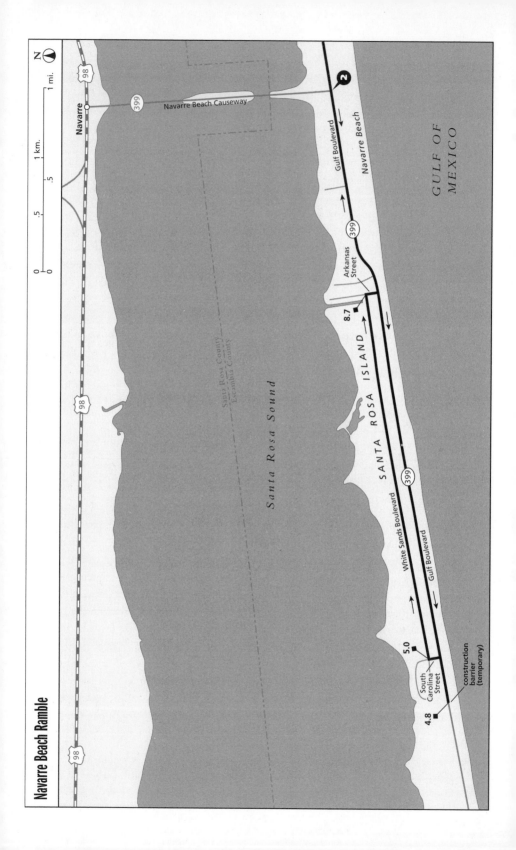

Navarre Beach Ramble

N

1 mi.

0   .5   1 km.

0   .5

98

Navarre

399

Navarre Beach Causeway

98

Santa Rosa County
Escambil County

Santa Rosa Sound

Gulf Boulevard

399

Navarre Beach

2

Arkansas
Street

8.7

SANTA ROSA ISLAND

399

White Sands Boulevard

Gulf Boulevard

5.0

South
Carolina
Street

4.8

construction
barrier
(temporary)

*GULF OF
MEXICO*

in real life and once in film. A storm surge is just as deadly as a tsunami, but it rushes toward the land with an unhurried but irrepressible pressure. With each passing minute the water level creeps higher in your home, so you take refuge on the second floor. And then it comes up the stairs, one at a time, as the wind howls with the screech of a thousand locomotives, and the windows blow out; and still the water creeps higher, and you place the ladder into the hole leading to the crawl space below the roof, happy that you put a hatchet there so you cannot be trapped and drowned, for no rescue is possible now, although you still do not quite believe. . . . And as your friends ascend into the attic with their flashlights and pillows, perhaps a beer in hand, chuckling in terror, not quite believing what is happening, screaming to be heard above the roar of their fear, the wind begins to rip the roof away and you look down, but water is already up to the second rung of the ladder and the house shudders violently. . . .

So this is what you will not see, the hurricane that is at the root of such wonderful construction and gives all of these workers jobs. And the smooth pavement you are cycling is the result of a storm surge so almighty that the Great Wall itself, perhaps a dozen Great Walls, could not have withstood its power. Have a nice ride.

Miles and Directions

0.0 Begin this ride on the east end of Navarre Beach. You will find plenty of public parking and facilities. Ride west on Gulf Boulevard. The road ends not far to the east before it reaches the boundary of Eglin Air Force Base.

4.8 The road ends at a construction barrier. Turn around and ride back east.

4.9 Turn left (north) on South Carolina Street.

5.0 Turn right (east) on White Sands Boulevard.

8.7 Turn right (south) on Arkansas Street.

8.8 Turn left (east) on Gulf Boulevard.

9.8 Arrive at the beginning and end of this ride.

Local Information

Santa Rosa County Chamber of Commerce, 5247 Stewart Street, Milton; (850) 623-2339; www.srcchamber.com.

Santa Rosa County Sheriff's Department, 5755 East Milton Road, Milton; (850) 983-1100; www.santarosasheriff.org.

Local Events/Attractions

Florida's Gulfarium, 1010 Miracle Strip Parkway, Fort Walton Beach; (850) 243-9046 or (800) 247-8575; www.gulfarium.com. Since 1955, sea-life shows and dolphin encounters. Open seven days a week.

Indian Temple Mound Museum, inside the City of Fort Walton Beach Heritage Park and Cultural Center, 139 Miracle Strip Parkway SE, Fort Walton Beach; (850) 833-9595; www.fwb.org. Hours are 10:00 a.m. to 4:30 p.m. Monday through Saturday, Sunday afternoons only in June and July.

National Museum of Naval Aviation, 1750 Radford Boulevard, Naval Air Station, Pensacola; (850) 453-2389 or (800) 327-5002; www.navalaviationmuseum.org. If you like to see fantastic flying and fighting machines, this is the place for you. Admission is free. Museum (9:00 a.m. to 5:00 p.m.) and an IMAX theater.

Restaurants

Cocodries, 8649 Gulf Boulevard, Navarre; (850) 939-8777; www.cocodries.com. It's cute and on the route! With a slogan like "Bringing the Bayou to the Beach," it has to be relaxed and fun. Daiquiri spoken here.

Devinci's Italian, 8097 Navarre Parkway, Navarre; (850) 939-2089; www.devincis.com. Pictures of plates of food on top of beer coasters. So how bad could it be!

Tropical Smoothie Cafe, 8646 Navarre Parkway, Navarre; (850) 936-1320; www.tropical smoothie.com. It's a chain, but I like it. . . .

Accommodations

The Breakers of Fort Walton Beach (on Okaloosa Island), 381 Santa Rosa Boulevard, Fort Walton Beach; (850) 244-9127 or (800) 395-4853; www.breakersfwb.com. About 15 miles east and quite pricey, but it is on the beach.

Comfort Inn, 8700 Navarre Parkway, Navarre; (850) 939-1761; www.choicehotels.com. All of the usual motels are present and accounted for.

Navarre Beach Campground, 9201 Navarre Parkway, Navarre; (850) 939-2188; www.navarrebeachcampground.com.

Bike Shops

There are no bicycle shops in Navarre, but there are shops about 15 miles away in both directions along US 98.

Bikes Plus, 3477 Gulf Breeze Parkway, Gulf Breeze; (850) 932-0706; www.bikesplus.com.

Dragon Sports, 233 Racetrack Road, Fort Walton Beach; (850) 863-8612; www.dragon sports.net.

Restrooms

At the east end of Navarre Beach in the neighborhood of the public parking areas.

Maps

DeLorme: Florida Atlas & Gazetteer: Page 43 A 3.

3 Highest Ride Ramble

Ride this mild loop on a summer eve and you will agree there's no sweeter country-road ride in America. To make this pedal more inviting, you can picnic or just sit and enjoy the view of fields and cattle and woods from the highest point in the state—345 feet above sea level—and then continue into Florala, which has to be one of the friendliest small towns in the region.

Start: The Florala (Alabama) Public Library at 1214 North 4th Street. (Google had this one spotted incorrectly in the summer of 2007. The library is "right down town.")
Length: An 11.4-mile loop.
Terrain: Hilly!

Traffic and hazards: Traffic is moderate to light, but the road is all two-lane and without a shoulder. Plus, it is hilly, so a pickup coming over a hill at high speed could crowd you. Be visible, and hang to the right.

Getting there: From Interstate 10, which runs east-west through the panhandle of North Florida, take exit 85 and drive north on U.S. Highway 331. It is about 30 miles through DeFuniak Springs to Florala. If you are driving from the west, take exit 70 north on County Road 285 to U.S. Highway 90; turn right (east) to Mossy Head, where you will turn left (north) onto County Road 1087. After about 20 miles CR 1087 dead-ends on State Road 2. Turn right for a mile and then left on US 331 and it will be a dozen miles to the start of the ride in Florala.

The Highest Ride Ramble is one of the shortest but sweetest rides in Florida. Summer evening air is warm and aromatic with the smell of country. Cicadas sing and traffic is light.

If you are annoyed by the frenzy to turn America into a giant subdivision, this is the perfect ride. It may renew your faith in the theory of inherent goodness. You will pedal through countryside as lovely as countryside gets, and as serene as it must be to relax into the road. It is a short loop, one you may want to cover in both clockwise and counterclockwise directions.

Your trip across the highest point in Florida begins in Florala, the southernmost town in Covington County, Alabama. It is a town of only a couple thousand people, and the people I met in this low-income area could not have been friendlier. "Nice" is probably the operative adjective, and I expect that you will find it to be the same.

The horizontal slice of Florida north of I-10 is the least-visited area in the state. That in itself is an excellent reason to make this ride. Traffic is light, and because there are no attractions or special reasons to be here other than family, you can sit on the steps of the Florala library, walk on the grass around Lake Jackson, or occupy a chair beneath the awnings on Main Street to your heart's content. ("We call it Main Street, but it is really just Highway 331," the librarian said.)

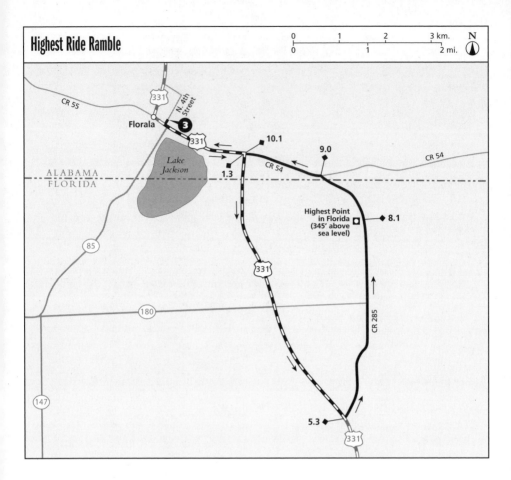

Highest Ride Ramble

0   1   2   3 km.   **N**
0   1   2 mi.

And you will not have to worry about crowds of tourists at the highest point, 345 feet above sea level. Chances are that no matter how long you dither, you'll be the only one there. Heck, Disney has rides higher than this!

I pedaled these highways on a late afternoon in early summer. Shadows were long. Cicadas were singing. (Some taxonomists consider cicadas to be the loudest and most efficient sound-producing insects in the world.) The ride was fragrant with country, animals, and fields. Wildflowers on the sides of the roads—my grandmother, a country girl born and raised on the remnants of a plantation not far from here, called the odorless purple bloom "phlox"—include wild daisies and buttercup and clover. And in the evening, when I returned to the highest point in Florida to simply "set a spell," spears of sunlight tinted the deepening curves of cumulus clouds with multiple shades of gray and highlighted luxurious green fields and feeding cattle. It was magic, a real magic kingdom.

As you might expect, this ride is hilly, although if you are a rogue biker who tackles California's mountains without huffing like a Lamaze graduate with a crowning infant, Florida's highest point will make you giggle. Nevertheless, it is one fine hill, and even though there are no paved shoulders—much less bike lanes—the local traffic should not be difficult. Watch for tractors pulling wagons loaded with hay—you should be able to outrun them—or pickups pulling boats, as the trailers will be extra wide. Otherwise, simply enjoy. . . .

Miles and Directions

0.0 Turn left (southwest) from the front of the Florala Public Library on North 4th Street.

0.1 Turn left (southeast) onto US 331/5th Avenue.

1.3 Turn right (south) at the stop sign and continue on US 331.

5.3 Turn sharply left (north) at the intersection with Walton County (Florida) CR 285.

8.1 Turn into the small parking lot at Littlewood Park, on the left (west) side of the road, and enjoy the highest point in Florida, 345 feet above sea level. Then turn left (north) out of the parking lot back onto CR 285.

9.0 Turn left (west) at the stop sign onto County Road 54 in Alabama.

10.1 Continue straight ahead at the flashing light in Florala. CR 54 ends, merging with US 331/5th Avenue.

11.3 Turn right (northeast) on North 4th Street.

11.4 End of ride at the Florala Public Library.

Local Information

Chamber of Commerce, 405 South 5th Street, Florala, AL 36442; (334) 858-6252.
Walton County (Florida) Sheriff's Department, 21527 US 331, Paxton; (850) 834-458; www.waltonso.com.

Local Events/Attractions

Florala State Park, 22738 Azalea Drive, Florala, AL 36442; (334) 858-6425; www .alapark.com/parks/park.cfm?parkid=16. Camping, fishing, swimming, and facilities in this small park on the shores of Lake Jackson in Florala.

Restaurants

Bean's Diner, 1310 6th Street, Florala, AL 36442; (334) 858-3393.
Country Folks Buffet, 1301 East 5th Avenue, Florala, AL 36442; (334) 858-3196.
Sara's Big R Restaurant, East 5th Avenue, Florala, AL 36442; (334) 858-7581 or (850) 830-0810. Just right with restrooms out back . . . but attached.
Starlight Grill, 300 East 3rd Avenue, Florala, AL 36442; (334) 858-8515.

Accommodations

Lake House Bed & Breakfast, 23622 5th Avenue, Florala, AL 36442; (334) 858-2070.
Lakeview Motor Lodge, 431 3rd Street, Florala, AL 36442; (334) 858-3544.
Sara's Big R Restaurant, Bed & Breakfast and RV Park, East 5th Avenue, Florala, AL 35442; (334) 858-7581 or (850) 830-0810.

Bike Shops

The closest bicycle shops are an hour from Florala in Enterprise, Alabama, and Niceville, Florida.

Restrooms

Mile 0.0: The Florala Public Library at the beginning and end of the ride.
Mile 8.1: Littlewood Park on the west side of CR 285 in Walton County, Florida.

Maps

DeLorme: Florida Atlas & Gazetteer: Page 29 A 1.

4 Panama City Ramble

This ride in downtown Panama City is dedicated to cyclists who enjoy block-by-block twists and turns. The principal challenge will be to keep one eye on the map and the other eye on the roadway while watching for street signs and enjoying the view of bays and quaint older homes.

Start: In the free parking areas of the Marina Civic Center, 8 Harrison Avenue, downtown Panama City.
Length: A 20.2-mile multiple figure-eight loop.

Terrain: Relatively flat with minor hills.
Traffic and hazards: Traffic similar to residential areas in suburbia.

Getting there: From Interstate 10 in North Florida, drive south to Panama City via any of a number of roads. If you were going into that city on the most direct route from the interstate via U.S. Highway 231/State Road 75, for instance, you would take exit 130, which is between Chipley and Marianna. In Panama City turn left on Harrison Avenue and follow it to the parking area behind the Marina Civic Center; it juts out into the Intracoastal Waterway/St. Andrew Bay.

This is just an old-fashioned in-town ride for those who enjoy puttering around the bays and older neighborhoods of a small, tourist-friendly city. Most of the neighborhoods date from the 1920s to the 1960s, so everything has a patina of quaint.

Imagine that you are a kid again, riding your old J. C. Higgins two-speed—stop and go—down to the playground on a Saturday morning, maybe looking for a pickup game of baseball or for some kids to ride the teeter-totter with. That's the kind of ride this is—a relic of the mid-twentieth century, before we had to worry about growing up. It is a ride for the kid inside, when we didn't insist on riding so fast and could actually look into people's yards for our buddies or maybe toss the weekly paper deep into the bushes next to the front porch.

Then there is the downtown segment of the ride, around small businesses and those miscellaneous areas that make a city, places where a Subway sandwich shop pops up next to a refurbished gas station converted to a Starbucks coffee emporium.

Locally, this area is referred to as the "Emerald Coast," but it is really and truly part of the "Redneck Riviera" (and we say that with love). Everyone here understands that term . . . and no, it isn't a slight. The Riviera is roughly bounded by Pensacola to the west and Panama City Beach on the east, and it has some of the most stunning beaches in the world, famous for sugar white sand and warm, emerald green waters. This sand actually squeaks when you walk on it. Contrary to popular belief, I am told that this beach sand is not bleached by the sun, but comprises Appalachian quartz that filtered down to the coast from the mountains. The emerald green color of the water is due to the reflection from the sugar white sand that lies beneath the clear water. And this water is clear!

When you complete the trek through downtown Panama City, head for the beach. Rent a fat-tire bike and see what comes alive!

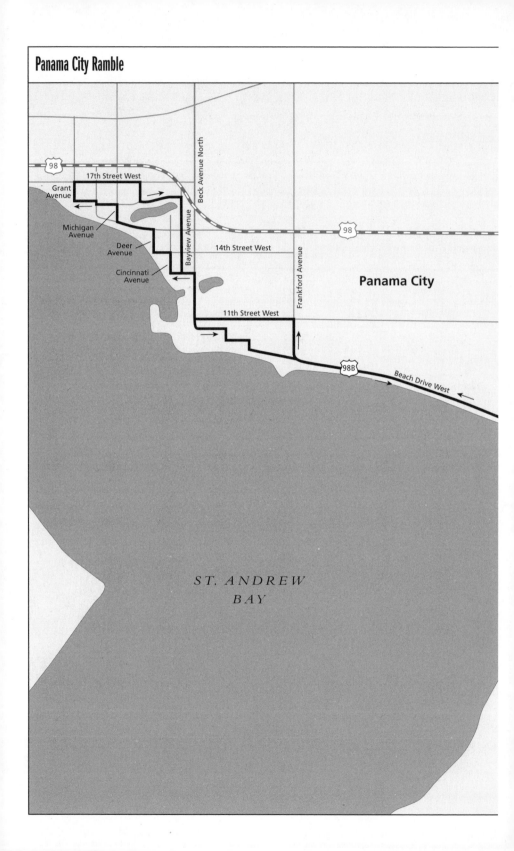

Panama City Ramble

17th Street West

Grant Avenue

Beck Avenue North

Michigan Avenue

Deer Avenue

Bayview Avenue

Cincinnati Avenue

14th Street West

Frankford Avenue

Panama City

98

98

11th Street West

98B

Beach Drive West

ST. ANDREW BAY

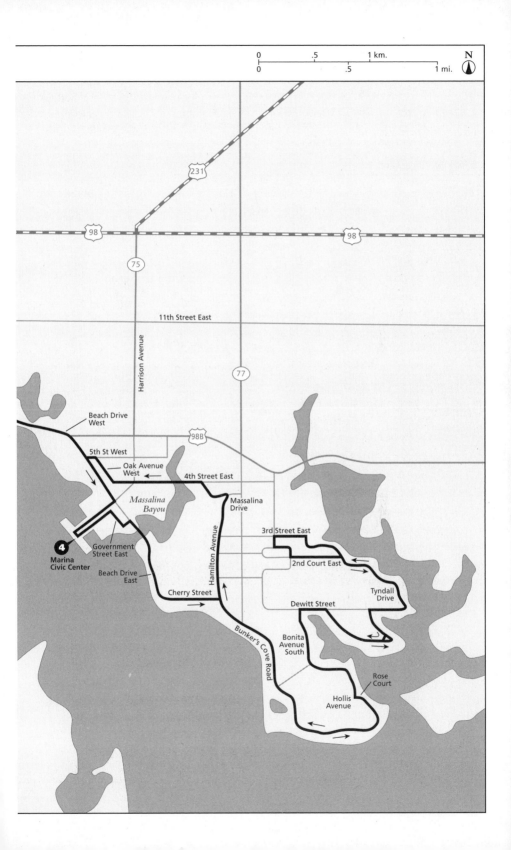

The Panama City ride is locally popular, even with people who possibly have not heard Tom T. Hall's country song "Redneck Riviera," which says that "Nobody cares if gramma's got a tattoo or Bubba's got a hot wing in his hand." Hot wing, flip-flops, a T-shirt, and a cold brew. You're on vacation now, Bubba. Enjoy. We'll do the putt-putt golf "here in a bit."

Miles and Directions

There are so many block-by-block twists and turns that for this ride only, we are suspending the established criteria for route travel, which links mileage with specific turns.

0.0 Begin in the parking lot of the Marina Civic Center.
- Turn right on Government Street East, which after 2 blocks bends 90 degrees.
- Turn right on Beach Drive East and cross the bridge over Massalina Bayou.
- Beach Drive East bends 90 degrees left and becomes Cherry Street.
- Turn right on Bunker's Cove Road and follow as it twists around the bay. Past the small "pocket park," the name changes to Rose Court for half a block.
- Turn right on Hollis Avenue, which, after a 90-degree turn left, becomes Bayou Court.
- Turn right on Bonita Avenue South.
- Turn right on Dewitt Street.
- Turn right on Cove Terrace Drive South.
- Turn left on Cove Lane South.
- Turn right on Dewitt Street East.
- Dewitt Street bends more than 90 degrees left and becomes Tyndall Drive.
- Turn left on 2nd Court East.
- Turn right on 2nd Plaza East.
- Turn right on Bonita Drive North.
- Turn right on 3rd Street East.
- Turn right on Tyndall Drive, which follows the water and, becoming Dewitt Street, takes a more-than-90-degree turn right.
- Turn left on Cove Lane South.
- Turn right on Terrace Place.
- Turn right on Cove Terrace Drive South.
- Turn left on Dewitt Street.
- Turn left on Bonita Avenue South.
- Turn left on Bayou Court.
- Turn right as Bayou Court becomes Hollis Avenue.
- Turn left on Rose Court, which makes a 90-degree turn into Bunker's Cove Road, which turns gradually to the right around this small peninsula.
- Continue straight across Cherry Street where Bunker's Cove Road becomes Hamilton Avenue.

- Continue straight as Hamilton Avenue becomes Massalina Drive.
- Stay to the left on Massalina Drive, following the water's edge.
- Turn left on 4th Street East.
- Veer to the right on West Oak Avenue, behind the post office.
- Turn left on 5th Street West.
- Turn right on Beach Drive West, which becomes Business U.S. Highway 98. Continue left.
- Turn right as US 98 swings right and becomes Frankford Avenue.
- Turn left on 11th Street West.
- Turn right on Beck Avenue North/Business US 98.
- Turn left on 13th Street West.
- Turn right on Cincinnati Avenue.
- Turn left on 14th Street West.
- Turn right on Deer Avenue.
- Turn left on 15th Street West, which turning right becomes Michigan Avenue.
- Turn left on 16th Street West.
- Turn right on Drummond Avenue.
- Turn left on 16th Street West.
- Turn right on Grant Avenue.
- Turn right on 17th Street West.
- Turn right on Billings Avenue.
- Turn left on 16th Street West.
- Turn right on Bayview Avenue.
- Turn left on 13th Street West.
- Turn right on Beck Avenue North/Business US 98.
- Turn left on 10th Street West.
- Turn right on Chestnut Avenue. The road bends around Truesdell Park.
- Turn left on 9th Street West.
- Turn right on Frankford Avenue.
- Turn left on Beach Drive West/Business US 98.
- Stay on Beach Drive West as Business US 98 veers off to the left.

20.2 Turn right on Harrison Avenue to your parking space and the end of the ride.

Local Information

Bay County Sheriff's Department, 3421 Highway 77, Panama City; (850) 747-4701; www.bayso.org.

Panama City Beach Convention and Visitors Bureau, 17001 Panama City Beach Parkway, Panama City; (850) 233-5070 or -6503; www.thebeachloversbeach.com.

Local Events/Attractions

The beach: Let's face it. The beach is the reason people flock to this area to spend their time and money. Miles and miles of white sand, tons of sunshine. They don't call it the "Redneck Riviera" for nothing. This is a true Florida beach destination, as good as Daytona or Fort Lauderdale, with dozens of rentals available for jet skis, miniature golf, restaurants, motels, arcades, fishing charters, snorkeling and scuba gear, and, of course, the beach.

Diving: The water is wonderful and there are numerous shipwrecks for scuba diving. Check these places on Panama City Beach: Dive Locker, (850) 230-8006; Diver's Den, (850) 234-8717; Down Time Diver Charters, (850) 896-DIVE; and Panama City Dive Center, (850) 235-3390. There are diving and snorkeling opportunities in St. Andrews State Park, too.

Restaurants

30 Degree Blue, 3900 Marriott Drive, Suite G, Panama City; (850) 236-1115; www.30 degreeblue.com. "Casual fine dining" means somewhere between bathing suits and ties. Dinner only.

Lady Anderson Dining Yacht, 5550 North Lagoon Drive, Panama City; (850) 234-5940; www.ladyanderson.com. Only $44.50 for the adult dinner/dance cruise.

Schooners, 5121 Gulf Drive, Panama City; (850) 235-3555; www.schooners.com. Calls itself the "Last Local Beach Club." Open every day "from 11:00 in the morning till the wee, wee hours of the night." Music. Casual. Sunsets. More beer than you can drink . . . at least in one night.

Sonny's Real Pit Bar-B-Q, 2400 Saint Andrews Boulevard, Panama City; (850) 763-5114; www.sonnysbbq.com. This barbecue is Southern-style.

Accommodations

The Pensione at Rosemary Beach, 78 Main Street, Panama City Beach; (850) 231-1790; www.rosemarybeach.com. An eight-room "European bed and breakfast" with an emphasis on "European simplicity just steps away from the beach."

Sugar Beach Inn, 3501 East Scenic Highway 30A, Seagrove Beach; (850) 231-1577; www.sugarbeachinn.com. Five "Victorian-inspired" rooms, all with full baths. No pets. It's halfway to Fort Walton Beach driving west.

Sunset Inn, 8109 Surf Drive, Panama City Beach; (850) 234-7370 or (888) 275-1205; http://yp.bellsouth.com/sites/sunsetinnfl/. On the beach with a view. Rates vary by time of year.

Bike Shops

Po Man's Bike Shop, 430 School Avenue, Panama City; (850) 522-6601.

Steve's Bike Shop, 1926 West 23rd Street, Panama City; (850) 769-6808; www.steves bike.com.

Restrooms

There are no public facilities along this route, so you must ferret out the private WCs. This route is in-town suburban riding and there are many places of business with restrooms.

Maps

DeLorme: Florida Atlas & Gazetteer: Page 46 C 3.

5 St. Joseph Bay Cruise

This is not a beautiful ride: It is a magnificently beautiful ride. For much of the time, you will be riding on narrow peninsulas with vistas of the Gulf of Mexico or St. Joseph Bay. All roads are two-lane, and toward the end of the state park, the road narrows to a single lane.

Start: The parking area of Constitution Convention Museum State Park adjacent to U.S. Highway 98/County Road 30 in the old town of Port St. Joe.
Length: 51.8 miles, but there are many side roads, variations, and start-stop points that make this a flexible biking experience.

Terrain: Flat.
Traffic and hazards: The short stretch along US 98 can be very busy, depending upon the day and time, and CR 30 is two-lane and narrow. Alert riding, especially when the scenery is elegant, is always advised.

Getting there: This ride along the Gulf of Mexico can most easily be reached by taking exit 142 on Interstate 10 and driving south on State Road 71 until it dead-ends on US 98 on the Gulf in Port St. Joe. The beginning of the ride will then be a few blocks left (east).

Beginning in Port St. Joe, this ride is centered in what some consider Florida's "forgotten coast." Residents of the region should consider themselves lucky. They still have spectacular views of wide Gulf waters and virtually unlimited free access to unspoiled white "sugar sand" beaches.

Port St. Joe is an old town sheltered by St. Joseph Peninsula. Study it on the map and it is like a southern mirror image of Cape Cod. The St. Joe peninsula is thinner, more delicate, but a ride along it and then to the Indian Pass area of Indian Lagoon is filled with as much charm as one can expect on a bicycle in the Sunshine State.

A significant portion of this ride around the elbow of Cape San Blas and then north on St. Joseph Peninsula offers picturesque views of the bay on one side and sand dunes topped with waving sea oats on the other. This leads directly to St. Joseph Peninsula State Park; only the "lower," or southern, 2 miles are lightly developed with beaches and camping areas. The "upper," or northern, 7.5 miles are a designated wilderness area, accessed on foot or by kayak. The park offers tent, RV, and primitive camping and has a few cabins for rent as well. Snorkeling, swimming, and fishing are high on the to-do list . . . once you have finished your ride.

Florida's scalloping season runs from June 1 to September 10, and the St. Joseph Bay area is prime for scooping up these delicacies. Here you can wade into the water and swim to snatch the scuttling bivalves, or snorkel from your kayak. Baked or just microwaved in butter, these are the original "u-pick" seafood. If you have not chased scallops before, you may doubt that shellfish can run from you. That's why a swim with snorkel, fishing license, and net bag is a must-do.

The high, shifting white dunes on the peninsula are nature's buffer between the ocean and the land. A major effort is being made statewide to preserve the remaining dunes, keeping people and pets off of them, from casual tourists picking the now-rare sea oats to developers who would prefer to build on them. Consequently, wooden boardwalks are common here and along much of Florida's fragile coastline. Boardwalks help people access the beach without destroying the dunes and the dune ecosystem of shy rabbits, snakes that feed on them, and nesting shorebirds. The coastal communities along this section of Florida are alive with white-tailed deer, fish eagles and kites, and doves and mockingbirds, and you can see them at almost any time of year. Of course, there are also cranes and herons galore, all visible from your spinning bicycle.

At the eastern end of the ride is Indian Pass and the Indian Peninsula, where you will be treated to a fine view of St. Vincent Island, a barrier island that is now a national wildlife refuge. St. Vincent is loaded with alligators, white-tailed deer, and migratory birds, and an interesting exotic deer species not native to the United States, the sambar deer. This sturdy Asian deer species is not the only animal that is exotic on the island, as it also boasts populations of armadillos, coyotes, domestic cats, and feral old-world swine as well as one exotic fish, the ever-popular carp.

A ride during the late summer and fall needs to take into account the instability of weather that produces hurricanes. While that may generally be true of any coastal zone in the Southeast, it is especially true of this Gulf Coast region because its low elevation makes it prone to extreme flooding and real battering from wind and water. (An interesting map of hurricanes that have affected Florida since 1970 can be found at www.environmentaldefense.org/article.cfm?contentid=5363&campaign=486.)

CR 30, by the way, is a bit narrow both on the mainland and on the respective peninsulas. Be alert to traffic and realize that drivers in coastal zones may often be distracted—as, indeed, you may be—by the views of white sand, sparkling water and salt marsh, soaring eagles, and brown dune rabbits. Ride safely and defensively.

Miles and Directions

0.0 Turn left (south) from the beginning of this ride in the parking area of Constitution Convention Museum State Park onto US 98/CR 30.

1.0 Veer right onto CR 30A.

7.7 Turn right on Cape San Blas Road/CR 30E.

16.5 Pay $1 (cyclists) at the entrance to T. H. Stone Memorial St. Joseph Peninsula State Park and continue straight on the park road.

19.5 The road forks here. Take the left fork for a quick cruise through the camping area or the right, longer fork, a single-lane road to the end of the pavement and a locked gate.

◄ *Florida's Gulf Coast offers wonderful opportunities for outdoors enthusiasts. At day's end a fisherman brings his kayak to shore in St. Joseph Peninsula State Park.*

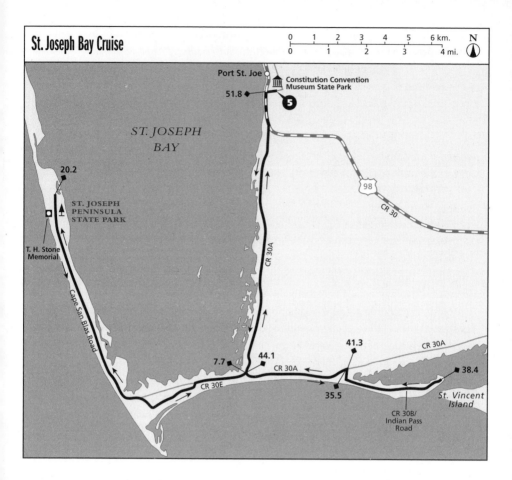

St. Joseph Bay Cruise

20.2 Turn around at the locked gate and return south and then east through the park on CR 30E.

32.7 At the stop sign, take the shallow right turn—you will still be going east—at this intersection of Cape San Blas Road with CR 30A.

35.5 Turn right (south) on CR 30B/Indian Pass Road.

38.4 Turn around at the end of this peninsula and return along Indian Pass Road.

41.3 Turn left (west) on CR 30A.

44.1 Follow CR 30A north at this sharp right turn. (Cape San Blas Road continues west).

51.8 Turn right (east) into the parking area of Constitution Convention Museum State Park.

Local Information

Gulf County Chamber of Commerce, 155 Capt. Fred's Place, Port St. Joe; (850) 227-1223 or -9684; www.gulfchamber.org.

Gulf County Sheriff's Department, 1000 Cecil G. Costin Senior Boulevard, Port St. Joe; (850) 227-1115 or (850) 639-5717; www.gulfsheriff.com.

Gulf County Tourist Development Council, (850) 229-7800 or (800) 482-GULF; www.visitgulf.com.

Local Events/Attractions

Constitution Convention Museum State Park, 200 Allen Memorial Way, Port St. Joe; (850) 229-8029; www.floridastateparks.org /constitutionconvention/default.cfm. Landscaped 14 acres and a museum.

St. Vincent National Wildlife Refuge, PO Box 447, Apalachicola, FL 32329; (850) 653-8808; www.fws.gov/saintvincent. Undeveloped, this is how the entire coastline could look: hunting, fishing, birding, hiking, canoeing, and wildlife in the dunes and swamps of this coastal treasure. Look for sambar deer. Take the ferry and enjoy.

T. H. Stone Memorial St. Joseph Peninsula State Park, 8899 Cape San Blas Road, Port St. Joe; (850) 227-1327; www.floridastate parks.org/stjoseph. Nine miles of white sugar sand, camping, cabins, fishing, snorkeling, swimming . . . what's not to like?

Restaurants

Amanda's Bistro, 2904 US 98, Suite 3A, Mexico Beach; (850) 648-5102. Breakfast, lunch, and dinner Tuesday through Saturday. Friday and Saturday dinner by reservation. Ten miles west of Port St. Joe on US 98.

Billy Bowlegs Grill and Grog, 108 1st Street, Port St. Joe; (850) 227-3500.

Indian Pass Raw Bar, 8391 CR 30A, Port St. Joe; (850) 227-1670.

Loggerhead Grill, 980 Cape San Blas Road, Port St. Joe; (850) 229-9703. Open for dinner Wednesday through Monday.

Sisters', 236 Reid Avenue, Port St. Joe; (850) 229-7121.

Accommodations

MainStay Suites, 3951 East US 98, Port St. Joe; (850) 229-6246. It is outside of town, east on US 98.

Port Inn Hotel, 501 Monument Avenue, Port St. Joe; (850) 229-7678; www.portinnfl.com. Each of the twenty-one rooms is a little different. Friendly staff. View of the Gulf.

Whispering Pines of Cape San Blas, 1177 Cape San Blas Road, Port St. Joe; (850) 227-7252; www.capesanblas.com/whispine. Fully equipped cottages.

Bike Shops

There are no bike shops in the Port St. Joe vicinity. The closest are in Panama City. Try **Steve's Bike Shop** at 1926 West 23rd Street, Panama City; (850) 769-6808; www.steves bike.com.

Restrooms

Mile 18.4: Visitor center, St. Joseph Peninsula State Park.

Maps

DeLorme: Florida Atlas & Gazetteer: Pages 59 B-C 2-3, 60 C 1-2.

6 Bridges of Apalachicola Ramble

This is a splendid ride—one of the finest in Florida—and it is mostly over water on bridges with high center spans to accommodate sailboats with high masts. Below, in Apalachicola Bay, notice the oystermen wielding long, heavy tongs scraping the bay bottom for oysters. The old town of Apalachicola is picturesque and the beaches on St. George Island are exactly what you imagine for an exquisite Florida vacation.

Start: In one of the public parking lots on St. George Island, which is in the Gulf of Mexico, just off the coast of Florida's Panhandle, immediately south of Eastpoint and Apalachicola and southwest of Tallahassee.
Length: A 22.4-mile loop, a there-and-back-again ride.
Terrain: Flat, except that the bridges have high center spans.

Traffic and hazards: This is all two-lane riding. The Bryant Grady Patton Bridge over Apalachicola Bay/St. George Sound has wide turnoff/emergency lanes on both sides; the emergency lanes on the older John Gorrie Memorial Bridge are narrower. In either case, these emergency lanes tend to be littered and this warrants cautious riding.

Getting there: Franklin County is located on the Gulf of Mexico in North Florida's panhandle, 80 miles southwest of Tallahassee. Apalachicola and Eastpoint are accessible via U.S. Highway 98/319, which runs east-west along the Gulf Coast. St. George Island is due south of Eastpoint.

Psychiatrists and biological geneticists report that we humans, of whatever race, family, or nationality, are more similar than we are different. After all, we have a common point of origin. So it should be no surprise that such things as food preferences or housing styles, which we imagine are as wide as the earth itself, are actually rather narrowly defined within cultural and geographic groups. Dreams fall into a narrow category as well.

I have dreamed that I could fly. Chances are that you have had similar dreams. Slipping the bonds of gravity, we soar free of the earth, gliding above the surface of the material world like birds. Sometimes in these dream states, we struggle to stay airborne and then sense or feel regret when the dream ends and we wake in bed.

On the Apalachicola Bridges Ramble, you will feel as though you have taken off into a dream, soaring above a world of water.

From St. George Island in the Gulf of Mexico, begin this pedal traveling north over the $71-million 4.1-mile Bryant Grady Patton Bridge, constructed less than ten years ago. This curving bridge separates, at least on maps, the waters of Apalachicola Bay from St. George Sound and connects the island with the mainland. The center span is nosebleed high, and it is sufficiently distant from the rippled water below to give one a feeling of vertigo, that eerie sense of being drawn over the edge.

Rest on your bike for a moment on the top of the center span of this two-lane bridge, and before you is an unbroken sweep of water for miles in almost all direc-

Riding uphill, this young cyclist seems to be taking the high span over St. George Sound in stride. Anglers use the old bridge in the distance behind him.

tions, except due north toward the mainland. The pull-off lanes on either side are sufficiently wide to allow stopping for a few minutes without excessive worry about being clipped by traffic (total bridge width is 44 feet).

In the shallows you may see licensed oystermen using large tongs to scrape the bottom of the bay for the justifiably famous Apalachicola oysters. In an electronic world, the collection process is somewhat primitive, though: one man, alone in a small, open boat wielding a pair of homemade wooden tongs that must be 18 feet long. It is hard work, but the manner of harvest is designed to preserve the resource.

Difficult as this work seems, the wild natural oyster beds are quite fragile. On one side, they are continually hammered by hurricanes and on the other, by increasing consumer demand. So in the Apalachicola area, one can watch as oysters are harvested, and then suck down (Does one chew an oyster? Or grits?) a couple dozen freshly shucked bivalves in a bayside restaurant where the brew is cold and the breeze is steady.

After a mile of curving two-lane on the mainland, exit west onto the causeway leading to the 4-mile John Gorrie Memorial Bridge. This bridge is named for the physician who, in 1851, received the first patent for mechanical refrigeration. A

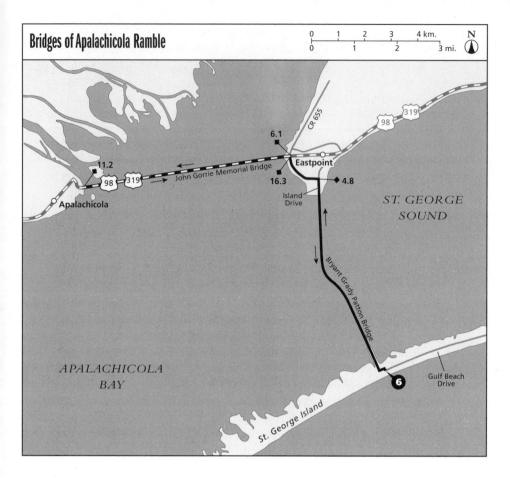

museum/state park is dedicated to the good doctor in Apalachicola, where he lived for much of his life.

Gorrie did not one day decide to invent air-conditioning and get rich. His interest in "conditioned air," meaning cooler air, came about as a result of his concern for patients suffering from the region's frequent epidemics of malaria and yellow fever in the nineteenth century. He observed that cooler temperatures seemed to moderate the effects of these diseases—which were thought to be caused by foul airs released as vegetation decayed—and built a machine that made ice to cool the air in his infirmary. A decade before the Civil War, this was an amazing accomplishment for an unknown country doctor from Apalachicola (even though it was at that time a busy, cotton-exporting seaport).

The bridge named for Gorrie is older than the Bryant Grady Patton Bridge, and narrower, so an additional dose of vigilance is advisable. I rode these bridges in both directions and found the side lanes of the Gorrie Bridge to be cluttered with gravel, fast-food trash, and miscellaneous auto scrap. Do be careful.

The view from the high span of the Gorrie Bridge includes the Apalachicola River and the old town itself. Watch for birds as you come sweeping down off the high span into this lovely little town and remember that you are not flying after all, but riding. This is such a sweet ride, though, that you may have to pinch yourself to make sure you are not dreaming and that a tiny slice of "old Florida" still exists.

Miles and Directions

0.0   Turn right (or perhaps left, depending upon the parking lot) out of the public parking lot onto Gulf Beach Drive, which is on the beach on St. George Island.

0.1   Turn left (north) on Franklin Boulevard, which is the approach to Bryant Grady Patton Bridge, the bridge that will carry you across Apalachicola Bay/St. George Sound.

0.6   At this point the southern causeway ends and you are officially over water.

4.8   You are over the northern causeway and on Island Drive.

5.1   Veer left (west) onto County Road 655/South Bay Shore Drive. This two-lane road bends to the north.

6.1   Turn left (west) onto U.S. Highway 98/319.

6.9   The eastern causeway ends and, again, you are over water, this time on the John Gorrie Memorial Bridge.

11.2   Circle the Franklin County Courthouse at 34 Forbes Street and return east on US 98/319 over the Gorrie Bridge.

16.3   Turn right (south) onto CR 655/South Bay Shore Drive.

17.3   Veer right (south again) onto Island Drive, which takes you to the Bryant Grady Patton Bridge and then to Franklin Boulevard.

22.4   Arrive in the parking areas on St. George Island.

Local Information

Apalachicola Bay Chamber of Commerce & Visitor Center, 122 Commerce Street, Apalachicola; (850) 653-9419; www.apalachicolabay.org. **Franklin County Sheriff's Department**, 270 State Road 65, Eastpoint; (850) 670-8500; www.franklinsheriff.com.

Local Events/Attractions

Constitution Convention Museum State Park, 200 Allen Memorial Way, Port St. Joe; (850) 229-8029; www.floridastateparks.org /constitutionconvention/default.cfm. Celebrates the times and events as Florida's people marched toward statehood.

Dr. Julian G. Bruce St. George Island State Park, 1900 East Gulf Beach Drive, St. George Island; (850) 927-2111; www.floridastate parks.org/stgeorgeisland/default.cfm. The best of swimming, fishing, boating, and relaxing on Florida's Forgotten Coast.

John Gorrie Museum State Park, 46 Sixth Street, Apalachicola; (850) 653-9347; www.floridastateparks.org/johngorriemuseum /default.cfm.

Restaurants

Caroline's River Dining and Boss Oyster are affiliated with Apalachicola River Inn, 123 Water Street, Apalachicola; (850) 653-8139; www.apalachicolariverinn.com. Caroline's features seafood and serves breakfast, lunch, and dinner seven days a week. Boss Oyster is an oyster bar but also serves pasta dishes and casual fare.

Tamara's Cafe Floridita, 17 Avenue East, Apalachicola; (850) 653-4111; www.tamaras cafe.com. Florida flavors with South American flair.

That Place on 98, 500 US 98, Eastpoint; (850) 670-9898; www.thatplaceon98.net. On the bay for seafood lunches and dinners.

Accommodations

Apalachicola River Inn, 123 Water Street, Apalachicola; (850) 653-8139; www.apalachicolariverinn.com. Downtown, with rates from $95 to $150 per night.

Gibson Inn, 51 Avenue C, Apalachicola; (850) 653-2191; www.gibsoninn.com. Tin roof, wraparound porches, thirty guest rooms, bar, and restaurant. Pet friendly.

St. George Inn, 135 Franklin Boulevard, East-point; (850) 927-2903 or (800) 824-0416; www.stgeorgeinn.com. Wraparound verandas, new pool, and great views of the beach.

Bike Shops

The closest bike shops to the Apalachicola/Eastpoint/St. George Island area are in Panama City (60 miles west) and Tallahassee (65 miles northeast).

Restrooms

Mile 0.0: Beach kiosks adjacent to the parking areas on St. George Island.

Mile 11.2: The Franklin County Courthouse in Apalachicola from about 8:00 a.m. to 5:00 p.m. Monday through Friday.

Maps

DeLorme: Florida Atlas & Gazetteer: Pages 61 C 1, 60 C 3.

7 Two Egg Cruise

This is a great ride through the country, a country that folks from New York and Los Angeles consider "flyover land" because there is "nothing there." Well, they just might be surprised at the spacious beauty and fresh air that abounds in this slice of "empty space."

Start: The parking area of Three Rivers State Park, 2 miles north of the intersection of U.S. Highway 90 and County Road 271 in Sneads.
Length: A 44.7-mile loop.

Terrain: Flat to gently rolling.
Traffic and hazards: Little to none except on US 90, which can be busy.

Getting there: Take exit 158 north from Interstate 10 onto County Road 286 and drive 7 miles north to US 90 in Sneads. Turn left (west), drive a few blocks, and turn right (north) at the flashing yellow light onto CR 271. It is about 2.5 miles to Three Rivers State Park and the beginning of the ride.

Are you searching for lonely back roads with long straightaways and very little traffic? If so, do not neglect riding in the least populated region of Florida, that thin, ,east–west slice of the Panhandle north of I-10 essentially, from U.S. Highway 301 west of Jacksonville to the Alabama border.

Almost halfway between Jacksonville and Mobile, Alabama, the Two Egg Cruise is undiscovered from start to finish. And yes, the ride actually rolls through a hamlet called Two Egg, supposedly so named for children who bartered eggs for candy

His name is Bob Carter, or CrazyManOnABike.com. We stopped along U.S. Highway 90 in Florida's Panhandle for a friendly chat even though we were riding in opposite directions.

when cash was scarce. Two Egg is in Jackson County in the central time zone and, except for its curious name, is of no particular commercial or social interest . . . except to the few hundred area residents and their extended families.

The star of this ride—and it is reminiscent of the ride up the east side of the Okefenokee Swamp—is its solitude, and that begins almost as soon as one exits Three Rivers State Park. In the first 5 miles, marsh and lakefront predominate, and there are anglers and birds aplenty. After that, however, although you ride parallel and close to the Chattahoochee River, you will not see that arm of the artificially impounded Lake Seminole and your ride is country through-and-through.

Florida has a reputation for outstanding state parks, and Three Rivers is a good one even though it does not have a fort or a pretty beach or a summer pageant. Three Rivers is situated on Lake Seminole, the very spot where Florida's border suddenly lurches due north for 20 miles, before continuing its ruler-straight march to the Perdido River and the great state of Alabama.

Three Rivers is all about camping and fishing and boating and hunting, because

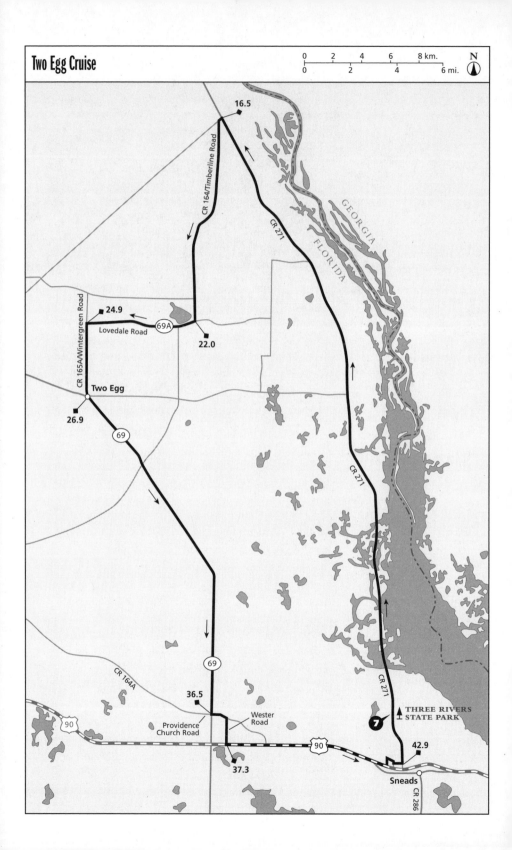

Two Egg Cruise

0 2 4 6 8 km.
0   2   4   6 mi.

N

16.5

CR 164/Timberline Road

CR 271

GEORGIA
FLORIDA

24.9

Lovedale Road

69A

CR 165A/Wintergreen Road

22.0

Two Egg

26.9

69

CR 271

69

CR 164A

36.5

Providence
Church Road

Wester
Road

90

37.3

90

7

THREE RIVERS
STATE PARK

CR 271

42.9

Sneads

CR 286

although three rivers do flow south into the lake—the Chattahoochee, the Flint, and Spring Creek—only one flows south from the dam: the Apalachicola. And the waters of the Apalachicola/Chattahoochee are the boundary between the eastern and central time zones. And lest it be misunderstood among snickers about catfish (a delicious, firm white meat without an oily fish flavor) or bream (also called red bellies and sunnies or occasionally mistaken for crappies), the king of fish in these parts is the largemouth bass. Every one of the hundreds of thousands of fishing boats being trailered to Florida and Georgia lakes and rivers is after "lunker" bass—big bass, sow-belly bass—the 15- or 20-pound females of that species capable of pulling a careless angler right out of his boat.

Ninety-nine percent of this ride is on long stretches of trafficless two-lane. Take plenty of water and do not let the whir of your tires on the roadway dull your sensibilities to the occasional speeding pickup truck. The 5 miles of east–west ride on US 90 west of the town of Sneads does have sufficient traffic to make you pay attention, but there are also paved shoulders there.

Look for acres of peanuts and cantaloupe and watermelon. Look for distinctive types of cattle. Enjoy the lonely solitude available on these long roads. Similar to the ride around the Suwannee River, if you are in trouble, people will help you and not ask for money. If you become lost, people will give you directions, even offer to put your bicycle in the back of their pickup and drive you to the route, no charge, just glad to help, thanks. It is quiet and a little lonely, the way life ought to be, and it won't last long, so ride and then get a fishing license. See what you can catch.

Miles and Directions

0.0 Begin by turning right out of Three Rivers State Park onto CR 271.

16.5 Turn left (west) on County Road 164/Timberline Road. The road bends due south almost immediately.

22.0 Bend right (west) on State Road 69A/Lovedale Road.

24.9 Turn left (south) at the intersection with County Road 165A/Wintergreen Road.

26.9 Turn left (southeast) on SR 69 in Two Egg.

36.5 Turn left (east) on CR 164A/Providence Church Road.

36.6 Turn right (south) on Wester Road.

37.3 Turn left (east) on US 90, at this point a four-lane divided highway.

39.1 US 90 narrows to two lanes.

42.1 Turn left (north) on Gay Avenue. After 2 blocks turn right (east) on Jenkins Street, after another 2 blocks turn right (south) on DeSoto Avenue, then make an immediate left (east) on Sherry Street.

42.9 Turn left (north) on River Road/CR 271.

44.7 Turn right (east) into Three Rivers State Park and cycle to the parking area.

Local Information

Jackson County Chamber of Commerce, 4318 Lafayette Street, Marianna; (850) 482-8060; http://jacksoncounty.com.

Jackson County Sheriff's Department, 4012 Lafayette Street, Marianna; (850) 482-9624; www.jcsheriff.com.

Capital City Cyclists, www.cccyclists.org.

Local Events/Attractions

There are no events or attractions in the immediate area except fishing on Lake Seminole.

Chipola College, 3094 Indian Circle, Marianna; (850) 526-2761; www.chipola.edu.

Florida Caverns State Park, 3345 Caverns Road, Marianna; (850) 482-9598; www.floridastateparks.org/floridacaverns. One of Florida's most magnificent state parks—in a string of magnificent parks. Stalactites! A dry cave system, the only caves open to the public in the Panhandle.

Restaurants

Homeplace Restaurant, 415 West Washington Street, Chattahoochee; (850) 663-4040.

Parramore Restaurant, 8141 US 90, Sneads; (850) 593-0138.

There are three additional tiny restaurants in Sneads—Pappy Tom's, Shoe Strang's, and Lighthouse Café.

Accommodations

Admiral Benbow Morgan Lodge, 116 East Washington Street, Chattahoochee; (850) 663-4336 or (800) 451-1986; www.admiralbenbowmorganlodge.com.

Hinson House Bed & Breakfast, 4338 Lafayette Street, Marianna; (850) 526-1500; http://phonl.com/hinson_house/. A refurbished bungalow in Marianna, about 20 miles west of Sneads on US 90.

Seminole Lodge & Marina, 2360 Legion Road, Sneads; (850) 593-6886; www.seminolelodge.com. Campground, modest room rates, and pets welcome.

Bike Shops

The closest bike shops are in Tallahassee.

Higher Ground Bicycle Shop, 3185 Capital Circle NE, Tallahassee; (850) 562-2453.

Sunshine Cycles, 2784 Capital Circle NE, Tallahassee; (850) 422-1075; www.bikesunshine.net.

Tec's Bicycle Sport, 672 West Gaines Street, Tallahassee; (850) 224-1122.

University Cycles—Tallahassee, 668 West Gaines Street, Tallahassee; (850) 222-1665; www.universitycyclesoftallahassee.com.

Restrooms

Other than the restrooms at Three Rivers State Park, there are no public facilities along this ride. There are plenty of woods and deserted highway, however. . . .

Maps

DeLorme: Florida Atlas & Gazetteer: Page 32 A-B-C 2-3.

8 Quincy Cruise

Only 15 miles west of Florida's growing state capital and two major universities, you can still enjoy one of the finest country cruises in the South. Wind through fields and farms, with stretches of quiet open countryside—and just enough hills—alternating with enormous live oaks draped with Spanish moss and, in the spring, mounds of pink and white azalea blossoms.

Start: The parking lot of Midway City Hall, 2.1 miles from the intersection of Interstate 10 and U.S. Highway 90 exit 192 west of Tallahassee. City Hall is on the south side of US 90 at the intersection of Martin Luther King Boulevard.

Length: A 37-mile loop.

Terrain: Flat to gently rolling countryside with an occasional easy hill.

Traffic and hazards: Traffic is moderate on this loop, and the pavement alternates between tight two-lane roads with no shoulder and spacious two-lanes with paved shoulders. Most riders out early on weekend mornings should miss the weekday-morning commuter traffic into Tallahassee entirely.

Getting there: This ride begins 2.1 miles west of the intersection of I-10 and US 90 (exit 192), a dozen miles west of Tallahassee. Turn or continue west on US 90, a four-lane divided highway. Midway City Hall will be on your left, on the south side of the highway, a relatively new but unpretentious single-story brick building across from a convenience store/gas station at the intersection of US 90 and Martin Luther King Boulevard.

You will not finish this ride sitting on the fence. You will love it.

On the plus side, the countryside is pleasant, with broad views of farms and livestock in pastures; and miles unroll beneath the shade of enormous spreading oaks hung with Spanish moss. It is picturesque, this slice of old Florida. Tobacco grows here and old wooden barns dot the farmsteads. Of course, this countryside is also in transition. The suburbs of Tallahassee have begun to creep west with charming suburban names like Falcon Heights, Blueberry Glenn, and Gnarly Hill Ridge.

This loop is a chance to experience the essence of the nineteenth-century South before it disappears, because northwest Florida—called "the Panhandle"—and South Florida are a very different species, and this ride reflects that.

Midway has made the transition to the twenty-first century, but you will be in and out before you recognize it. A little town without a specific center, it is scattered through a couple miles of pine trees and sandy oak hammocks, born between the interstate and a U.S. highway. When you cross US 90 and pedal north along Dover Road, be attentive to the roar of traffic. In Midway that roar becomes a part of the background, more familiar than the song of a cicada or the drumming of rain on the roof.

This route into the country does not go to Havana—the one in Florida, not the one in Cuba—although you could extend it by 4 miles and make that loop by staying on Dover Road north to U.S. Highway 27. (To rejoin the route, you would simply slip out of town west on State Road 12.) Havana is a small town with a lot happening. A bona fide antiques and art mecca with parades and fireworks and bead festivals and a slow but emotionally moving lawn mower parade. A unique and picturesque small town that still works, even though it is only 15 miles from Tallahassee and suburban development can be spotted in the surrounding countryside like a drop of paratroopers scattered by wind.

Traffic will be light on Shady Rest, Post Plant, and Woodward Roads. If the day promises to be hot, as most Florida days do from mid-April through October, you may be happy to slow down in Quincy, the county seat of Gadsden County, for a leisurely pedal through its historic district. After a cup of joe and a donut at Reynolds Donut Shop on North Madison (Monday through Friday 5:30 a.m. to 3:00 p.m., Saturday 5:30 a.m. to noon; closed Sunday), you can walk around the beautifully preserved courthouse and pay homage at the memorial to Gadsden's fallen Confederate heroes of the War Between the States.

As an aside, Gadsden County was home to dozens of families who purchased stock in Coca-Cola in the early 1900s and became wealthy by virtue of its explosive popularity. One estimate suggests that sixty-seven such families became millionaires and that, at one time, more stock in this beverage was held in the Quincy area than in the rest of the United States combined!

With 7,000 residents, Quincy is the largest town on the route, and it can be congested, illustrating an irreversible dynamic at work in Florida. The vigorous life and business structure along US 90, with its fast-paced traffic, contrasts vividly with the quiet charm of historic district bed-and-breakfast inns.

US 90 is the principal east–west corridor through Quincy and the county. Once you cross it in the very heart of town, be extra wary for several blocks until you break free of traffic and commercial intersections, as the several blocks south of that highway may be the most hectic along the route.

The swing from Quincy south and east to Midway is an easy pedal. Woods, planted pines, grazing dairy goats, and the ever-present signs advertising backhoe work and stump grinding. You will pass north of Lake Talquin State Recreation Area, which is well worth a visit for a picnic and cool swim. Enjoy the woods and the miles of planted pines, row by row, but there is no reason to speed through this last leg, except for the last half mile, which abruptly turns 90 degrees left (north) and crosses a railroad track in a semi-intersection in Midway (ride carefully through the sand and gravel at this intersection). Enjoy this slice of old Florida—and please see it before it becomes a suburb of the state capital.

◀ *The Quincy Cruise takes in some of Florida's loveliest country terrain and features a number of authentic hills!* PHOTO COURTESY OF GADSEN COUNTY TOURISM DEVELOPMENT

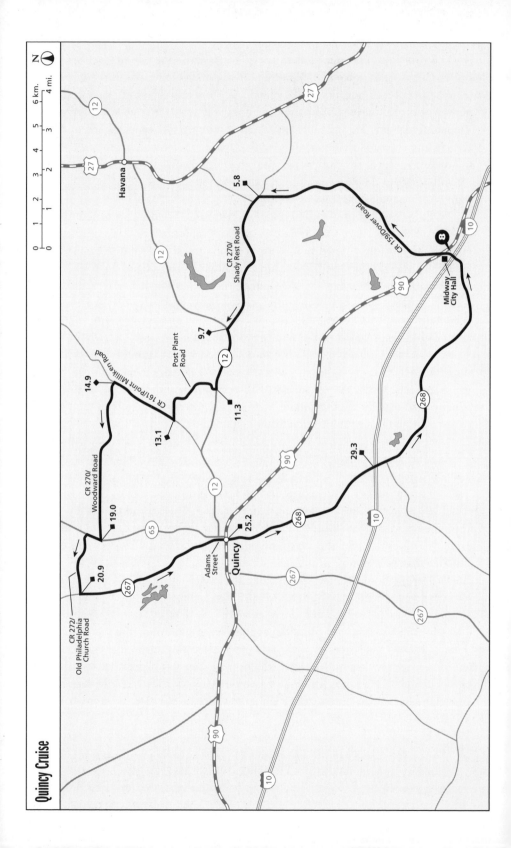

Quincy Cruise

Miles and Directions

0.0 From the Midway City Hall parking lot, ride north across US 90 onto County Road 159 (Dover Road). This intersection is dangerous. Traffic is fast and caution here is advised, but once you are on CR 159 north, traffic will be light.

5.8 At the stop sign, turn left (west) on County Road 270 (Shady Rest Road).

9.7 At this stop sign, also turn left (west) on SR 12 (Havana Highway), a wider road with paved shoulders.

11.3 Turn right (north) after only 1.6 miles onto a narrow, twisting, but shady road without shoulders. This is Post Plant Road. It will appear suddenly; the street sign may not be standing so watch your odometer. (If you miss this turn, go straight 1.8 miles and turn right on County Road 161. You will only have added a mile to the route.)

13.1 At the stop sign, turn right (northeast) onto CR 161, called Point Milliken Road.

14.9 Take a left (west) onto CR 270, now called Woodward Road.

19.0 At the dead end and stop sign, turn right (north) on State Road 65.

19.3 Turn left (west) onto County Road 272, Old Philadelphia Church Road.

20.9 Turn left (south) at the stop sign onto State Road 267. This road takes you into Quincy, the county seat of Gadsden County. Just before town the road narrows suddenly and veers steeply, but briefly, uphill. In Quincy this becomes North Adams Street.

25.2 At the traffic light at US 90, the picturesque county courthouse will be on your left. SR 267 actually jogs briefly west on US 90 before continuing south, but you will forge straight ahead on South Adams Street, through this small town's congestion zone, and emerge from town on State Road 268 (High Bridge Road), which swings gradually to the southeast. Halfway to the interstate overpass, you will cross a railroad track.

29.3 This point marks the overpass over I-10. SR 268 begins to swing due east as it passes north of Lake Talquin and the Lake Talquin State Recreation Area. SR 268 turns sharply left 2.5 miles from the end of the ride. A gravel road meets this elbow-turn from the right, so watch for sand and loose gravel here. You will cross the railroad tracks again just before the end of this ride.

37.0 Arrive at the parking area, which will be on your left.

Local Information

Capital City Cyclists, www.cccyclists.org.

Gadsden County Chamber of Commerce, PO Box 389, Quincy; (850) 627-9231; www.gadsdencc.com.

Gadsden County Sheriff's Department, 339 East Jefferson Street, Quincy; (850) 627-9233.

Gadsden County Tourist Development Council, 208 North Adams Street, Quincy; (850) 627-0344; www.visitgadsden.com.

Midway, Florida, www.midwayfl.com.

Quincy, Florida, www.quincyflorida.com.

Local Events/Attractions

Challenger Learning Center, 200 South Duval Street, Tallahassee; (850) 645-STAR; www.challengertlh.com. Features state-of-the-art space mission simulator, IMAX theater, and domed, high-definition planetarium. A cooperative effort of Florida State and Florida A&M Universities.

Down on the Farm, usually held in November; www.spanishmossproductions.com. Southern bands in three-day festival on 450-acre grassy field perfect for camping. Spreading oaks, pine forest with trails and ponds. Benefits Habitat for Humanity, Gadsden County Board of Education Music Programs, and local food banks.

Havana, Florida: Small town east of the bike trail at the SR 12 intersection with US 27 that's known for its charm and its antiques shops; www.havanaflorida.com.

Restaurants

The Last Cast at Lake Talquin, 3129 Cook's Landing Road, Quincy; (850) 875-2605. Known by locals as "The Whip," this restaurant sits beside picturesque Lake Talquin. Casual dining. Ever-changing menu, but Friday night low-country shrimp boil is popular. Hours: 11:00 a.m. to 9 p.m. Closed Monday. About 20 miles south out of Quincy on SR 267.

Nicholson's Farmhouse Restaurant, 200 Coca Cola Avenue, Havana; (850) 539-5931. Any dinner that begins with boiled peanuts can't be bad. Small-town restaurant consistently praised for hand-cut, aged steaks. Open Tuesday through Saturday 4:00 to 10:00 p.m. Take SR 12 east from Quincy about 12 miles.

Accommodations

Allison House Inn, 215 North Madison Street, Quincy; (850) 875-2511; www.allisonhouse inn.com. Beautiful rooms filled with antiques, plus television and Internet access.

Howard Johnson Express Inn, 56 Fortune Boulevard, Midway; (850) 574-8888. One of several dozen motels along I-10 toward Tallahassee within 30 miles of the start of this ride.

McFarlin Bed & Breakfast, 305 East King Street, Quincy; (850) 875-2526; www .mcfarlinhouse.com. Restored 110-year-old three-story house nestled in the heart of Quincy's historic district.

Bike Shops

All area bicycle shops are east of this ride and south of I-10 in Tallahassee.

Great Bicycle Shop, 1909 Thomasville Road, Tallahassee; (850) 224-7461.

Higher Ground Bicycle Company, 1319 East Tennessee Street, Tallahassee; (850) 942-2453.

Sunshine Cycles, 2784 Capital Circle NE, Tallahassee; (850) 422-1075; www.bike sunshine.net.

Restrooms

Mile 0.0: City of Midway City Hall, 60 Martin Luther King Boulevard, Midway; (850) 574-2355; www.midwayfl.com. Hours: 8:30 a.m. to 5:00 p.m. Monday through Friday. City Hall is on the south side of US 90, 2.1 miles from the intersection of US 90 and I-10. It is also the start of the Quincy Cruise route.

Mile 25.2: Gadsden County Court House, 10 East Jefferson Street, Quincy; (850) 875-8601. Hours: 8:30 a.m. to 5:00 p.m. Monday through Friday.

Maps

DeLorme: Florida Atlas & Gazetteer: Pages 33 D 3-4, 34 D 1, 50 A 1.

9 Florida Flatwoods Classic

This wonderful and awfully flat ride affords marvelous miles of wheeling through several distinct Floridas in what is colloquially known as the "flatwoods." Beginning in one of the most beautiful state parks in Florida's Panhandle, the route comprises a figure eight through sandy countryside to the Gulf of Mexico and back. On the way, expect wonderful views of bays and inlets.

Start: The parking lot near the lodge at Edward Ball Wakulla Springs State Park south of Tallahassee. An alternate start on the same route, if you choose to camp, is Ochlockonee River State Park.

Length: A 73.9-mile figure eight.

Terrain: Flat.

Traffic and hazards: Traffic is light to moderate on most of the state and county roads and in the towns and hamlets through which you will pedal. On holidays and during the summer, traffic can be quite heavy on U.S. Highway 98, which parallels the coast.

Getting there: From Tallahassee, drive due south on State Road 363/61. About 4 miles south of the state capital, stay on SR 61 as it veers left and watch for signs to Wakulla Springs State Park. It is slightly less than 6 miles to the intersection with State Road 267, and then a block east to the entrance.

This ride comprises a figure eight through the countryside south of Tallahassee, the state capital of Florida, to the Gulf of Mexico. Along the way it passes some of the most interesting wild scenery in all of Florida, particularly the two state parks that are the linchpins of the ride: Wakulla Springs and Ochlockonee River.

Indeed, the 73.9 miles chosen for this tour are but a fraction of the great biking available in this region. Although FOR SALE signs are everywhere, people have not yet flocked to this area, but they are on the way and that gives a cycle through this region a special urgency.

The ecological envelope here is referred to as "flatwoods," low pine woods with oak thickets, and once you put two and two together on the ride, you will understand why. Folk wisdom says that if it thunders in the Gulf, the water level in the flatwoods rises. Much of this area, many miles of which are in the Apalachicola National Forest and bordering Tate's Hell State Forest and St. Marks National Wildlife Refuge, is nominally underwater. And there are plenty of alligators and moccasins out there as well.

In the old days, seeing plumes of smoke rise for days on end, apparently from the deep woods, people believed there must be a volcano lost in the dark fastness of the swamp. If you find that volcano, someone will surely come forward with a substantial reward. The smoke was probably caused by a peat fire, which could smolder for weeks and even go underground to flare up again miles away.

Florida is a wonderland for bird-watchers. This yellow-crowned night heron politely posed on its way to lunch in the flatwoods. PHOTO BY DAVID SCHINDLER

While the flatwoods is tolerable on a warm spring day (until the mosquitoes come out), you would not want to be here during a hurricane (hurricane season officially begins June 1). Storms come ashore along the Florida Panhandle with depressing frequency, although ground zero for nasty blows is typically a little farther west, from Panama City to Pensacola. One of these big storms hits and the flatwoods for a hundred miles in all directions is neck-deep in sharks . . . and this land doesn't drain all that fast, either. During a hurricane, the quaint little towns along and near your path—Panacea and Sopchoppy, west to Apalachicola and east to Shamrock—can be subject to intense flooding.

Assuming that you have sense enough to stay out of the area when a hurricane is tracking north, the pedaling is great. All of the roads are two-lane, many are well shaded, and the few miles on Jack Crum Road/County Road 375 are ultra-narrow, but traffic is ultralight.

You may experience very heavy traffic on U.S. Highway 98 along the Gulf Coast. And we know that when broad vistas of water come into view, drivers let their attention stray: "Hey, momma, look at that-there water. Shore is purty, ain't it!" (Of course it's pretty, dear. Now keep your eyes on the road!) That is probably no different than biking along Chesapeake Bay, the shores of Lake Superior, or Big Sur,

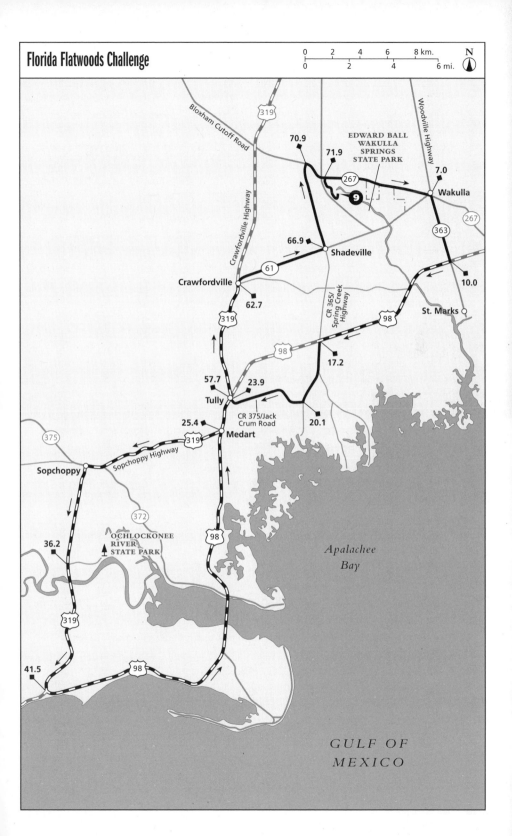

Florida Flatwoods Challenge

so even though the shoulders of US 98 are marked and paved, one must exercise additional traffic awareness and defensive riding.

Outdoor recreation and nature-viewing opportunities in this area are legion, and the myriad of intersecting deserted roads, mostly well paved and only nominally occupied by cars and trucks, are practically infinite, so take a map or GPS. Campers will want to check out Ochlockonee River State Park, and those who prefer a more comfortable evening setting will be pleased with the fine old lodge in Wakulla Springs. From fishing to hunting, hiking, photography, snorkeling, and trekking through the deep woods, you can do it all in this little slice of Florida.

A minor, but not to be ignored, suggestion is to take all-purpose paper (TP, toilet paper) and extra water, because clean facilities, public or private, along this particular route are scarce. While there are plenty of gas stations, their toilets can be rustic, even intimidating. Sometimes a comfortable and private location leaning against a pine tree, even with water oozing around your cycling shoes, is preferable . . . and sometimes it isn't, especially for the double-X chromosomally inclined. Enjoy!

Miles and Directions

0.0 Begin at the parking lot near the lodge in Edward Ball Wakulla Springs State Park and ride the twisting park road to the entrance.

2.0 At the entrance to the state park, turn right (east) on SR 267/Bloxham Cutoff Road.

7.0 Turn right at the intersection with SR 363/Woodville Highway, just a tenth of a mile after crossing the Tallahassee-St. Marks Historic Rail-Trail in the hamlet of Wakulla.

10.0 Turn right (west) on US 98.

17.2 Turn left (south) on CR 365/Spring Creek Highway.

20.1 Turn right (west) on CR 375/Jack Crum Road.

23.9 Turn left (south) on US 98 in the hamlet of Tully.

25.4 Turn right (west) on U.S. Highway 319/State Road 375/Sopchoppy Highway. Stay on US 319, bending south, in the town of Sopchoppy. At 36.2 miles, riders pass the entrance to Ochlockonee River State Park, an alternate start if you choose to camp.

41.5 Veer left to the stop sign and proceed forward and left (east) with caution onto US 98. The Gulf of Mexico is ahead and on your right.

57.7 Turn left (north) onto US 319/SR 61/Crawfordville Highway.

62.7 Veer right (northeast) onto SR 61/Shadeville Road as it separates from US 319 in the town of Crawfordville.

66.9 Turn left (north) on CR 365/Spring Creek Highway.

70.9 Turn right (east) on SR 267/Bloxham Cutoff Road.

71.9 Turn right (south) into the entrance to Edward Ball Wakulla Springs State Park.

73.9 End the ride at the parking lot near the lodge.

Local Information

Franklin County Sheriff's Department, 270 SR 65, Eastpoint; (850) 670-8500; www.franklin countyflorida.com.
Franklin County Tourism Development Council, PO Box 819, Apalachicola, FL 32329; (850) 653-8678; www.franklincountyflorida .com/tdc/.
Wakulla County Sheriff's Office, 15 Oak Street, Crawfordville; (850) 926-0800; www .wcso.org.

Local Events/Attractions

Edward Ball Wakulla Springs State Park, 550 Wakulla Park Drive, Wakulla Springs; (850) 224-5950; www.floridastateparks.org /wakullasprings/. One of largest, deepest freshwater springs in the world, with lots of wildlife, riverboat tours, and a lodge.
Gulf beaches: Secluded and public beaches for swimming and water sports, plus some deep bogs for wildlife viewing and complete serenity. Plenty of rentals available. Begin searching at www.wakullacounty.org/wakulla-37.htm or www.wakullacountyfla.com.
Ochlockonee River State Park, PO Box 5, Sopchoppy, FL 32358; (850) 962-2771; www.floridastateparks.org/ochlockoneeriver /default.cfm. Fishing, boating, and camping in fresh and salt water.
Sopchoppy Worm Gruntin' Festival, www .wakullacounty.org/worm_festival.htm. An early-April weekend festival with musicians, arts and crafts, and worm gruntin'!

Restaurants

Edward Ball Wakulla Springs State Park, 550 Wakulla Park Drive, Wakulla Springs; (850) 224-5950; www.floridastateparks.org/wakulla springs/. Dining in the lodge is a fine experi-ence: three meals a day and fresh seafood.
Hamaknockers BBQ, 3123 Crawfordville High-way, Crawfordville; (850) 926-4737. It's bar-becue—greasy, salty, delicious—and it's right on the route.

Harbor House Restaurant and Lounge, 107 Mississippi Avenue, Panacea; (850) 984-2758.
The Landing, 1168 Coastal Highway, Panacea; (850) 984-4996; www.wakulla.com/Dining _Guide/Dining_Guide/The_Landing _Restaurant_in_Panacea,_Florida _20051219797/. Moderately priced and on the route.

Accommodations

Inn at Wildwood, 3896 Coastal Highway 98, Crawfordville; (850) 926-4455 or (800) 878-1546; www.innatwildwood.com.
Shell Island Fish Camp and Marina, PO Box 115, St. Marks, FL 32355; (850) 925-6226; www.shellislandfishcamp.com. Superbly down-scale!
Sweet Magnolia Bed and Breakfast, 803 Port Leon Drive, St. Marks; (800) 779-5214 or (850) 925-7670; www.sweetmagnolia.com.
Wakulla Springs Lodge in Edward Ball Wakulla Springs State Park, 550 Wakulla Park Drive, Wakulla Springs; (850) 224-5950; www.florida stateparks.org/wakullasprings/Lodge.cfm. The lodge dates from 1937. You can enjoy a fine weekend getaway here.

Bike Shops

Tec's Bicycle Sport, 672 West Gaines Street, Tallahassee; (850) 224-1122.
University Cycles—Tallahassee, 668 West Gaines Street, Tallahassee; (850) 222-1665; www.universitycyclesoftallahassee.com.

Restrooms

Sopchoppy City Hall, 100 Municipal Avenue, Sopchoppy; (850) 926-4611. A block off the route.
There are no public restrooms on this ride except those at the two state parks. Take toilet tissue and remember that venomous snakes are rare in the flatwoods.

Maps

DeLorme: Florida Atlas & Gazetteer: Pages 50 C-D 1-2, 61 A 3 and Inset.

10 Maclay Gardens Cruise

A pleasant ride north of Tallahassee, state capital and university city, that includes urban, suburban, and rural stretches. NOTE: The shortcut on Proctor Road trims the ride by a third.

Start: The parking lot of Alfred B. Maclay Gardens State Park in Tallahassee.
Length: 36.5 miles (alternately, a 23-mile route).
Terrain: Flat to gently rolling.

Traffic and hazards: Make this ride early in the day and traffic problems will be virtually nonexistent. On the eastern end of the ride, traffic is always light; on the western end, it is moderate and can sometimes be heavy.

Getting there: Maclay Gardens State Park is located one-half mile north of Interstate 10 on U.S. Highway 319 in the city of Tallahassee, Florida.

Our ride begins in one of Florida's most beautiful state parks, Alfred B. Maclay Gardens, which is also easily accessible. It is only minutes from downtown Tallahassee, the state capital and center of one of the most active road-biking groups in the Sunshine State, Capital City Cyclists.

Florida is widely recognized as a leader in the development and maintenance of its state park system. According to Florida's Department of Environmental Protection, Florida's state parks are recognized as the nation's best. Many of these parks have trails for both road and off-road riding, and they welcome cyclists who are not "trail terrorists": cyclists who enjoy the trails and ride in harmony with other users, and at safe speeds.

Maclay Gardens is practically downtown, located near one of the heaviest-trafficked intersections in the area. However, on early weekend mornings when you will likely take this ride, traffic will be light. Even here.

One crosses US 319 and leaves, almost immediately, the hectic urban setting of the state park entrance for Ireland . . . or at least roads and golf courses given Irish names: Shannon, Shamrock, Killarney, Killearn, Lake Sheelin, Fern's Glen, Roscommon, and so on. No orange here. Green only.

This first (and last) section of the ride through "Little Ireland" can be confusing, so be sharp. Carry a "cheat sheet" on your handlebars and check a map before pedaling off into the sunrise. Better yet, find someone from Capital City Cyclists and follow them. Once you have turned onto Centerville, however, you will have made a successful transition from urban to suburban to rural. Whew. Cows and corn and FOR SALE signs abound as Tallahassee expands in all directions. The rural ride is wonderful. Many sections of shade. Hills alternating with long flat stretches of highway.

If you have limited time and cannot ride the full 36.5 miles, an abbreviated version, also beginning at Maclay Gardens, can trim about 13 rural miles. It turns left

Florida's disaster-preparedness and -response command center is located just a few miles south of Maclay Gardens in Tallahassee, the state capital.

onto Proctor Road/County Road 0345 rather than right on Crump Road/CR 0345. (As far as I am concerned, you should probably start a short ride by cutting out the urban/suburban section. Begin at the Miccosukee country store, after asking permission to park in their not-so-large lot, and ride the rural two-lane roads. This will give you a 10.4-mile ride west–southwest to the intersection of Centerville and Roberts Roads, and then 12 miles east–south–northeast back to the store.)

Miles and Directions

0.0   Turn left (east) out of the parking lot of Maclay Gardens onto Maclay Road and ride to the stoplight at US 319. Continue straight across as the road name changes to Killarney Way.

1.6   Turn right (east) on Shamrock Street South.

2.8   Turn left (north) on Shamrock Street East. (You will have a tendency to look forward to the larger intersection with Centerville Road/County Road 151; do be careful not to miss this turn.)

3.8   Turn right (northeast) on McLaughlin Drive.

3.9   Turn left (north) on North Shannon Lakes Drive.

Maclay Gardens Cruise

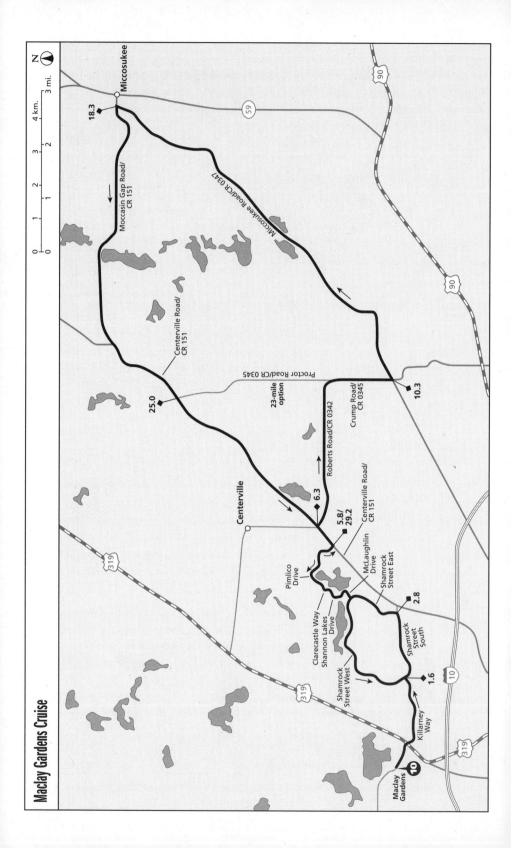

4.2 Turn right (north) on Clarecastle Way.

4.4 Turn right (northeast) on Pimlico Drive and follow it as it winds around the lakes and through the subdivision.

5.8 Turn left (northeast) on Centerville Road/CR 151.

6.3 Turn right (east) on Roberts Road/County Road 0342.

9.2 Turn right (south) onto Crump Road/CR 0345. **Option:** Alternately, for the short ride, turn left and ride north on Proctor Road/CR 0345—the road is named differently from this point, depending upon whether you ride north or south—3.1 miles to the intersection with Centerville Road/CR 151 and turn left. This shortened ride takes you back through the lakes subdivision.

10.3 Turn left (northeast) onto Miccosukee Road/County Road 0347. A little over a mile along Miccosukee, the road turns abruptly to the left. You will not be able to ride straight ahead as the road has been terminated at this point. This is not what is indicated on your Google maps or even in the *DeLorme Atlas*, as it is a recent development.

18.3 Turn left (west) onto Moccasin Gap Road/CR 151. (If you are out of water or just need a break, you may want to turn right to the country crossroads store, which is only a 2-block ride on your left.)

25.0 This point is the intersection with Proctor Road/CR 0345.

29.2 Turn right (north) onto the winding Pimlico Drive.

30.1 Turn left (south) onto Clarecastle Way.

30.3 Turn right (west) onto North Shannon Lakes Drive.

32.4 Continue through the roundabout as the road name changes to West Shannon Lakes Drive.

33.4 Turn left (west) onto Shamrock Street West.

34.9 Turn right (west) onto Killarney Way.

36.5 Arrive at the turn into the parking area at Maclay Gardens.

Local Information

Capital City Cyclists, www.cccyclists.org.
Greater Tallahassee Chamber of Commerce, 100 North Duval Street, Tallahassee; (850) 224-8116; www.talchamber.com.
Leon County Sheriff's Department, 2825 Municipal Way, Tallahassee; (850) 922-3300; http://lcso.leonfl.org.
Tallahassee Visitors Bureau, 106 East Tallahassee Street, Tallahassee; (850) 413-9200; www.visittallahassee.com.

Local Events/Attractions

Alfred B. Maclay Gardens State Park, 3540 Thomasville Road, Tallahassee; (850) 487-4556; www.floridastateparks.org/maclay gardens. Popular for sculptured gardens, blooming from December to April; swimming in Lake Hall, hiking, picnicking.

The Mary Brogan Museum of Art & Science, 350 South Duval Street, Tallahassee; (850) 513-0700; www.thebrogan.org. Art, bones, antiques, and the host of the Florida Wine Festival in April.

Tallahassee Antique Car Museum & Unique Collectibles, 3550A Mahan Drive, Tallahassee; (850) 942-0137; www.tacm.com. Ohhhhhh—they have my 1966 cherry Twister Mustang.

Restaurants

Bradfordville Blues Club, 7152 Moses Lane, Tallahassee; (850) 906-0766; www.bradford villeblues.com. Follow the tiki torches along dirt roads to this unique experience—hot bonfire and cold beer: "jook joint under the stars." Near the route!

Outback Steakhouse, 1820 Diehl Road, Tallahassee; (850) 385-1998; www.outbacksteak house.com. A chain, but you know what you're getting and it is close to Maclay Gardens.

Paradise Grill, 1406 North Meridian Road, Tallahassee; (850) 224-2742; www.paradise grillandbar.com. Supper Saturday, closed Sunday, and otherwise lunch and supper. Music on Friday nights.

Accommodations

Dawson Street Inn, 324 North Dawson Street, Thomasville, GA 31792; (229) 226-7515; http://dawsonstinn.com. It is 150 years old but has a pool and cable TV. Thirty miles north of the ride.

Governor's Inn, 209 South Adams Street, Tallahassee; (850) 681-6855 or (800) 342-7717; www.thegovinn.com. A "boutique hotel" within walking distance of the capitol, the Supreme Court, Florida State University, and the Challenger Learning Center.

Millstone Farms Bed & Breakfast Inn, 3895 Providence Road, Quincy; (850) 627-9400. Located on a working cattle ranch 30 miles west of your ride.

Bike Shops

Higher Ground Bicycle Shop, 3185 Capital Circle NE, Tallahassee; (850) 562-2453.

Sunshine Cycles, 2784 Capital Circle NE, Tallahassee; (850) 422-1075; www.bike sunshine.net.

Restrooms

Public restrooms are located at the beginning and end of this ride at Maclay Gardens State Park.

Maps

DeLorme: Florida Atlas & Gazetteer: Pages 34 D 3, 35 D 1.

11 Chaires Shady Lane Cruise

What a delightful ride through the countryside east of Tallahassee. Gently rolling, even hilly in a few places; shady and cool as well. There is not much traffic on these two-lane roads, and at popular ride times—early on weekend mornings—you ought to see plenty of cyclists.

Start: Waukeenah, a virtually unmarked hamlet east of Tallahassee on U.S. Highway 27/19. There are no public facilities here so find a good place to park and trust that you are among friends.
Length: A 38.1-mile loop.

Terrain: Flat to hilly and often shaded.
Traffic and hazards: These are two-lane country roads with no shoulders or bike lanes. While traffic is light, there are numerous intersections with dirt roads and occasional stray dogs.

Getting there: From the east or west on Interstate 10, take exit 225 onto US 19 and drive south for almost 5 miles to US 27. Turn right (west) and Waukeenah will appear in about 2.5 miles. Alternatively, you could drive straight east from Tallahassee and begin your ride at Chaires Crossroads, where you will find other cyclists parked.

It is possible to learn a great deal about Florida just by being observant as you enjoy this ride. Long stretches of shade connect wide-spreading live oaks older than your

Every active biking group will have good volunteer leaders. Nancy and Ewen, who live in Gainesville, organize cycling tour groups in North Florida.

granddaddy's granddaddy, and the route is lined with farms and ranches. It is both hilly and flat and runs through a delightful area of hamlets with little traffic early on Saturday and Sunday mornings. This is one of the reasons the area around Chaires is such a popular nexus for Tallahassee area cyclists.

Certainly, there is an abundance of FOR SALE signs in this lovely country east of the state capital. Without them, it simply would not be Florida. So the occasional cement driveway and new home notwithstanding, this remains a fine rural ride. It is close to town, but it is still country. Country "before country was cool."

One stretch of these two-lane roads is much like another. No paved shoulders and no bike lanes, but by Florida statute, cyclists must be given 3 feet of clearance by motorized vehicles. Of course, by Florida statute, people must not spit on the street or sacrifice animals in religious ceremonies, either, but folks insist on chewing tobacco and practicing Santeria, a New World variation of an old Yoruba African cult.

Nevertheless, folks are accustomed to cyclists here and they do make room for them. On several stretches of road along this ride, shaded stretches where the oaks reach entirely over the pavement and form a roof of leaves and branches, vehicular

Chaires Shady Lane Cruise

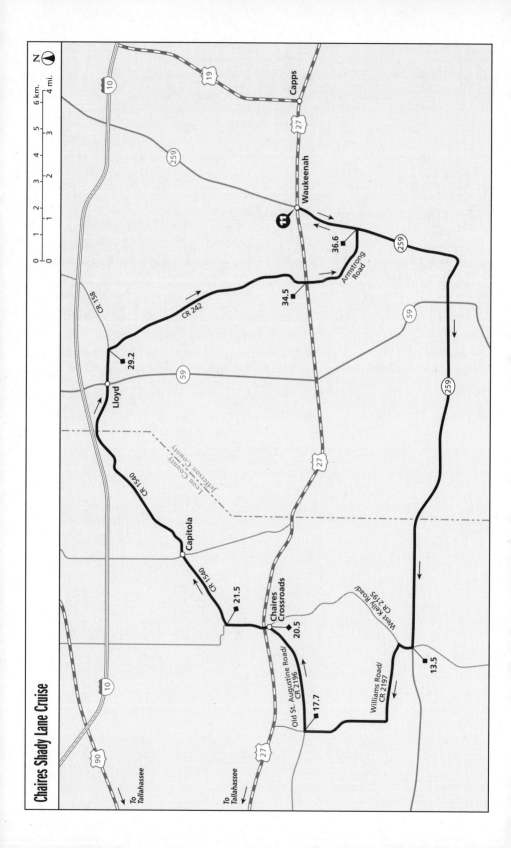

speeds will actually be a mile-a-minute less than the speeds you encounter on I-10 just to the north.

Cattle along this ride may strike you as quite variable, but there are no dairies here so the smells will be fresh air and mown hay. You may recognize the Black Angus from advertisements for popular steakhouses, and perhaps the reddish brown, white-face beef cattle, the Herefords and "polled Herefords," which are a naturally occurring mutation without horns. Cattlemen consider these basic breeds to be relatively docile and rapidly maturing, which is to say they move rapidly from grass chewers to the barbecue grill. The average big red cow will be Santa Gertrudis, a breed developed on the King Ranch in Texas.

Keep your eyes open and you will occasionally be rewarded with glimpses of even more exotic livestock. By reputation, you know the humpbacked Brahman, India's "sacred cattle," which have the ability to withstand drought, heat, and poor-quality food and water. They also have a reputation for prickly personalities. The herds of white cattle are Charolais; they originated in France, where meat is typically tough and stringy. At some point your cycling mate will point and shout "Longhorn! Texas longhorn." While there are a few certified Longhorns on Florida pastures, on this ride you will see real horns, the granddaddy of cattle horns. Ankole-Watusi cattle were brought to Florida from East Africa as both curiosities and to help build genetic diversity. The horns on this cow will cause you to stop for photos.

Cattle are not the only livestock on the ride—you will see a surprising number of donkeys and mules. Not being a jackass expert, I couldn't tell these apart, but in the old days when a farmer could not afford a fine horse and when his reputation depended on being able to plow a straight furrow, he would rather hitch a mule into the traces than a horse. No less an expert than my grandfather Lemmer (110 years ago in rural Florida someone could not spell "Lamar") told me that a mule was less likely to balk and would keep working when a horse would simply lie down and die. Let it be so, Lemmer.

And since I have spent so much time educating you about the appearance of cattle, look for the few "flue-cured" tobacco barns still standing. As recently as twenty-five years ago, farmers were still happily working their government tobacco allotment, convinced by the words of tobacco representatives that there was no evidence cigarette smoking harmed your health. Area boys performed much of the work and it was hard work, picking ("cropping") leaves from the bottom of the plant, working their way up as leaves ripened from the big coarse lugs at bottom—cigar wrapper—to the smaller, more delicate, and aromatic leaves at top.

Tobacco was a way of life here once, just as cotton had been. Men drove the tractors or, before tractors, the wagons, and boys cropped and women and girls strung the leaves on long sticks for the men to hang high in the wooden barns. It was a social affair, but deadly earnest because they sold the tobacco for cash. After the leaves were strung on sticks and hung in the barns, fires were set beneath them to "cure," or dry, them. Then they were tied in 200-pound burlap bundles and hauled to warehouses for auction. Entire families attended the summer auctions and then they went shopping, buying once-a-year dresses and shoes, new straw hats, and coveralls.

Ride with your eyes, mind, and heart open and there is no limit to your adventure.

Miles and Directions

0.0 From the parking area in the tiny hamlet of Waukeenah, turn south onto County Road 259. This road will twist and turn from due south to due west.

13.5 Turn right (north) on West Kelly Road/County Road 2195.

13.8 Turn left (west) on Williams Road/County Road 2197.

15.6 Williams Road bends right 90 degrees and continues north.

17.7 Turn right (east) on Old St. Augustine Road/County Road 2196.

20.5 Your road merges with CR 2195 at Chaires Crossroads and turns left (north) to cross US 27/19.

21.5 At the stop sign, turn right (east) before the railroad tracks on County Road 1540.

24.6 Cross single railroad tracks. (About a mile before the hamlet of Lloyd, CR 1540 becomes County Road 158, designated CR 158A on some maps.)

29.2 Turn right (south) on County Road 242, which may be unmarked, but look for the sign to St. Rilla Missionary Baptist Church. This turn is about half a mile past the hamlet of Lloyd, in which you will cross State Road 59. This road begins as Lloyd Creek Road, but within a few miles becomes Cherry Tree Road.

34.5 Cross US 27/19.

34.8 The pavement ends. The map indicates that you simply turn left (east) on Old St. Augustine Road and ride into Waukeenah, but in reality that segment of road does not exist. You have a choice: Either return to US 27/19 and ride 2 miles into Waukeenah or plunge forward, staying in the center of the hard-packed clay and crushed limestone path called Armstrong Road.

36.6 Turn left (north) on CR 259.

38.1 Arrive at the start of your ride in Waukeenah.

Local Information

Capital City Cyclists, www.cccyclists.org.

Greater Tallahassee Chamber of Commerce, 100 North Duval Street, Tallahassee; (850) 224-8116; www.talchamber.com or www.visittallahassee.com.

Jefferson County Sheriff's Department, 171 Industrial Park, Monticello; (850) 997-2523.

Leon County Sheriff's Department, PO Box 727 (2825 Municipal Way), Tallahassee, FL 32304; (850) 922-3300; http://lcso.leonfl.org.

Monticello/Jefferson County Chamber of Commerce, 420 West Washington Street, Monticello; (850) 997-5552; www.monticello

jeffersonfl.com or www.mainstreetmonticello.com.

Local Events/Attractions

Challenger Learning Center, 200 South Duval Street, Tallahassee; (850) 645-4629; www.challengertlh.com. They have an IMAX theater and a planetarium.

Florida A&M University, South Adams Street, Tallahassee; www.famu.edu. Florida A&M began as a fundamentally black college and now has 12,000 students on a 419-acre campus in downtown Tallahassee. Their specialty is their fabulous marching band, The Rattlers.

Florida State University, Tallahassee; http://fsu.edu. State research and teaching university with 40,000 students on a 451-acre campus in downtown Tallahassee. Known as the Seminoles.

Restaurants

Chez Pierre, 1215 Thomasville Road, Tallahassee; (850) 222-0936; www.chezpierre.com. Opens for lunch at 11:00 a.m., then a "bistro menu" is served until dinner at 5:30.

Jasmine Cafe & Lounge, 109 East College Avenue, Tallahassee; (850) 681-6868; www.jasmine-cafe.com. Sushi specialists for lunch and dinner.

Kool Beanz Cafe, 921 Thomasville Road, Tallahassee; (850) 224-2466; www.koolbeanz-cafe.com. Lunch Monday through Friday, dinner Monday through Saturday. Funky neighborhood restaurant with a good reputation.

Accommodations

Cottage B&B Inn, 295 West Palmer Mill Road, Monticello; (850) 342-3541. In case you were driving from the east and did not want to spend the night in Tallahassee.

Hilton Garden Inn, 3333 Thomasville Road, Tallahassee; (850) 385-3553; www.hilton gardeninn.com. Located next to I-10 north of Tallahassee.

Little English Guest House, 737 Timberlane Road, Tallahassee; (850) 907-9777; www.littleenglishguesthouse.com. Tallahassee's only "traditionally English" bed-and-breakfast inn. With rates beginning at $85 and only ten minutes north of downtown.

Quality Inn, 2020 Apalachee Parkway, Tallahassee; (850) 877-4437; www.choice hotels.com. Downtown, but mom-and-dad square.

Bike Shops

Tec's Bicycle Sport, 672 West Gaines Street, Tallahassee; (850) 224-1122.

University Cycles—Tallahassee, 668 West Gaines Street, Tallahassee; (850) 222-1665; www.universitycyclesoftallahassee.com.

Restrooms

There are no public restrooms along the length of this ride.

Maps

DeLorme: Florida Atlas & Gazetteer: Pages 50 A 3, 51 A-B 1-2.

12 Ray Charles Challenge

You won't believe you are cycling the fastest-growing state in America on most of this ride through Madison and Jefferson Counties . . . certainly not with the Confederate battle flags flying from trailers and small homes. This is old Florida, and people remember, especially along a ride that features miles and miles of "empty" woods on every side.

Start: The parking area of Jefferson County High School/Jefferson County Public Library, 1 block south of U.S. Highway 90 and 3 blocks west of the Jefferson County Court House square on South Water Street in Monticello.
Length: A 65.3-mile loop.
Terrain: Flat to gently rolling countryside with an occasional easy hill.

Traffic and hazards: Except for a 2.5-mile stretch on US 90 and a 5-mile stretch on U.S. Highway 27/19, traffic is light. While the pavement alternates between tight two-lane roads with no shoulders and spacious two-lanes with paved shoulders, riders should not feel squeezed by the traffic.

Getting there: The ride begins in the parking lot of the public high school and library on South Water Street in downtown Monticello. If you spend the night at a motel in Tallahassee and/or bike with members of Capital City Cyclists, you will most likely reach Monticello by driving east on Interstate 10 and then north on US 19 or by taking the more scenic, albeit slower, route east on US 90.

Ray Charles Robinson never biked this strip of highway, although the famous American pianist and soul musician grew up near it in the small town of Greenville. Of course, by the age of 4 he was going blind and by 7 he could see none of the wild roses or yellow daisies, wild turkeys, and whitetail deer that populate the area.

Born in 1930, Ray Charles could not see the Confederate battle flags that, more than 75 years after his birth and 140 years after the demise of that rebellion, still hang from trees and trailers in this colorful section of natural Florida. Flapping "Stars and Bars" sprinkle the route of the Ray Charles Challenge. The flags are probably fewer than in Ray's time, but I could not attest to that. I believe, however, that they now signal a mind-set of "leave-me-alone" independence in the face of a complex, corporate, and marginally comprehensible world, rather than the unfortunate racism of Ray's time.

In commemoration of this African American's life and musical genius, a bronze statue of Charles sits in Hayes Park in Greenville. It is a pleasant rest stop on what can be a hot, dry ride.

Pianist and soul musician Ray Charles (Robinson) grew up in ▶
Greenville, Florida, where his bronze statue resides. This ride
through unrepentantly rural countryside is named for him.

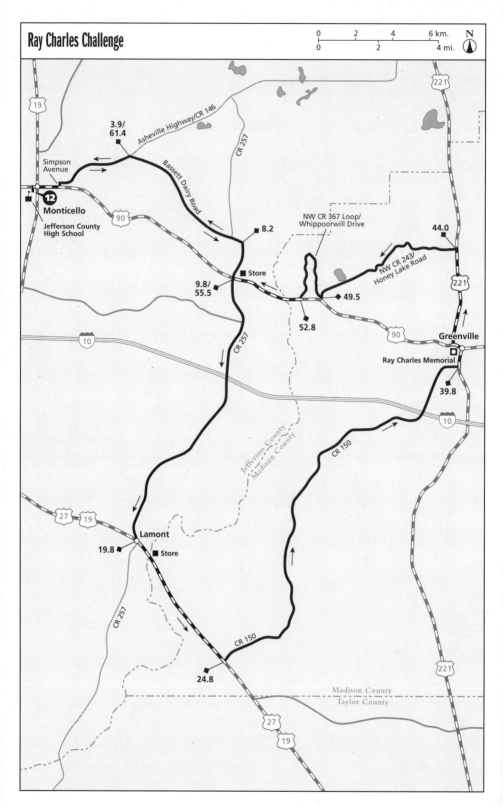

Ray Charles Challenge

3.9/61.4

Asheville Highway/CR 146

CR 257

Simpson Avenue

Bassett Dairy Road

12

Monticello

Jefferson County High School

90

8.2

NW CR 367 Loop/ Whippoorwill Drive

44.0

NW CR 243/ Honey Lake Road

Store

9.8/55.5

49.5

221

52.8

90

Greenville

CR 257

Ray Charles Memorial

10

39.8

CR 150

10

221

27 19

Lamont

19.8

Store

Jefferson County

Madison County

CR 257

CR 150

24.8

CR 150

Madison County

Taylor County

27

19

19

221

221

This trip begins 16 miles west of Greenville, in Monticello, the county seat of Jefferson County. In less than 2 miles, you are solidly out of Monticello, however, and cruising through the country. The pedal loops into Madison County before returning to Monticello. Overall, it is a beautiful and pleasant ride through countryside that is almost 100 percent pine forest, oak hammock, cow pasture, and flatwoods. Traffic congestion is not a problem, and there is no "rush" hour.

So it's country, all right. The Ray Charles Challenge takes you through an unapologetic region of the South. If you are lucky, you might see a tall yellow pine that still bears the slashing imprint of the turpentine axe, a bitter way of life that has now disappeared. You may also see a field of cotton or tobacco, although those crops are infrequent and, these days, economically impracticable. And the woods are dotted with the remnants of sharecropper cabins, because farming "on shares," while still a viable part-time economic proposition, is no longer the way of life that it was in Charles's childhood and during the Great Depression.

Today these lonely two-lane roads plow through fields of memories because the future for the sweet rural life is no longer bright. Small but independent rural holdings are increasingly entwined in the net of corporate cattle raising or silviculture (planting pine trees) or even the cultivation of acre upon acre of suburban homesteads.

But the ride, the long pedal itself, is delightful, and if you can navigate the barbed-wire fences without incident, the woods are a wonderful place for a potty break. Other than Monticello, there are no public—and few accessible private— toilet facilities along this ride: a small business at the intersection of US 90 and County Road 257 at mile 10 and another on US 27/19 at about mile 20. A convenience store may be open when you pedal through Greenville at mile 40, and there is the store at 90 and 257 once again, this time at mile 55.

On this ride you are virtually on your own and must carry what you need for a flat tire, to communicate for help, and water. If you are thirsty and a store is open when you pass, fill up, because there are long empty stretches of highway ahead.

On the 15 miles of County Road 150, the only sound you hear will be your own tires and a very rare truck. From the hamlet of Lamont (CR 257 and US 27/19) to Greenville, a distance of 20 miles, you are riding in the open sun on hot pavement. Hope for a slight overcast and that your application of sunscreen does not wilt in perspiration. Any deeper in the country and you would be pedaling in coveralls.

While Monticello and Greenville are interesting in their own ways, the loveliest section of this ride is Honey Lake Road and the curious north–south loop made by County Road 367/Whipporwill Drive. Here, there is shade, handsome countryside, sparse traffic, wildlife, and abundant wildflowers. Halfway along Honey Lake Road, thin-tire cyclists will groan at a sudden half mile of crushed lime rock, but it does not last, and the pleasantness of this section of Ray's ride is worth a steady but cautious approach.

Country rides are disappearing throughout America. With the persistence of memory, they are the fabric of our nation that cannot be appreciated through the windows of an automobile. Hot, lonely, and thirsty, we are lucky to take this bicycle challenge.

Although Ray Charles may not have ridden this route, he was a prolific progenitor and his dozen children (from seven wives), twenty-one grandchildren, and (at this writing) five great-grandchildren would surely appreciate it.

Miles and Directions

0.0 From the parking lot of the Jefferson County High School or Public Library, head north on South Water Street toward US 90. It will only be a couple blocks.

0.1 Turn right (east) on US 90 and ride around the Jefferson County Court House square.

1.1 Turn left (north) on Simpson Avenue and ride the 2 blocks to Asheville Highway/County Road 146.

1.2 Turn right (east) on CR 146.

3.9 Turn right (southeast) on Bassett Dairy Road.

8.2 Turn right (south) on CR 257.

9.8 Stop at the flashing red light at the intersection of CR 257 and US 90. Continue straight ahead when the traffic is clear. After 1.6 miles you will cross rough railroad tracks; it is 3.5 miles farther to the I-10 underpass.

19.8 Turn left (southeast) in the hamlet of Lamont at the intersection with US 19/27, when the traffic is clear.

24.8 Turn left (northeast) at the intersection with CR 150 or SW Overstreet Avenue. It is 12.7 miles to I-10 and another 0.2 mile to the railroad tracks.

39.8 Turn left (north) at the stop sign onto U.S. Highway 221 and ride into Greenville.

40.5 Turn left (west) at the stop sign onto US 90. Hayes Park, with the statue of Ray Charles, will be on your left.

40.8 Turn right (north) onto US 221.

44.0 Turn left (west) onto NW County Road 243/Honey Lake Road. Watch carefully, as Honey Lake Road dead-ends on US 221 and, not being a wide road, this would be an easy intersection to miss.

49.5 Veer sharply back to the right (north) 1 block before the intersection with US 90 on Whippoorwill Drive (NW 367th Loop).

51.2 Turn sharply back to the left (south) where NW 85th Avenue intersects. Stay on Whippoorwill Drive/NW 367th Loop.

52.8 Turn right (west) on US 90.

55.5 Turn right (north) at the flashing yellow light. This point completes the loop section of the route and you are returning from this point over familiar ground.

56.9 Turn left (west) on Bassett Dairy Road.

61.4 Turn left (southwest) toward Monticello on CR 146/Asheville Highway.

64.1 Turn left (south) on Simpson Avenue and ride the 2 blocks to US 90.

64.2 Turn right (west) on US 90 and ride into Monticello and around the court house to Water Street.

65.2 Turn left (south) on South Water Street. It should only be a couple blocks to your car.

65.3 Arrive back at the start of your ride.

Local Information

Capital City Cyclists, www.cccyclists.org.
Jefferson County Sheriff's Department, 171 Industrial Park, Monticello; (850) 997-2523.
Madison County Sheriff's Department, Court House, Madison; (850) 973-4151.
Monticello, Florida, ww.monticelloflorida.com.
Monticello/Jefferson County Chamber of Commerce, 420 West Washington Street, Monticello; (850) 997-5552; www.monticello jeffersonfl.com or www.mainstreet monticello.com.

Local Events/Attractions

The Challenger Learning Center, 200 South Duval Street, Tallahassee; (850) 645-STAR/644-IMAX. A 32,000-square-foot facility designed to "foster a long-term interest in math, science and technology, create positive learning experiences, and motivate students to pursue careers in these fields." Features a state-of-the-art space mission simulator, an IMAX theater, and a domed high-definition planetarium to create a "holistic educational and entertaining experience."

Jefferson County Watermelon Festival: Begun more than fifty years ago to recognize county watermelon growers, the festival includes beauty pageants, dinners, street dances, barn dances, arts and crafts shows, a melon run, sports events, and a parade. It is held annually the third week of June. (850) 997-5552; www.co.jefferson.fl.us/rectour/melonfest03.htm.

O'Toole's Herb Farm, Rocky Ford Road, Madison; (850) 973-3269. A certified commercial herb grower with greenhouses and large display gardens. Also a gift shop where you can take tea and rock on the front porch.

Restaurants

Jake's Sub & Grill, 180 West Washington Street, Monticello; (850) 997-0388. Opens at 10:00 a.m. and closes at 8:30 p.m. Monday through Thursday; closes at 9:30 p.m. Friday and Saturday.

The Rare Door, 229 North Cherry Street, Monticello; (850) 997-3133. Steak and potato fare. Open from 7:00 a.m. to 9:00 p.m. Monday through Saturday.
Three Sister's Restaurant, 370 South Jefferson Street, Monticello; (850) 342-3474. Featuring white tablecloths and family cooking. Open Wednesday through Saturday from 11:30 a.m. to 2:00 p.m. and also on Friday and Saturday from 5:30 p.m. to closing.

Accommodations

1872 John Denham House, 555 West Palmer Mill Road, Monticello; (850) 997-4568; www.johndenhamhouse.com. Any B&B where the official policy is "children and pets are welcome" is okay in my book! One block from the start of the ride.

Grace Manor Bed & Breakfast Victorian Inn, 117 SW US 221/PO Box 87, Greenville, FL 32311; (800) 750-6305; www.gracemanor inn.com. Wonderfully restored and more than a century old. Features murder-mystery nights. Modern motels are available in Monticello if you are shy about the pampering and Victorian fluff of a B&B: **Day's Inn,** (850) 997-5988, **Super 8;** (850) 997-8888; and the bike-friendly **Capri Lazy Days Motel and Lounge;** (850) 997-5712.

Bike Shops

Area bicycle shops are west of the start of this ride in Tallahassee (or north in Thomasville or Valdosta, Georgia).
Great Bicycle Shop, 1909 Thomasville Road, Tallahassee; (850) 224-7461.
Higher Ground Bicycle Company, 1319 East Tennessee Street, Tallahassee; (850) 942-2453.
Sunshine Cycles, 2783 Capital Circle NE, Tallahassee; (850) 422-1075; www.bike sunshine.net.

Mile 0.0: Jefferson County Public Library, the beginning and end of the Ray Charles Challenge, opens at 9:00 a.m. Tuesday through Saturday. Closing hours vary, although on Saturday, the day most bicyclists will take this ride, it closes at 3:00 p.m.

Maps

DeLorme: Florida Atlas & Gazetteer: Pages 35 D 3, 51 A, 52 A-B 1.

13 On-the-Gulf Challenge

Begin anywhere along the route, but for heaven's sake begin it soon. This little slice of Florida won't be undiscovered for long. Enjoy scenic tiny villages lost in Florida's Big Bend. There's fishing and scalloping, and you will be one of the first bikers to take this underappreciated challenge.

Start: The small parking lot of Hodges Park Enhancement Project, which is on the Gulf in Keaton Beach. Even on Memorial Day there is plenty of parking. There are public restrooms and picnic pavilions to serve the tiny beach.
Length: 59.4 miles.
Terrain: Flat, very flat.

Traffic and hazards: This ride is entirely two-lane and some of it even has paint down the middle, perhaps a recent concession to out-of-towners. Not a lot of traffic except on holidays, but watch out for pickups pulling boats with trailers that are wider than the truck bed, as there isn't much room on some of County Road 361.

Getting there: From east–west Interstate 10 about an hour east of Tallahassee, take U.S. Highway 221 south (the Greenville exit) through Perry where the road intersects with U.S. Highway 98/19/27A. Locally, the four-lane divided highway south is the Byron Butler Parkway. About 5 miles south of Perry, turn right onto CR 361 and continue to Keaton Beach. Heading south on Interstate 75, turn west on County Road 247 about ten minutes south of Lake City (an hour and a quarter south of the Florida-Georgia state line) and it is about a half hour to Branford (on the Suwannee River); then twenty minutes south on County Road 349 and then turn right on County Road 351 to Cross City. Another fifteen minutes on US 98/19/27A to County Road 358 and south to the hamlet of Jena, where a bridge crosses the Steinhatchee River to the intersection of State Road 51 and CR 361. Take CR 361 to Keaton Beach and begin the ride.

I got married here once, and several other places, too, but this is not about me. Still, when the wedding party sat down at Roy's Restaurant for the pre–ceremony family breaking-of-bread in Steinhatchee, the Big Bend area of Florida's coast on the Gulf of Mexico was a lonely place. Not deserted, just not desirable. That isolation ended almost as quickly as the marriage.

A farsighted person could have predicted the end of lazy days in Florida's Big Bend. It began about the time of the image reorientation of the area immediately to the south, Florida's freshwater paradise. Various citizen groups and state tourism offi-

The Nature Coast offers terrific rides along the Gulf of Mexico, among tiny no-name coastal fishing villages that are in the process of "being discovered" at this very minute.

cials changed the Big Bend image from the "Mud Coast" to the "Nature Coast." That has made all the difference.

Normally, change in Florida means more people, more government, and more commercial establishments. All of that is probably going to happen here, in the Big Bend or Nature Coast area, but in this case it may not be an altogether bad thing, especially for bike riders.

A supersized development is scheduled for Keaton Beach. It is called Magnolia Bay, and the area is truly divided about whether this is a step forward. Many are for it and many are "agin it." As in Yankeetown to the south and other places whose way of life is about to change, this fight is far from over.

Anyway, an old girlfriend, a talented potter who still throws and fires up on the Suwannee River, once told me that the area from Panama City to Clearwater was only good for kids who wanted to drink beer and smoke cigarettes on the muddy beaches at night. Otherwise, the entire area of low-lying flatwoods and tidal marsh wasn't useful for much except growing pine trees after it was drained, and launching fishing boats. She was wrong. We should have taken our life savings—which at that time,

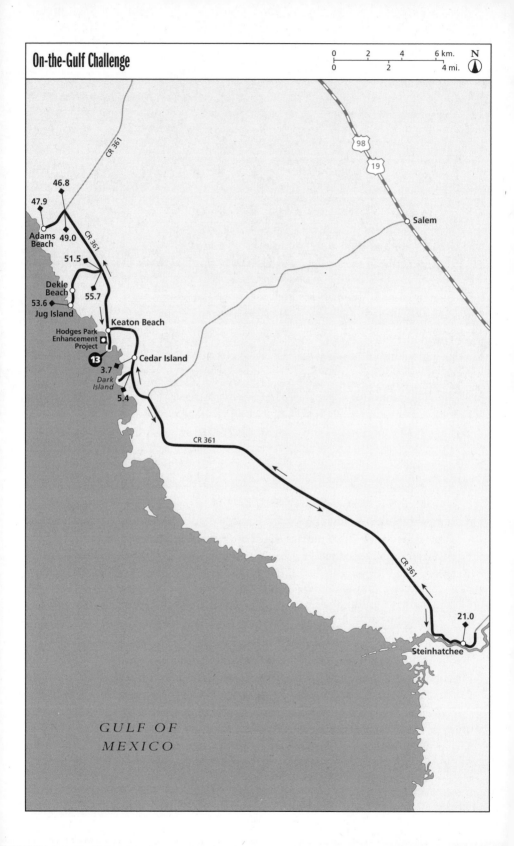

On-the-Gulf Challenge

0 2 4 6 km.
0   2   4 mi.
N

CR 361

98
19

Salem

46.8
47.9
Adams
Beach
49.0
CR 361
51.5
Dekle
Beach
55.7
53.6
Jug Island
Keaton Beach
Hodges Park
Enhancement
Project
13
3.7
Dark
Island
5.4
Cedar Island

CR 361

CR 361

21.0
Steinhatchee

GULF OF
MEXICO

lumped together, wouldn't have bought a good bicycle seat—and purchased as much land on or near the water as we could afford. We would today be rich.

Speaking of "as soon as possible," you must pedal the On-the-Gulf Challenge right away because you will be able to watch development progress, neighbor fighting neighbor tooth and fang: See culture change and democracy in action. It all began with the bridge over the Steinhatchee River, built just a few years ago, that now has attracted a couple of motels, a couple of marinas, a couple of curio shops, and a horde of new and expensive homes, all crowding on or near the water . . . and the plans for Magnolia Bay (a wall of interlocking condominiums, chain motels, and more shops and marinas).

I am talking about the ride out of sequence, I'm afraid, and yet you can park practically anywhere along the route—Steinhatchee, Dekle Beach, Keaton Beach, even the virtually deserted Adams Beach—and take this ride. I have suggested starting in Keaton Beach only because there is relatively secure public parking, not because it is otherwise especially logical.

This wonderful and interesting ride itself can begin anywhere and run the full spectrum from southeast to northwest, from "developing now" (Steinhatchee) to "developing soon" (Adams Beach). The progression on the land and over the water is logical. Wherever you begin, Taylor County 361 is your thoroughfare, and from this two-lane road, you exit toward the Gulf to check out the individual communities. Because most of them—Dark Island, Cedar Island, Jug Island—are out in the Gulf, you will ride the same road back after exploring.

Between Steinhatchee and the turn to Dark Island is a long stretch of pinelands and flatwoods. Boring, but purposeful in that it serves to focus your mind on pedaling. Once you are past this 16-mile stretch, which—unless you pre-positioned a vehicle—you will ride both directions, you can begin turning off and exploring the coastal villages.

Most habitations are on stilts out here—the houses, the motels—because anything that isn't underwater, come a good storm soon will be. After all, this land is only inches above sea level.

Although the Big Bend area isn't Ground Zero for hurricanes—that's a good thing, because flat as the land is, a powerful storm would flood all the way to Atlanta—it suffered from the "Storm of the Century." That powerful March 1993 "white hurricane," or super-cell, thundered ashore in this area with no warning. Resulting in the death of forty-seven people in Florida, the event is considered one of the "Top Ten Weather Events" of the twentieth century in the Sunshine State (www.srh.noaa.gov/TLH/topevents/). The fast-moving storm struck with ferocity, produced an enormous storm surge—every road you will bike on was a dozen feet underwater—and was followed by snow and freezing cold. It devastated this area and caused an old way of life to begin to die once the newscasters brought the old Mud Coast to the attention of the outside world.

Our little wedding restaurant, Roy's, went under, by the way, but so did the marriage. Life goes on and you can be a part of that resurgence on this unusual and marvelous ride with long views of water and marsh, birds and manatees. It is the perfect setting for a Carl Hiaasen novel. Maybe you will be in it!

Miles and Directions

0.0 Begin by turning left (north) out of the parking lot of the Hodges Park Enhancement Project on the Gulf in Keaton Beach.

0.7 Turn right (east) at the stop sign on CR 361.

3.7 Arrive at Cedar Island (ride in island area).

5.4 Arrive at right turn (west) to Dark Island (ride in island area).

21.0 Arrive in Steinhatchee and, after touring the area, return to CR 361 and loop back north and northwest.

46.8 Turn left (southwest) from CR 361 onto the narrow two-lane road toward Adams Beach.

47.9 Turn around at the dead end on the Gulf beach and return to CR 361 (after riding around in Adams Beach area).

49.0 Turn right (southeast) on CR 361.

51.5 Turn right (west) at sign to Dekle Beach (all paved highways in this area seem to be CR 361, as is this one).

53.6 Dead-end on Jug Island and turn back.

55.7 Turn right (south) on CR 361 toward Keaton Beach.

58.7 Do not turn left on CR 361, but continue straight into Keaton Beach.

59.4 Arrive at the beginning of the ride.

Local Information

Web site of interest: www.taylorflorida.com.
Perry-Taylor County Chamber of Commerce, 428 North Jefferson Street, Perry; (850) 584-5366 or (800) 257-8881; www.taylorflorida.com.
Steinhatchee.Com, PO Box 994, Steinhatchee, FL 32359; (352) 498-8002; www.steinhatchee.com.
Taylor County Sheriff's Department, 108 North Jefferson Street, Suite 103, Perry; (850) 584-7017.

Local Events/Attractions

There are no events or attractions of special note along this ride. It is an area known for **fishing and scalloping,** all from your own boat, and more recently for its **birding.** There have been until recently few places to rent a kayak or bicycle. It is all very small, very "down home," and the chance to see it before it develops local events and attractions is part of the fascination of the Big Bend area of Taylor County . . . that and the marvelous views of the Gulf and the sunsets.
Florida Forest Festival in Perry: The fifty-second-annual October festival took place in 2007; (850) 584-8733.
Check out www.floridastatebluegrass.com for the **Florida State Bluegrass Festival,** presented by the Taylor County Chamber of Commerce.

Restaurants

Keaton Beach Hot Dog Stand: Look for this local establishment at the end of the road, across from Hodges Park Enhancement Project in Keaton Beach. Opens at 11:00 a.m. but closing hours vary. Closed Monday.
Roy's Restaurant, 100 1st Avenue SW, Steinhatchee; (352) 498-5000; www.roys-restaurant.com. A very good seafood restau-

rant on the north bank of the Steinhatchee River and overlooking the Gulf of Mexico. (If you see my ex, say Hi!)

Accommodations

Paradise Suites, Highway 51, PO Box 403, Steinhatchee, FL 32359; (352) 498-5005. **Sea Hag Marina:** Multiple options from cottages to motor homes in Steinhatchee. Check www.seahag.com or call (352) 498-3008. **Steinhatchee Landing,** 203 Ryland Circle/PO Box 789, Steinhatchee, FL 32359; (352) 498-3513 or (800) 584-1709; www.steinhatcheelanding.com. Multiple styles of new cottages—Victorian to Florida cracker—with kayaking, tennis, fishing, and a chapel on-site. Cottages have kitchens and pets are welcome in select units.

Bike Shops

You must be self-sufficient, because at this time there are no bicycle shops near this ride.

Restrooms

Mile 0.0: There are very few public facilities in the area and, indeed, few facilities at all along this marvelous ride. Public toilets are available beside the parking lot at Hodges Park Enhancement Project, the start/end of the ride in Keaton Beach.

Maps

DeLorme: Florida Atlas & Gazetteer: Pages 62 A 2, B 2, C 3.

14 Hatch Bend Ramble

From Branford, Florida's self-proclaimed cave-diving capital on the fabled Suwannee River, through "Hatch Bend" farm-and-ranch country in Lafayette County, you will enjoy this rural slice of life. Hatch Bend is named for the Hatch family, a prolific country family from the days when Florida was governed by the rural north rather than the urban south.

Start: There is ample on-street parking in Branford so parking almost anywhere is fine. Alternatively, leave your vehicle in the developed park on the Suwannee River in Branford just south of U.S. Highway 27.
Length: A 27.9-mile loop.
Terrain: Flat.

Traffic and hazards: Whether you are on county, state, or federal highways, every inch of this ride is two-lane without shoulders. Along US 27, traffic can be fast, but this stretch is short. Otherwise, traffic is light. Watch for trucks carrying crates of chickens!

Getting there: Take exit 399 on Interstate 75 north of Gainesville and proceed west on U.S. Highway 441 about 5 miles to High Springs, where you will follow the signs and veer to the left onto US 27. Stay on 27 for about a half hour to arrive in Branford. From Interstate 10, take exit 283 and drive south through Live Oak on U.S. Highway 129 for about forty minutes to arrive in Branford.

One of my relatives was involved in a notorious shooting not far from this ride, although using the word "involved" may seem as if I am sugarcoating the deed. It happened a long time ago. More than a hundred years, I imagine, since Marshal McLane shot "Bully Bob" Sullivan on Main Street, just up the road in Live Oak.

These chicken houses are situated along the roadway in Hatch Bend. Bordering the fabled Suwannee River, these residents grow much of the food that you and I take for granted.

In those days, this area of the American nation was deeply rural, fundamentally suspicious of outsiders, and obdurately introspective. Two generations after the Civil War ended, the region still seethed with the fervor of battles won and wars lost, and hung on to its isolated and segregated way of life with intense passion. Now those times are truly a distant memory and this area of the world is sliding rapidly toward modernity.

Today the people of Hatch Bend and similar rural communities would openly forswear any temptation to talk publicly about "Yankees" or "negroes." A bike rider could stop at virtually any farm or home in the region and, once past the customary packs of inquisitive porch dogs, ask for help . . . and get it.

Despite our lingering impressions from the movie *Easy Rider* (or *Deliverance*), there is little to fear today from the old stereotype of "rednecks in pickups." Although at one time in the early 1970s, after I had shaken foreign soil off my boots and changed from Army green to civvies, I had just such a dustup not far from here. It sent me to the hospital, my Chevy Nova to a junkyard, and a highway patrolman to the office scratching his head about just how he would write a report so that no one was at fault. But that was thirty years ago, and you will definitely not hear banjo music in the background as you ride these country roads. More like the ghost of John Denver, although this is far from his normal haunts.

Hatch Bend country roads are straight and easy, and the Suwannee River is an absolutely delightful stream of golden brown water filled with catfish and huge jumping sturgeon. And even though Stephen Foster never saw the river, I believe he would have enjoyed a picnic at the boat ramp (mile 17.3) in the middle of the ramble. A few crows, perhaps a blue jay or a soaring buzzard, and the deep, powerful silence of the flowing water. A masterful place to meditate. Lightly visited. One imagines Siddhartha listening to the voices of the river here.

With no historic battlefields to keep alive the pain of war, the past truly has been allowed to dissolve. And what remains is straight road and speeding pickups with dogs, tools, spare tires, and miscellaneous junk in the truck bed that give you a wide berth as you sweat. Local drivers will even raise a hand from the steering wheel to wave. Rows of poultry houses and the acrid smell of chickens compete with Angus, Charolais, Brahma, polled Hereford, and the pure, almost sweet odor of open-air cow plops.

It is possible to pedal this Hatch Bend Ramble and think about strong families clinging to the land, adjusting and persisting through time. Outlasting the government and shifting market forces and all the thousand-and-one things that can ruin or destroy families. Families so strong they give their names to an area . . . or an era.

So Marshal McLane shot Bully Bob Sullivan dead long ago. Sullivan, the ruthless "quarters boss" who had only minutes before stepped out of the narrow-gauge LOP&G railcar with casual murder on his mind. When McLane plugged the desperado that Saturday morning, market morning in Live Oak, the county seat, he sent a signal down through the generations. As McLane drilled Sullivan, he signaled that the era of the "quarters boss" who ruled rural communities through sheer intimidation was over. He signaled that poverty and ignorance could come to an end.

In a way, he signaled that the road would be safe for cyclists, too. That whatever one's persuasion or personality, the old ways of intolerance could change to acceptance, and that the black-and-white painted church signs one sees at every intersection could point not just to a black or white congregation, but to a new future of broadmindedness and sharing the road.

Miles and Directions

0.0 From on-street parking in Branford, head south on US 129.

0.1 Turn right (west) on US 27 and cross the Suwannee River.

1.5 Turn left (south) on State Road 349.

8.8 Turn left (east) on County Road 500/342. (The maps, the street signs, your GPS, and Google may all vary, so look for the signs to "Hatchbend Volunteer Fire Department" and "Hatchbend Baptist Church." If you notice a street sign marking the boundary between Lafayette and Dixie Counties, you have pedaled too far. You will need to turn around and pedal back about a mile.)

11.8 Follow the 90-degree turn left (north) at the church.

12.0 Follow the 90-degree turn left (west).

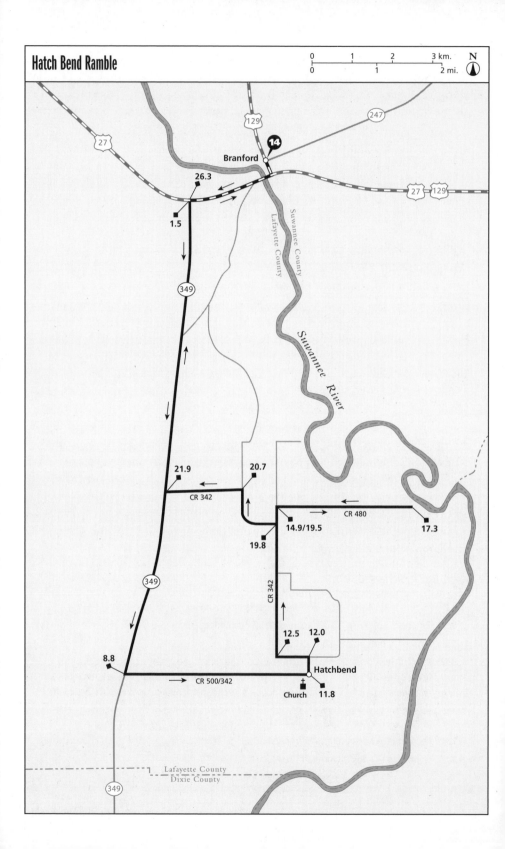

12.5   Follow another 90-degree turn right (north). (At 14.7 the signs change to County Road 480.)

14.9   Follow the 90-degree turn right (east).

17.3   The road dead-ends at an infrequently used boat ramp and picnic area on the Suwannee River. Turn around here and return the way you came, west on CR 480 (labeled CR 138 on some maps).

19.5   Turn left (south) on CR 500.

19.8   Turn right (west) on CR 480. The road gradually turns north in a sweeping curve.

20.7   Follow the 90-degree turn left (west).

21.9   Turn right (north) at the intersection with SR 349. (Here the sign will read HATCH BEND APOSTOLIC CHURCH.)

26.3   Turn right (east) on US 27 toward Branford.

27.9   Cross the Suwannee River into Branford and return to the parking area.

Local Information

Lafayette County Chamber of Commerce, Highways 27 and 51, Mayo; (386) 294-2705.
Lafayette County Sheriff's Department, Courthouse, Highways 27 and 51, Mayo; (386) 294-1222.
Suwannee County Chamber of Commerce, Branford Office, 701 Suwannee Avenue, Branford; (386) 935-3722.

Local Events/Attractions

Ichetucknee Springs State Park, State Roads 47 and 238, Fort White; (386) 497-2511; www.floridastateparks.org/ichetucknee springs/.
Suwannee Expeditions Canoe and Kayak, 26201 77th Place, Branford; (386) 935-9299; www.canoeflorida.com.
Troy Springs State Park, 674 NE Troy Springs Road, Branford; (386) 935-4835; www.florida stateparks.org/troyspring/default.cfm.

Restaurants

Nell's, 403 Suwannee Avenue, Branford; (386) 935-1415.
Sister's Café, 208 Suwannee Avenue, Branford; (386) 935-6989.
Suwannee River Cove, 8749 288th Street, Branford; (386) 935-1666.

Accommodations

Grady House B&B Inn, 420 NW 1st Avenue, High Springs; (386) 454-2206; www.grady house.com. Half an hour southeast of Branford on US 27.
Le Chateau de Lafayette, 136 North Fletcher Avenue, Mayo; (386) 294-2332. Half an hour east of Branford on US 27.
Steamboat Dive Inn, Corner US 27 and 129, Branford; (386) 935-2283.
Suwannee River State Park, 20185 County Road 132, Live Oak; (386) 362-2746; www.floridastateparks.org/suwanneeriver /default.cfm. Camping about half an hour northwest of Branford.

Bike Shops

Keaton Bike Shop, 327 North Marion Avenue, Lake City; (386) 752-8788. Lake City is half an hour from Branford, northeast on State Road 247.
Santa Fe Bicycle Outfitters, 10 North Main Street, High Springs; (386) 454-2453. High Springs is half an hour from Branford, south on US 27.

Restrooms

Restrooms both public and private are plentiful in Branford.

Maps

DeLorme: Florida Atlas & Gazetteer: Page 64 A-B 1.

15 Suwannee River Ramble

Although you do not get many actual peeks at the Suwannee on this ride, it is a sweet little ramble through the countryside on the north and south sides of the fabled river. Not much traffic. Smooth, wide two-lane roads and an interesting start/end in White Springs and the Stephen Foster Folk Cultural Center State Park. One way to enjoy it is to ride it in both directions. You will be amazed at how different the country-side looks from an opposite bearing.

Start: The parking lot of the Florida Nature and Heritage Visitor Center on the north bank of the Suwannee River in "downtown" White Springs, at the intersection of U.S. Highway 41 and County Road 136.

Length: A 32.3-mile loop.

Terrain: Flat to gently rolling.

Traffic and hazards: Except at the intersection of Interstate 75 and CR 136, this ride is wonderfully free of traffic.

Getting there: From the intersection of Interstates 75 and 10 north of Lake City in north-central Florida, drive north to the first exit, #439. Leave the interstate and drive east 3 miles on CR 136, crossing the Suwannee River into the town of White Springs. After 1 to 2 blocks, the Florida Nature and Heritage Visitor Center will be on your left.

If you enjoy long stretches of good road with little traffic and interesting places to visit, any bike route originating in White Springs will provide an excellent ride. At the time of this writing, this little jewel of an old and threadbare town on the north bank of the Suwannee River has not been "discovered" . . . yet. This is Florida, though, so anonymity of place won't last, and that fact alone is one superior reason to find White Springs on the map, fill the auto's tank with gas and the stomach with an energy drink, and go find it.

Our ramble from and to White Springs could be classified as a ramble or a challenge or even a classic—there are so many fine riding options in the immediate area. Most roads are devoid of heavy traffic (a pickup truck or tractor pulling a hay baler will be the worst you encounter) and all seem to have recently been paved and smoothed. There are no bike lanes, though, and except for the U.S. highways, no paved shoulders, but that should not impair riding comfort or safety here.

This area of Florida is extraordinarily hospitable to people who enjoy the outdoors: biking (on- and off-road), hiking, camping, canoeing and kayaking, even cave diving in the multitude of springs along the river. And this is outdoor Florida at its best. As a kid, if I had not owned a canoe, the only way to navigate the Suwannee would have been to swim to the Gulf of Mexico—all 170 miles from White Springs or 266 miles from the river's origin in the Okefenokee Swamp—and to camp stealthily on its banks at night. Today there are scores of outfitters, bed-and-breakfast inns, and campgrounds. So in that way, perhaps, the area has been "discovered."

Cyclists string out along a highway near the Suwannee River. The Suwannee Bicycle Association promotes rides and ride safety, and lobbies for increased awareness of cyclists on Florida roadways.

The Suwannee River Ramble circles a section of the famous river, but unless you get off your bike and/or take a few side rides, your glimpses of that golden brown stream will be brief. So I suggest doing the ride and then circling back to explore. Actually, at 32 flat, easy miles you will make good time; and this is a short ride, so have an energy bar and a swig of PowerAde, then ride it in the opposite direction. I am convinced that, except perhaps for the I-75 overpass with its fast-food outlets and gas stations, it will feel like an entirely different route.

Of course, this area is famous for Stephen Foster's song "Way Down Upon the Suwannee River" or "Old Folks at Home," which he wrote in 1851. The Pennsylvanian never saw the river, though; never, in fact, visited Florida. Too bad for him!

Stephen Foster's absence, however, takes nothing away from the remarkable charm of the Suwannee. The river seeps south out of the Okefenokee Swamp toward the Gulf of Mexico. Along its route, the tannin-laced freshwater is continuously fed by cold and crystal clear springs ranging in size from hundreds of mere trickles to first-magnitude floods, millions of gallons welling upward through the porous and fragile limestone that serves Florida as bedrock. Through eons, the

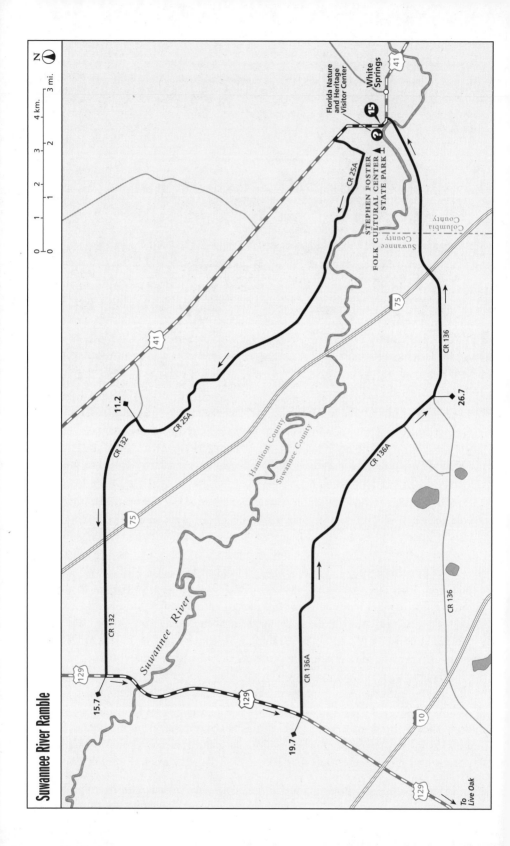

Suwannee River Ramble

river has cut its way downward into the stone until a kayak or canoe trip on it sometimes feels lush and tropical, sometimes walled with jagged cliffs and collapsing oak and cypress. This river is the defining characteristic of the region, but it is not all that is here.

North Florida is rich in pioneer culture—black, white, and Native American—and that diversity and richness is celebrated at the Stephen Foster Folk Cultural Center State Park in White Springs. There, folk arts such as weaving and broom making and potting are kept alive and the public is welcome to enjoy and, on occasion, to participate. Thus, riding this route back and forth, one finally recognizes the purposes of the bales of sticks—they are tomato stakes—and the wooden barns that seem too small for livestock and too old for the twenty-first century—flue-cured tobacco—and the humpback cattle called Brahma (brought from India at about the same time Foster wrote the song), and the red hogs called Durocs.

So there is much to experience and learn along this route, and although there are few places to pull over for water and no immediately available services should your bicycle blow a tire, remember that this area is still natural. People along the route will help you without asking for money. Stop at most homes and ask for water and you may be invited to sit in the porch swing and sip iced tea; walk up to practically any mobile home and the occupants will help you fix a flat tire, let you use their phone if they have one, and offer you (and your bike) a lift back to White Springs.

If this is what "undiscovered" means, count me in.

Miles and Directions

0.0 Start in the parking lot of the Florida Nature and Heritage Visitor Center in White Springs and pedal north on US 41.

0.3 Turn left (west) onto County Road 25A. There will be a stop sign after 0.3 mile on this in-town stretch, but the route is obvious. Turn left and stay on CR 25A. At 0.5 mile there is another stop sign at the old entrance to Stephen Foster Folk Cultural Center State Park. Continue straight.

11.2 Turn left (west) at this T onto County Road 132.

15.7 Turn left (south) at this T onto U.S. Highway 129. After just 0.7 mile, cross over the Suwannee River.

19.7 Turn left (east) onto CR 136A.

26.7 Turn left (east) onto CR 136. At 2.5 miles cross over I-75, and at 5.4 miles cross once again over the Suwannee River.

32.3 From the Suwannee River bridge, it is uphill to the parking lot of the Florida Nature and Heritage Visitor Center, the beginning and end of this ride.

Local Information

Lake City/Columbia County Chamber of Commerce, 162 South Marion Avenue, Lake City; (386) 752-3690; www.lakecitychamber.com.
Sheriff's Offices: This ramble takes you through three counties. White Springs and the initial half of the ride are in Hamilton, (386) 792-2004; after crossing the Suwannee River, the ride is in Suwannee—patrol (386) 362-2222; and just before White Springs, a couple miles are in Columbia—patrol (386) 719-2026.
Stephen Foster Folk Cultural Center State Park, PO Drawer G, White Springs, FL 32096; (386) 397-4331; www.floridastateparks .org/stephenfoster/.
Town of White Springs, Florida, PO Drawer D, White Springs, FL 32096; (386) 397-2310; www.whitesprings.org.

Local Events/Attractions

Florida Folk Festival, held at Stephen Foster Folk Cultural Center State Park, PO Drawer G, White Springs, FL 32096; (386) 397-4331; www.floridastateparks.org/stephenfoster/. The event celebrates Florida's history, cultures, and people, with food, music, and dance. www.floridastateparks.org/folkfest.
Ichetucknee Springs State Park, 12087 SW U.S. Highway 27, Fort White; (386) 497-2511; www.floridastateparks.org/ichetucknee springs/default.cfm. A National Natural Landmark. Snorkeling, tubing, and canoeing are the attractions of this cold, crystal clear river direct from the source!
Suwannee Bicycle Association, PO Box 247, White Springs, FL 32096; (386) 397-2347; www.suwanneebike.org. Maintains a full calendar of popular road and trail rides.
Suwannee River Wilderness Trail, (888) 868-9914; www.suwanneeriver.com. Plenty of outfitters are available to canoe or kayak the 170 miles of twisting golden river flowing past parks and springs to the Gulf of Mexico.

Restaurants

Country Cafe, 16750 Springs Street, White Springs; (386) 397-2040. Basic food (meat-

loaf, catfish . . .) for a good price, when it is open.
Suwannee River Diner, 16538 Springs Street, White Springs; (386) 397-1181. Even mo' basic food!
Telford Hotel/Restaurant, 16521 River Street/PO Box 407, White Springs, FL 32096; (386) 397-2000. A cut above the rest in the area . . . when it is open.

Accommodations

Adams House Bed and Breakfast, 16513 River Street, White Springs; (386) 397-1915 or (866) 397-1915.
America's Best Value Inn, 3119 County Road 136, White Springs; (888) 315-2378; www.americasbestvalueinn.com. Inexpensive rooms on I-75, 3 miles from White Springs.
Suwannee River Motel, 16502 Springs Street, White Springs; (386) 397-2822. Just across the street from the start of the ride.
Telford Hotel/Restaurant, 16521 River Street/PO Box 407, White Springs, FL 32096; (386) 397-2000.

Bike Shops

Keaton Bike Shop, 327 North Marion Avenue, Lake City; (386) 752-8788. Bicycle sales, repairs, and rentals.
Suwannee Bicycle Association, PO Box 247, White Springs, FL 32096; (386) 397-2347; www.suwanneebike.org. A nonprofit, membership organization formed to promote environmental awareness and family fitness through bicycling and other outdoor activities in the Suwannee region.

Restrooms

Restrooms inside, but via an outside door, at the beginning and end of the ride courtesy of the Florida Nature and Heritage Visitor Center (386) 397-4461 and at the Stephen Foster Folk Cultural Center State Park (386) 397-4331.

Maps

DeLorme: Florida Atlas & Gazetteer: Page 54 A-B 1-2.

The North Center

16 Amelia Island Cruise

This magnificent cruise on historic Amelia Island, the "Isle of Eight Flags," gives you miles of beachfront riding alternating with miles of intensely shaded and winding roads. There are shrimp boats in the harbor and a Civil War fort, too. What's not to like!

Start: The harbor parking lot at the foot of Atlantic Avenue in downtown Fernandina Beach on the west side of the island.
Length: 36.5 miles with loops.
Terrain: Flat, except for the sudden but brief hilly section on the north end of island. This is toward the end of the ride at about mile 32.3

on North 18th Street/Stanley Drive and North 14th Street.
Traffic and hazards: You will encounter occasional paved shoulders but few bike lanes. There are traffic issues on this picturesque island's roads except on those narrow shaded lanes in Fort Clinch State Park.

Getting there: From Jacksonville, drive north on Interstate 95 to the Highway A1A (State Road 200 or Buccaneer Trail) exit. Amelia Island is 13 miles straight ahead. Once on the island, keep to the left and follow the signs to downtown Fernandina. The road becomes South 8th Street. Turn left at the intersection with Atlantic Avenue and it is 8 blocks to the harbor.

This is one ride you will not regret taking. In fact, a long weekend or vacation on Amelia Island may be the high point of your year.

Beginning and ending at the magnificent, spacious harbor, this ride winds through the historic district and is lined with hundred-year-old homes that have been converted to bed-and-breakfast inns, ancient live oaks, and stately sycamores. Don't be surprised if you occasionally bump along on one of the town's nineteenth-century brick streets, either. After all, Europeans and Africans have lived under eight different national—or rebel—flags on this island since the 1600s. And yes, real pirates sailed from this harbor!

The charm of Fernandina and Amelia Island begins in the harbor, at the foot of Atlantic Avenue. This spacious expanse is often filled with cruising sailboats and shrimp boats bound for the Yucatan. You can find every kind of souvenir your heart desires along this main street, from silly T-shirts to excellent art by local painters.

The ride south to Nassau Sound can be eerily quiet if you swing onto the saddle early in the morning. Quiet, that is, if you consider a profundity of wading birds, countless shrimp and fish breeding in the marshes that march almost up to Highway A1A's two thin lanes, rolling dunes, marvelous swamp thickets filled with raccoons and opossums, and unspoiled beaches. Quiet and sweet!

Pedaling along Fletcher Avenue, which the chamber of commerce calls the "First Coast Highway," you find miles of broad, white beach, much of which is hospitable to our fat-tire cousins. Old island and new island are abundantly evident along Fletcher Avenue. Old-island stands out for its small homes (often rented to weekly

Construction on Fort Clinch at the north end of Amelia Island was begun 150 years ago. Across Amelia Sound is Tiger Island, Georgia.

visitors, perhaps you and your biking team), while new-island residents flash architecturally clever, multistory houses. Watch for the unusual as you cruise: homes built like lighthouses, a couple of old taverns, and a few stretches of beach still bordered by shifting dunes thick with waving sea oats. The magic has not deserted this stretch of Atlantic coastline.

And speaking of coastline, when you finally rack your bike and head to the beach, you can swim, walk, surf, and search for seashells the complete length of the island. Although the west side of Amelia is tidal marsh, the ocean side is one long, fabulous white-sand beach. It is so wide and firm at low tide that, years ago, auto races were held on the beach, and even today, for a small fee, you can drive on it.

Much of Amelia's beach is heavy with crushed shells called coquina. Compacted into a mass, coquina was the principal building material for the Castillo de San Marcos in St. Augustine. One of the historic two-story homes in downtown Fernandina is constructed entirely from blocks of coquina.

Two-thirds of the way south—or one-third of the way north—on Highway A1A, the ride loops east on Burney Boulevard to visit historic American Beach. During the years of segregation, American Beach was a separate beach and entertainment district

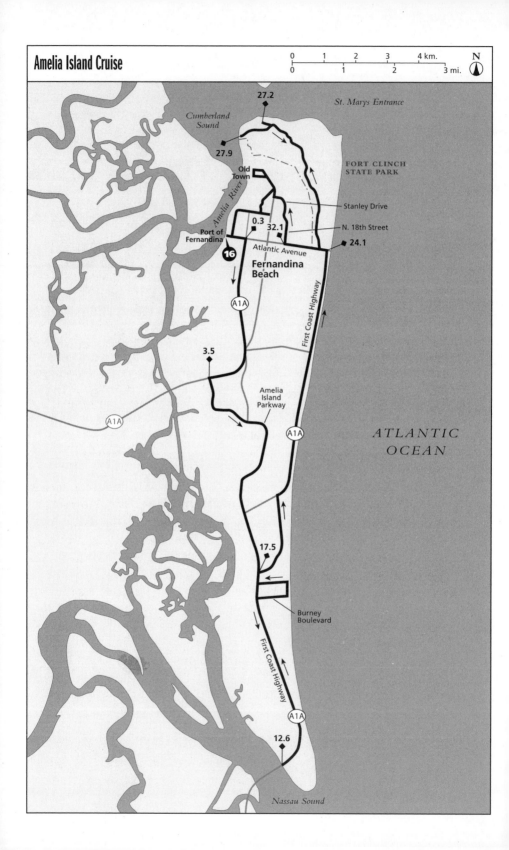

Amelia Island Cruise

0   1   2   3   4 km.

0   1   2   3 mi.

N

27.2

St. Marys Entrance

Cumberland Sound

27.9

FORT CLINCH
STATE PARK

Old Town

Amelia River

Stanley Drive

0.3   32.1

N. 18th Street

Port of
Fernandina

24.1

16

Atlantic Avenue

**Fernandina
Beach**

A1A

First Coast Highway

3.5

A1A

Amelia
Island
Parkway

A1A

*ATLANTIC
OCEAN*

17.5

Burney
Boulevard

First Coast Highway

A1A

12.6

Nassau Sound

for black residents and visitors. Regularly patronized by famous black entertainers, writers, educators, and intellectuals, American Beach is today a National Historic District. Mostly deserted these days, this broad beach still reflects the jazz era when it was one swinging place!

Now, the glory of this ride may be the miles of narrow and twisting but lightly trafficked road through Fort Clinch State Park. Park blacktop winds beneath a full canopy of oaks and palms, and even on the hottest day in midsummer, this part of the Amelia Cruise will be pleasant. Take time to walk the walls of the brick fortress, because the view across the mouth of the St. Mary's River to Cumberland and Tiger Islands, with sailboats, shrimp boats, and, if you are very lucky, a submarine in passage to or from King's Bay Naval Submarine Support Base, is just marvelous.

On the loop through Bosque Bello Cemetery and Old Town, you encounter one of the most unusual geographic formations on the island, a linked series of small but steep hills. Winding through older subdivisions, the Stanley Drive loop threads you past a marker for the battle of McClure's Hill, a Spanish fortress (Fort San Carlos) collapsing into the harbor, the tall homes of sailing-ship captains with their "widow's peak," and the cedar shade and calming breezes of Bosque Bello with four centuries of gravestones.

Miles and Directions

0.0 Begin the ride at the harbor parking lot on the west end of Centre Street (Atlantic Avenue) and ride east across the railroad tracks.

0.3 Turn right (south) on South 7th Street. The street bends left (east) and intersects with South 8th Avenue.

1.3 Turn right (south) on South 8th Street, which eventually bends southwest.

3.5 Turn left (southeast) onto Amelia Island Parkway and stay on this road without stopping as it bends south and changes names variously as A1A, Amelia Road, First Coast Highway, and Buccaneer Trail.

12.6 This is Nassau Sound, the south end of Amelia Island. Turn around here to return north.

15.9 Turn right (east) on Burney Boulevard for the American Beach loop.

16.5 Turn left (north) on Gregg Street.

16.8 Turn left (west) on Lewis Street.

17.4 Turn right (north) on Highway A1A.

17.5 Turn right (northeast) on Amelia Island Parkway (Julia Street). This is not well marked.

19.3 Turn right (north) on South Fletcher Avenue/Highway A1A.

24.1 Turn left (west) on Atlantic Avenue.

24.2 Turn right (north) into Fort Clinch State Park.

27.2 Turn around at the fort visitor center parking lot.

27.9 Turn around at the fort camping area overlook at St. Mary's River to return to the state park entrance.

31.3 Turn right (west) on Atlantic Avenue.

32.1 Turn right (north) on North 18th Street and ride over the highest point on the island. After the hill's peak, the road twists and turns and is also called Stanley Drive.

33.0 Stanley Drive turns west, becomes Leon Street for 2 blocks, and climbs to an intersection on McClure's Hill.

33.1 Turn right (north) on North 14th Street.

33.7 Turn left (west) on Ladies Street into Old Town.

33.9 Turn left (south) on Estrada Street.

34.0 Turn left (east) on White Street.

34.2 Turn right (south) on North 14th Street.

34.3 Turn right for a short ride through Bosque Bello Cemetery.

34.6 Turn right (south) on North 14th Street.

35.2 Turn right (west) on Franklin Street and wind around the entrance to Smurfit-Stone (old Container Corporation) factory.

35.7 Turn left (south) on North 8th Street.

35.8 Turn right (west) on Dade Street.

36.0 Turn left (south) on North 3rd Street.

36.3 Turn right (west) on Centre Street/Atlantic Avenue.

36.5 Recross the railroad tracks to arrive at end/beginning of this ride in the parking lot on the harbor in the Port of Fernandina.

Local Information

Amelia Island Chamber of Commerce, Railroad Depot, 102 Centre Street, Fernandina Beach; (800) 226-3542 or (904) 261-3248; www.islandchamber.com.

Fernandina Beach Police Department, 204 Ash Street, Fernandina Beach; (904) 277-7341 (emergency) or (904) 277-7342 (beach patrol or nonemergency); www.fernandinabeachfl.org.

Nassau County Sheriff's Department, 76001 Bobby Moore Circle, Yulee; (904) 548-4000; www.nassaucountysheriff.com.

North Florida Bicycle Club, www.nfbc.us.

Local Events/Attractions

Annual Tour of Bed & Breakfast Inns: The second weekend in December, Amelia Island's many bed-and-breakfast inns and historic buildings open their doors in the afternoon. Don't miss this as tickets are only $20.

Nassau Sport Fishing Kingfish Tournament: A four-day event in late June with cash prizes, this tournament is one of the largest of the Southern Kingfish Tournaments. Music and a community fish fry. Call (904) 277-3277 for information.

Shrimp Festival: Held the first weekend in May and officially named the Isle of Eight Flags Shrimp Festival, this event draws huge crowds to the island. Arts, crafts, antiques, clowns, and pirates! Begins with a parade that all the kids will love.

Restaurants

Brett's Waterway Café, 1 South Front Street, Fernandina Beach; (904) 261-2660. Brett's is casual dining at its best and the location and views of the harbor are superb, especially at sunset.

Frisky Mermaid Bar & Grille at the Florida House Inn, 20-22 South 3rd Street, Fernandina Beach; (904) 261-3300 or (800) 258-3301; www.floridahouseinn.com. Downtown in the historic district. Casual dress for seafood and steaks.

Slider's Seaside Grill, 1998 South Fletcher Avenue, Fernandina Beach; (904) 277-6652. Seafood, hot wings, and a Caribbean-themed restaurant.

Accommodations

The Fairbanks House, 227 South 7th Street, Fernandina Beach; (904) 277-0500; www.fairbankshouse.com. An excellent example of the many bed-and-breakfast inns in Fernandina. This one is on the route in the historic district (www.ameliaislandinns.com). **Hampton Inn,** 19 South 2nd Street, Fernandina Beach; (904) 491-4911; www.hampton innandsuites.net. At the foot of Centre Street next to the harbor. **Ritz-Carlton Amelia Island,** 4750 Amelia Island Parkway, Fernandina Beach; (904) 277-1100; www.ritzcarlton.com. For the upscale visit, this resort hotel is on the south beach off Amelia Island Parkway.

Bike Shops

Cycling & Fitness Center, 11 South 8th Street, Fernandina Beach; (904) 277-3227. One

block off the mapped route in downtown Fernandina; principal road bike brand is Raleigh.

Restrooms

Mile 9.5/16.1: While restrooms are available at many places along this route, public restrooms are available at Burney Park on American Beach (going, turn to the beach on Burney Road at mile 9.3: coming, the turn is at mile 15.9).

—Central Park on the south side of Atlantic Avenue between South 11th and South 13th Streets.

—Also available in Fort Clinch State Park Visitor Center.

Maps

DeLorme: Florida Atlas & Gazetteer: Page 41 C-D 3.

17 Edge of the Okefenokee Classic

Commencing with a marvelous stretch of rail-to-trail network, this ride loops through rural North Florida and south Georgia, crossing state lines—technically in the middle of the St. Mary's River—twice. Expect long stretches of lonely road bordered by endless rows of planted pines. Test yourself on this ride now, because this is as close to a big city as you can get while still being in the country for a hundred miles.

Start: The parking lot at the trailhead of the Jacksonville-Baldwin Trail just minutes west of Interstate 295 in Jacksonville/Duval County and east of Baldwin on Imeson Road.
Length: A 103.1-mile loop or alternate 63.2-mile ride that does not loop into Georgia.
Terrain: Flat to occasional gentle swells.

Traffic and hazards: Most of this ride takes place on two-lane roads with no paved shoulder. A few short stretches on U.S. four-lane divided highways can be hectic, but on these expect a little extra room with narrow paved shoulders beyond the white line.

Getting there: From Jacksonville, take Interstate 10 west to exit 53 (new exit 356) for Interstate 295. Drive north on I-295 to Commonwealth Avenue (exit 9). From exit 9, head west on Commonwealth Avenue approximately 1 mile to Imeson Road. Take a right on Imeson (heading north) and continue to the trailhead on the left (west) side of the road.

Southern planters, especially of the gentleman variety, meaning they do not rely on the farm for their sustenance, tend to overuse the term "plantation." In North Florida you will likely spend hours riding beside pine plantations. These slash pines have survived a few years but are still years from harvest size.

Classic describes the length of the ride and the endurance necessary to pedal 90 miles in a day. Of course, if you are clocking along at between 20 and 25 miles per hour, you can do the circuit in four to five hours. But that would just be wrong, not to mention exhausting. Head down, you wouldn't see a thing that you could remember—you might as well be on the stationary bicycle in your garage.

This ride features stretches of planted pines that seem to last for miles. A mind-numbing staccato of landscape without scenery. Between the endless rows are cut-over fields, hundreds of acres of stumps and scrub that, I admit, can't be too fascinating unless you are a tree farmer. Still, as on many rides in Florida, there is more here than meets the eye.

The folks who have engineered the rails-to-trails movement have done a terrific service to America. The Okefenokee Classic begins at the head of the Jacksonville-Baldwin Trail; a 12-foot strip of asphalt with another 12 feet of sculptured grass, shrubs, and trees on either side that runs east-and-west for 14.5 miles. It is easy to find. Expect joggers, hikers, skaters, and, on a side trail, horses.

Now, horses and bicycles do not mix. This is not as much of a problem for thin-tire riders as for off-road or mountain bikes. Still, inexperienced cyclists need to learn, and experienced cyclists who already understand often need a reminder. If horses are near your path, approach them very carefully. If you are coming up behind them, slow down and hail the riders; let riders and horses know you are coming. They may move to the side of their trail, so move to the far side of your trail. If a horse shows signs of fear, stop and walk your bicycle past them. Take off your helmet. Speak to them.

Go out of your way to be a good citizen and your actions will rebound positively. Thoughtlessness or a display of irritation at any inconvenience always sows seeds that at some future time, probably when we cyclists need support the most, will bear bitter fruit.

After you turn north from the trail onto Brandy Branch Road, you are in for a two-lane ride for virtually the balance of this classic. Sure, there are a couple stretches of hectic four-lane south out of Folkston on U.S. Highway 301, but they are short.

The good news is that traffic is light. Beware of log trucks, however, as it is understood in these parts that brakes, safety equipment, and driver's licenses are impediments to getting logs to mills. So if you hear a heavier rumble than the rattle of a pickup, move to the right and ride defensively.

This is a ride "in the sticks." Don't expect paved shoulders, and designated bike lanes are not on the horizon out here yet. You are riding on the edge of the Okefenokee Swamp—although little of the swamp is visible from the roadway—and it is traditionally hardscrabble country. There aren't even many country stores or gas stations along this route and therein lies its danger and its beauty. It is perfect for finding your rhythm and allowing the whir of wheels on asphalt to take you to that exalted mental place that cyclists sometimes find, a place where the body functions automatically and without effort.

Take extra water and a cell phone and make sure your patch kit is intact. Very little of this great ride is shaded and in the summer it will be hot. Because there are several stretches of long, empty road—and that's great, right?—you are on your own if you have a flat tire or twist a rim.

If you break this ride into two days with a night in Folkston, it can give you a deep breathing experience. You will have time to enjoy a visit to the Okefenokee National Wildlife Refuge; take pictures on the bridges over the golden brown St. Mary's River; sit in the porch swing of a bed-and-breakfast; and watch the trains go by.

Folkston, by the way, is a small and very old-fashioned Southern town. Unless you are saddle-sore after the 55 miles from the trailhead, or 65 miles if you ride to the refuge visitor center, do explore it to see what a country town is like. Be observant and you will be happy that you did.

A note about all the railroads you cross on this ride. People who love trains "come from all over" to enjoy the continual stream of rail traffic through Folkston.

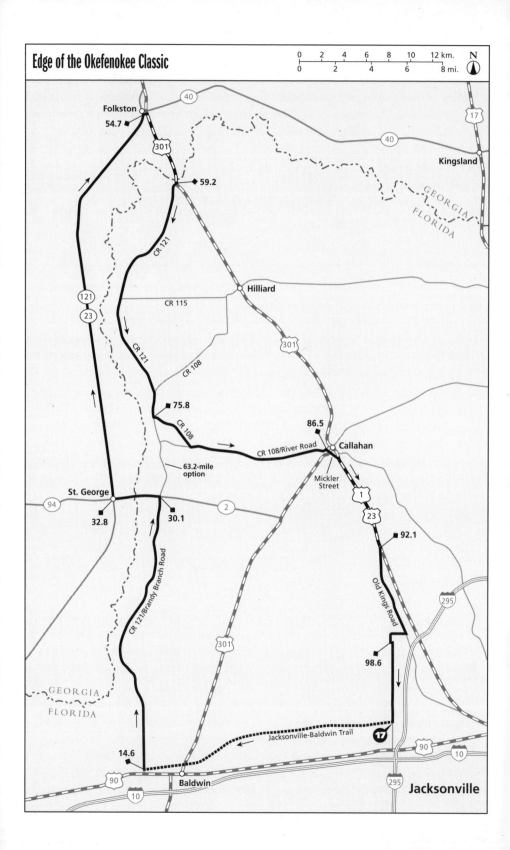

0   2   4   6   8   10   12 km.

0   2   4   6   8 mi.

N

Folkston
54.7

40

301

Kingsland

40

17

59.2

GEORGIA
FLORIDA

CR 121

Hilliard

121

23

CR 115

CR 121

CR 108

75.8

86.5

CR 108

CR 108/River Road

Callahan

63.2-mile
option

St. George

94

30.1

2

Mickler
Street

1

23

32.8

92.1

295

CR 121/Brandy Branch Road

301

Old Kings Road

98.6

GEORGIA

FLORIDA

Jacksonville-Baldwin Trail

17

90

10

14.6

90

Baldwin

295

Jacksonville

10

The area is a funnel for cargo north-to-south and also west from Savannah, Charleston, and Jacksonville. Train spotting is so popular that Folkston has earned something of a rep for the dozens of locomotives and freight cars that pass the town's special viewing platform each day. Standing near a rushing, rumbling train is the next best thing to standing near the space shuttle as it launches from Cape Canaveral. It will shake you to your core—without the burn—and this is one reason this ride is a classic.

Miles and Directions

0.0 Begin at the trailhead parking lot for the Jacksonville-Baldwin Trail and pedal west.

14.6 Turn right (north) at the western terminus of the trail onto CR 121/Brandy Branch Road. Just before the next turn onto State Road 2, you will cross a set of railroad tracks.

30.1 Turn left (west) onto SR 2 and cross the St. Mary's River into Georgia. The road becomes Georgia State Road 94. **Option:** For a shorter, 63.2-mile ride, continue north on CR 121 in Florida without turning west toward St. George, Georgia, on SR 2. It is 4.6 miles to the right turn east onto County Road 108 toward Callahan.

32.8 Turn right (north) in the hamlet of St. George onto Georgia State Road 23/121 (don't confuse Georgia State Road 121 with CR 121 in Florida).

54.7 Turn right (east) onto Martin Street in Folkston. After 1 block you cross double railroad tracks.

54.9 Turn right (south) on 2nd Street/US 301.

59.2 Turn right (west) 0.2 mile after recrossing the St. Mary's River into Florida on CR 121. At a mile you cross railroad tracks. Then, just 1.3 miles before you turn onto CR 108, CR 121 intersects with CR 108 (!); stop at the stop sign, but keep right on 121.

75.8 Turn left (southeast) on CR 108/River Road (some maps label this Drury Ferry Road). Then, a couple blocks before your turn on Mickler Street in Callahan, you will cross railroad tracks.

86.5 Turn right, again southeast, on Mickler Street.

86.6 Turn right (south) on U.S. Highway 1/23.

92.1 Angle right (still south) on Old King's Road at the sign for Dinsmore Community Correctional Center. (Don't be confused here. This may be a good time to watch your mileage, as you will pass an earlier Old King's Road on the right. If you take the wrong [first] turn, don't worry, though; it angles back into US 1/23 before the correct turn.) After a mile and a half, you cross railroad tracks.

97.1 Turn right (west) on Garden Street. At a mile, the road bends 90 degrees left (south). A few blocks from Imeson, you cross railroad tracks (again!).

98.6 Turn left (east) on Imeson Road. Imeson shortly bends 90 degrees right (south).

103.1 Arrive at end/beginning, the trailhead for the Jacksonville-Baldwin Trail.

Local Information

Greater Nassau County Chamber of Commerce, 45383 Dixie Avenue, Callahan; (904) 879-1441; www.greaternassaucounty.com.

Jacksonville & the Beaches Convention and Visitors Bureau, (904) 798-9111 or (800) 733-2668; www.jaxcvb.com/visiting_jax/.

Jacksonville/Duval Sheriff's Department, 711 North Liberty Street, Jacksonville; (904) 358-3678 or (904) 630-0500; www.coj.net/Departments/Sheriffs+Office/default.htm.
Jacksonville Regional Chamber of Commerce, 3 Independent Drive, Jacksonville; (904) 366-6600; www.myjaxchamber.com.
Nassau County Sheriff's Department, 76001 Bobby Moore Circle, Yulee; (904) 548-4000; www.nassaucountysheriff.com.
North Florida Bicycle Club, www.nfbc.us.

Local Events/Attractions

The **Folkston Funnel** in Folkston, Georgia, is a specially built viewing platform for train lovers. The double-track through Folkston concentrates East Coast rail traffic. The platform is built with ceiling fans, lights, electric outlets, and a scanner to listen to talk between trains and stations. Picnic tables, a grill, and new restroom facilities.
Okefenokee National Wildlife Refuge, Route 2, Box 3330, Folkston; (912) 496-7836; www.fws.gov/okefenokee/. The Land of the Trembling Earth refuge was established in 1936 to protect this enormous freshwater swamp and its rich ecological system.

Restaurants

Callahan Barbecue, 450009 State Road 200, Callahan; (904) 879-4675. Barbecue, fried chicken, and burgers just a couple blocks off the route.
Everybody's Lunch, 35 US 90 West, Baldwin; (904) 266-9458. A couple blocks off the route, but be on the lookout for authentic 1950s decor, food, and service.
The Grape at St. Johns Town Center, 10281 Midtown Parkway #119, Jacksonville; (904) 642-7111. Wine bar and restaurant offers eclectic continental dining. Can be pricey, but quite good.
Okefenokee Restaurant, 103 South 2nd Street, Folkston, GA 31537; (912) 496-3263.

Accommodations

Folkston Bed & Breakfast, 509 West Main Street, Folkston, GA 31537; (912) 496-6256; www.innatfolkston.com. Four uniquely deco-rated rooms on the ground floor with typical B&B pricing. Handicapped accessible.
Folkston House, 802 Kingsland Drive, Folkston, GA 31537; (912) 496-3445 or (904) 219-4240; www.folkstonhouse.com. Six rooms in easy walking range of antiques shopping and right in the heart of a naturalist's paradise. Canoeing and kayaking, too.
Hampton Inn, 548 Chaffee Point Boulevard, Jacksonville; (904) 783-8277; www.hampton inn.com. Anyone who travels understands this motel. Routine, but required.
Ship Inn, 542953 US 1, Callahan; (904) 879-3451. Right out of the 1940s, but clean and comfortable plus modest or reasonable prices! Pool and laundry; pets allowed.

Bike Shops

Bicycle Outpost, 3514 Citation Drive, Jacksonville; (904) 626-3062; www.bicycleoutpost.com. About 2 miles north of the County Road 228/Normandy Boulevard intersection with US 301. According to the Web site, they have "gone mobile! Call us, and we'll come to you. We offer bicycle assembly, on-site repairs, custom bicycle fitting, and a full line of accessories."
Open Road Bicycles, 3544 St. Johns Avenue, Jacksonville; (904) 388-9066; www.open roadbicycles.com. Full-service bicycle shop east of the route in downtown Jacksonville near the St. Johns River.

Restrooms

Mile 0.0: There are two portable toilets at the beginning/end of this ride, the trailhead of the Jacksonville-Baldwin Trail parking area.
Mile 14.6: West end parking area of the Jacksonville-Baldwin Trail; two portable toilets.
Mile 75.8: Greater Nassau County Chamber of Commerce in the Old Callahan Train Depot, Callahan; 8:00 a.m. to 4:00 p.m. Monday through Friday (904-879-1441). The old train depot is 2 blocks farther east, past the turn on Mickler Street, at the intersection of CR 108/River Road and US 1/23.

Maps

DeLorme: *Florida Atlas & Gazetteer:* Pages 57 A-B 1; 56 A-B 2-3; 40 B-C-D 1-2 and D 3.

18 Macclenny Cruise

This is an important ride in Florida, sociology happening all around. Of course, it is flat, very flat. The route, however, courses from one of the fastest growing cities—Jacksonville—to an old-fashioned town with a legacy of turpentine, pulpwood, and whiskey stills deep in the Baker County swamps—Macclenny. A delightful leg cruises the multipurpose Jacksonville-Baldwin Trail.

Start: The parking lot of the Cecil Recreation Complex & Jacksonville Equestrian Center, 13611 Normandy Boulevard, Jacksonville; (904) 573-3157.

Length: A 44.8-mile loop.

Terrain: Flat, very flat.

Traffic and hazards: Except for the brief but enjoyable 5 percent of the ride on the multipurpose trail, there is some danger of traffic. Keep your guard up on the U.S. highways, 90 and 301, and on those sections on Normandy Boulevard (County Road 228) east of US 301, which are being widened and repaved to accommodate the new subdivisions in West Duval. You will be able to pedal more freely on County Roads 217 and 218, on CR 228 between US 301 and Macclenny, and even on Yellow Water Road between Baldwin and Normandy Boulevard (CR 217). None of these roads have bike lanes, however, and even the paved shoulders are narrow.

Getting there: From Jacksonville, drive about 5 miles west on Interstate 10 past Interstate 295 to Chaffee Road. Exit and drive 3 miles south on Chaffee to Normandy Boulevard (CR 228). Turn right (west) and continue almost 4 miles to the start of the ride, which will be on the right.

Beware of this ride. Without the excitement of white-sand beaches or sunny lakes, without sweeping vistas of scenic countryside, even without wide bike lanes and the sweet comfort of shady country roads, you may end with a profound respect for the people and ways of life of old Florida.

Begin in the parking lots of the sprawling, new, and definitely upscale Cecil Community Center. This sparkling facility incorporates an aquatic center and the Jacksonville Equestrian Center. From here west, this ride along Normandy Boulevard is all dust and traffic as developers rush to reconfigure the West Duval landscape from low country with scrub oak thickets and pine barrens into suburbia.

Even as you turn south on CR 217, 6 miles from the community center, and west again on CR 218, you will be able to hear the busy rumbling of bulldozers, the steady beep as cement trucks back toward their wire-mesh targets, and the continuous bang of hammers. Nevertheless, by 218 the clamor is for the moment behind you, for on these narrow two-lane roads, you begin to see homes tucked into the woods—somewhat haphazardly, not arranged to maximize housing density as the new subdivisions. These homes are set between scrub oaks and tire swings (with real tires) next to rutted, sandy driveways that wind toward the front door through flats of palmetto that hide armadillos and rattlesnakes. Wide green lawns and wide paved driveways are not the fashion out here, for these are mobile homes and they have been a quiet presence in the landscape for many generations.

Scattered through the trees here and on CR 228 into Macclenny are literally thousands of mobile homes. You will rarely see wheels, but they must be there, by law. These homes belong to the children of the people living in small homes on large lots in towns like Macclenny and Baldwin, both of which are on this route, and Bryceveille and Raiford, which are not on the route but are nearby. Homes built before central heat and air, which distinguishes them from the homes of their children, which may be mobile and seem impermanent, but do have central units.

This sector of the United States has for centuries been known for "naval stores" (hard, straight yellow pine for masts), small farms, whiskey stills, and stringy cattle. The work and way of life is hard, a rough-and-tumble existence without a lot of sentiment outside the church.

North Florida played a pivotal role in the Civil War, but not for battles. The only engagement of significance resulted in the defeated Union army fleeing back to Jacksonville following the battle of Olustee (or Ocean Pond) in February 1864. Northern strategists believed that, with a lightning thrust from Jacksonville to Pensacola, they could cut Florida's beef and naval-stores industry away from the Confederacy. Starve that rogue state. The bluecoats' march across the state failed due to poor on-site leadership and a lack of precise intelligence about their enemy.

But all of that happened so long ago that no one remembers except the reenactors who gather annually in Lake City to celebrate and commemorate the event (www.olusteefestival.com). What the people here do remember is how their grandfathers cut the trees just so, not too deep, not too shallow, and what hard work that was six days a week with the curved blade of the heavy axe. They remember how their fathers cut the huge yellow pines, how they hauled long cables into the woods to hitch the logs to steam engines that pulled them out whole. They remember these stories as they drive to the pulp mills, but the stories are as irrelevant to their paychecks as is the battle of Olustee and the thousands of men who died there and along the Union army's retreat to Jacksonville.

So please return and ride the shady streets of Macclenny. There are tall pecan trees in the yards and broadleaf sycamores lining the neighborhoods and moss-draped live oaks with mistletoe high in the branches. People will be outside raking leaves and burning them by the curb. They may look up at you and wave. Poke around in the local stores, antiques markets, and junk emporiums in Baldwin and along US 301. This is a slice of small-town, neighborhood America that your children, who will grow up in the new subdivisions, will never see . . . or understand.

Miles and Directions

0.0 Begin in the parking lot of the Cecil Recreation Complex & Jacksonville Equestrian Center. Turn right (west) onto Normandy Boulevard/CR 228.

6.0 Turn left (south) on CR 217, a two-lane that will not be crowded.

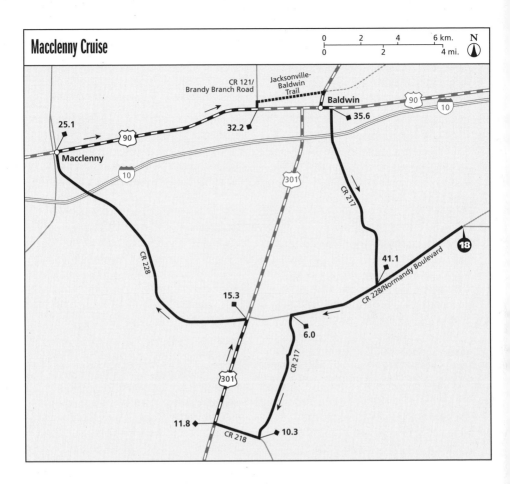

10.3 Turn right (west) on CR 218—ditto for this two-lane. Just before US 301, you will cross a rough railroad track.

11.8 Turn right (north) on US 301, a four-lane divided highway.

15.3 Turn left (west) on CR 228. Use exceptional care as this is a spaghetti intersection. CR 228, however, should be a fine ride through the pinewoods, palmettos, and planted pines with little traffic.

25.1 Turn right (east) on US 90. Again, traffic is heavy and there is a very narrow paved shoulder.

32.2 Turn left (north) on Brandy Branch Road (CR 121).

32.5 Turn right (east) into the parking lot at the west trailhead for the Jacksonville-Baldwin Trail. This rail-to-trail is a fine piece of engineering and a great ride.

34.9 Turn right (south) off the trail at Martin Luther King Jr. Drive. This is marked with stop signs on both sides of the trail. MLK is, of course, in a poor section of Baldwin—there are no other sections, really—and the street is not painted with lines. It is heavily, though very irregularly, patched.

35.5 Turn left (east) on US 90.

35.6 Turn right (south) on Yellow Water Road. It is a bit rough over the railroad tracks here, two-lane and no shoulders.

41.1 Turn left (east) on Normandy Boulevard (CR 228).

44.8 Turn left (north) into the parking area of the Cecil Recreation Complex & Jacksonville Equestrian Center.

Local Information

Baker County Chamber of Commerce, 20 East Macclenny Avenue, Macclenny; (904) 259-6433; www.bakerchamberfl.com.

Baker County Sheriff's Department, 56 North 2nd Street, Macclenny; (904) 259-2231; www.bakercountyfl.org/bcso/.

Jacksonville & the Beaches Convention and Visitors Bureau, (904) 798-9111 or (800) 733-2668; www.jaxcvb.com/visiting_jax/.

Jacksonville-Duval Sheriff's Department, 711 North Liberty Street, Jacksonville; (904) 358-3678 or (904) 630-0500; www.coj.net/Departments/Sheriffs+Office/default.htm.

Jacksonville Regional Chamber of Commerce, 3 Independent Drive, Jacksonville; (904) 366-6600; www.myjaxchamber.com.

North Florida Bicycle Club, www.nfbc.us.

Local Events/Attractions

The beaches! Drive straight east from Jacksonville (you don't need a map for this, just a compass, and it's all city driving, just different cities) to Florida's beautiful white-sand beaches. For hundreds of miles along the coast, there are restaurants, motels, attractions, and, of course, all those fabulous crashing waves.

The Cummer Museum of Art & Gardens, 829 Riverside Avenue, Jacksonville; (904) 356-6857; www.cummer.org. Unless a special exhibit is showing, this fine—and not overpowering—art museum is well worth a visit. Small fee for admission.

Florida's First Coast Birding & Nature Festival, usually held in April; www.getaway4florida.com/birdfestival/. An excellent time to see natural Florida, and many of the motels have special rates, but book early. Emphasis on photography. Google "First Coast Birding and Nature Festival" and follow numerous links set up by participating communities and organizations.

Olustee Battlefield State Historic Site, PO Box 40, Olustee, FL 32072; (386) 758-0400; www.floridastateparks.org/olustee/. Fifty miles west of Jacksonville and near I-10. Florida's largest and bloodiest Civil War battle took place here on February 20, 1864. It is commemorated with annual February reenactments.

Restaurants

Connie's Kitchen, 1199 South 6th Street, Macclenny; (904) 259-7535. Between Macclenny and the interstate, this spot is locally owned and gets very good reviews for its home-style fare, especially for breakfast.

Everybody's Lunch, 35 US 90 West, Baldwin; (904) 266-9458. A couple blocks off the route, but look for authentic 1950s decor, food, and service. I've been eating here since I was a kid, and it hasn't changed a bit.

Sand Dollar Restaurant & Marina, 9716 Heckscher Drive, Jacksonville; (904) 251-2449; www.sandollarrestaurantandmarina.com. Follow the signs east from Jacksonville on Atlantic Boulevard to the ferry ($3 and a quaint ten-minute ride) over the St. Johns River in Mayport. Seafood and more seafood. Moderately priced.

Sea Turtle Inn, 1 Ocean Boulevard, Atlantic Beach; (904) 249-7402; www.seaturtle.com. Once the height of fashion, now slumbers through multiple well-meaning renovations and new owners, but still offers excellent dining and accommodations. Lobster ravioli with shrimp . . . my mouth waters.

Accommodations

Day's Inn, 510 Lane Avenue South, Jacksonville; (904) 786-0500; www.daysinn.com. About 7 miles from the start/end of the ride.
Hilton Garden Inn Airport, 13503 Ranch Road, Jacksonville; (904) 421-2700 or (877) 924-2700; www.elitehospitality.com/cms /page.aspx?pageid=197. Near the airport and convenient to the interstate if you are traveling.
The House on Cherry Street, 1844 Cherry Street, Jacksonville; (904) 384-1999; www.bedandbreakfast.com/florida-jacksonville-houseoncherryst.html. Small B&B located on the west bank of the St. Johns River in downtown Jacksonville. Free use of bikes, canoes, and kayaks.
Travelodge, 1651 South 6th Street, Macclenny; (904) 259-6408. At the intersection with I-10.

Bike Shops

Bicycle Outpost, 3514 Citation Drive, Jacksonville; (904) 626-3062; www.bicycle outpost.com. About 2 miles north of the CR

228/Normandy Boulevard intersection with US 301. According to the Web site, they have "gone mobile! Call us, and we'll come to you."
Open Road Bicycles, 3544 St. Johns Avenue, Jacksonville; (904) 388-9066; www.open roadbicycles.com. Full-service bicycle shop east of the route in downtown Jacksonville near the St. Johns River.

Restrooms

Mile 0.0: Beginning and end—Cecil Recreation Complex & Jacksonville Equestrian Center, Monday through Friday 8:00 a.m. to 8:00 p.m. Weekend hours vary.
—Emily Taber Public Library in the Peg McCollum Building, 14 McIver Avenue West, Macclenny; (904) 259-6464. Hours vary, but Saturday 10:00 a.m. to 2:00 p.m.
Mile 32.5: At the west end parking area of the Jacksonville-Baldwin Trail; two portable toilets.

Maps

DeLorme: Florida Atlas & Gazetteer: Page 56 B-C 1-2-3.

19 Sweet Potato Challenge

There are short (35 miles), intermediate (43 miles), and long (55 miles) versions of this ride, which take you through the busiest of urban Florida and the most bucolic pastures. The highlight will be your glimpses of the only river in North America, and one of only two in the world, that flows from south to north, the wide and beautiful St. Johns.

Start: The parking lot of Lake Shore Schwinn Cyclery on the east side of U.S. Highway 17, 947 Park Avenue, Orange Park.
Length: A 54.5-mile loop with options for shorter 43- and 35-mile rides.
Terrain: Florida flat!
Traffic and hazards: Traffic on US 17, alternately a four- and six-lane divided highway, is

routinely heavy as is traffic in Orange Park. Much of this challenge is routed through side streets, which brings on its own hazards from drivers coming to rolling stops at intersections, doors of parked cars suddenly opening, and the urge to ride too fast. A quarter of the ride is routed on a multiuse trail and another quarter is two-lane country roads.

Getting there: This challenge begins in the parking lot of Lake Shore Schwinn Cyclery, 947 Park Avenue, on the east side of US 17 in Orange Park, Florida. The Cyclery is one-half mile south of Interstate 295 on the south side of Jacksonville and on the east side of the St. Johns River.

The North Florida Bicycle Club pioneered the Sweet Potato Challenge. A loop ride on the west side of the St. Johns River on and off US 17, it affords a little of everything the Sunshine State has to offer. Small towns to suburbs. Cow pastures to protected bike trails to frenetic highways.

A quick start from an ideal location—a bike shop—is just one of the benefits of this ride, which turns immediately toward the water. Unless you have sailed on it, you will be amazed by the immensity of the St. Johns River and this is an excellent place to appreciate its breeze and whitecaps.

The second excellent view of the water is from the top of the high bridge over Doctor's Inlet, which you will cross both going and coming. (Google Maps calls it Doctor Lake.) I succumb to vertigo in places like this and tend to hang on the inside of the lane, but adventuresome riders may want to look out and down from the railing. From this giddy vantage, one can see the skyscrapers of downtown Jacksonville, waves breaking on the shore of Atlantic Beach, and the tall masts of schooners delivering federal troops in the Civil War . . . well, almost.

Unless you are riding the Sweet Potato to meet a deadline, a rest stop at Spring Park in Green Cove Springs, about mile 41.6 on the 55-mile loop, is required. If you need a breather or are not in a hurry, this is a wonderful place to get out of the saddle and either relax in the shade by the side of the river or give your butt a rest while contemplating the purchase of a wide or padded seat.

Bricks are still the foundation for numerous town streets in Orange Park and Green Cove Springs. While I find this picturesque, bricks do make for a rough ride. The districts with these streets are littered with stop signs, parallel parking, and driveways. So it is best not to gawk at the homes and lawns as you ride, homes that, with flat roofs, carports, and picture windows, shout 1950s. Imagine pole lamps, Ward Cleaver, and lawn mowers before the two-cycle engine.

The southern portion of this ride evolves rapidly from suburban to pleasantly rural. That brings us to the question: Why do they call it the "Sweet Potato"? Jeanne Hargrave, doyenne of the North Florida Bicycle Club and the cyclist who originally mapped the route, says, "When we first started riding it, there was a sign on Highway 17, just before the left turn on CR 226 (at mile 21.5, the turn east for the 43-mile ride). The sign said SWEET POTATOES for sale. Our ride leader could never remember the number of the road, so he would just tell riders to turn left at the sweet-potato sign."

◀ *The Sweet Potato Challenge offers the option of riding on the shoulder of a very congested US 17 or employing a multiuse trail that parallels about 10 miles of the highway on the west side.*

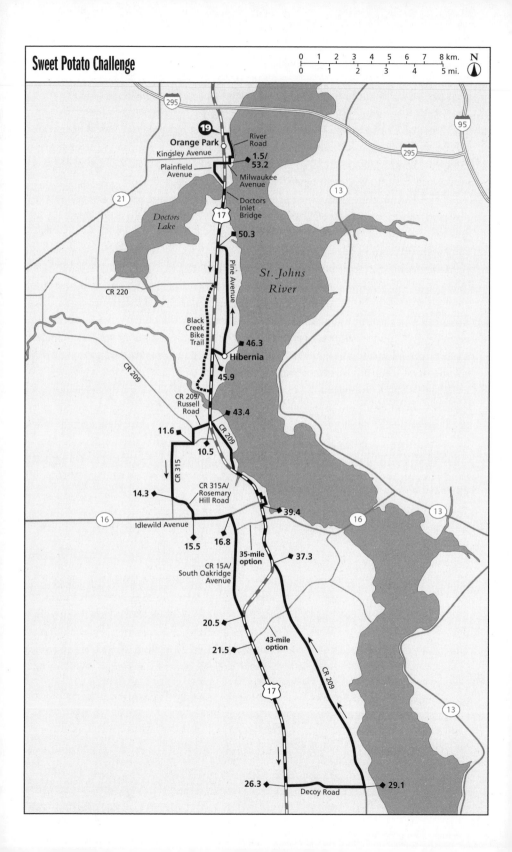

Sweet Potato Challenge

0 1 2 3 4 5 6 7 8 km.
0 1 2 3 4 5 mi.

N

19

Orange Park

Kingsley Avenue

River Road

1.5/ 53.2

Plainfield Avenue

Milwaukee Avenue

Doctors Inlet Bridge

17

Doctors Lake

50.3

Pine Avenue

St. Johns River

CR 220

Black Creek Bike Trail

46.3

Hibernia

45.9

CR 209/ Russell Road

CR 209

43.4

CR 209

11.6

10.5

CR 315

CR 315A/ Rosemary Hill Road

14.3

16

Idlewild Avenue

39.4

16

15.5

16.8

35-mile option

37.3

CR 15A/ South Oakridge Avenue

20.5

21.5

43-mile option

CR 209

17

26.3

Decoy Road

29.1

295

95

295

21

13

13

13

13

And by the way, she says, "The club has several other rides in Clay County, but the Sweet Potato has the least traffic. It's even pretty good on weekdays. The southern county roads—209, 315B, and 315, which are narrow and without paved shoulders—are a little too busy for my taste. There's a lot of new home construction in that area, and also the Rosemary Hill landfill off CR 315A. We sometimes refer to that part of the ride as the 'dump run.'"

You will cross railroad tracks several times on Jeanne's Sweet Potato. Each is rough and needs to be negotiated carefully; hit them vertically and at speed if possible. Otherwise, falling while twisting a rim in front of a vehicle could keep you from meeting the gang at Java's Brewin' on Highway 17 for a cappuccino and muffin.

Bikers who have pumped vertically on Oregon's hills or spun over the rolling knolls of Vermont during leaf season may not feel that Florida's rides are difficult or spectacular, but not every gully is a Grand Canyon, either. The trick on many Florida routes is to appreciate the details. The old Gustafson Dairy signs (featuring Ma and Pa Gustafson) on County Road 15A and the faint odor of cow manure. The sweet, clean aroma of pines along County Road 226. The salty scents of coconut-oil suntan lotion blowing in from the beaches—that's your imagination. Even the slightly sulfurous smell from the cool spring in Spring Park. Breathe deeply and pedal.

Miles and Directions

0.0 From the parking lot of Lake Shore Schwinn Cyclery, head east on Campbell Avenue toward the St. Johns River. It is only 2 blocks.

0.2 Turn right (south) on River Road and ride along the St. Johns River.

1.0 Turn right (west) on Kingsley Avenue.

1.1 Turn left (south) on Astor Street.

1.3 Turn right (west) on Milwaukee Avenue.

1.5 Turn left (south) on US 17. (Alternately, and better, continue ahead on Milwaukee to the stop sign at Plainfield Avenue. Turn left [south] and wind around to join US 17 a half mile south of the intersection with Milwaukee. This avoids a dangerous narrowing of 17 north of Doctor's Inlet Bridge and allows you to take the bike path over this high bridge on the west side of the highway. Once you are over the bridge, you have the choice of riding on the narrow paved shoulder of 17 or on the adjacent paved multiuse path, which connects to the Black Creek Bike Trail.)

10.5 Turn right (west) on County Road 209/Russell Road.

11.1 Immediately upon crossing railroad tracks, the road turns 90 degrees left (south) and becomes County Road 315B/Grant Avenue.

11.6 Turn right (west) on CR 315. In 0.6 mile the road turns 90 degrees left (south).

14.3 Angle left (southeast) onto CR 315A/Rosemary Hill Road.

15.5 Turn left (east) on State Road 16/Idlewild Avenue.

16.8 Turn right (south) on CR 15A/South Oakridge Avenue.

17.4 **Option:** Turn left on Green Cove Avenue for the short 35-mile ride. It is 1.2 miles to US 17, where you will turn left (north) and once again join the longer ride. You cross a railroad after 0.6 mile on Green Cove Avenue.

20.5 Turn right (south) as CR 15A merges with US 17.

21.5 **Option:** Turn left on CR 226/Bayard Road for the intermediate 43-mile ride. It is 1.8 miles to CR 209, where you will turn left (north) and once again join the longer ride. You cross railroad tracks immediately before stopping at CR 209.

26.3 Turn left (east) on Decoy Road. A quarter mile before the intersection with CR 209, you will cross railroad tracks.

29.1 Turn left (north) on CR 209/West Tocoi Road.

37.3 Turn right (north) as CR 209 merges with US 17.

39.4 Turn right (east) on Oak Street.

39.5 Turn left (north) on Magnolia Avenue.

39.8 Turn right (east) on Walnut Street.

39.9 Turn left (north) on St. Johns Avenue.

40.9 Turn left (west) on Governor Street.

41.0 Turn right (north) on US 17.

41.4 Angle right (north) on CR 209/Haven Drive.

43.4 Turn right (north) on US 17.

45.9 Turn right (southeast) on Hibernia Road. (You will pass Hibernia Forest Drive on the right one-half mile before you should turn. Do not be fooled!)

46.3 Turn left (north) on Pine Avenue, which, near the next intersection with US 17, becomes Raggedy Point Road.

50.3 Turn right (north) on US 17. (At this point, you should strongly consider crossing to the west side of the highway and rejoining Black Creek Bike Trail for the jaunt over the Doctor's Lake high bridge.)

53.2 Turn right (east) on Milwaukee Avenue.

53.3 Turn left (north) on Astor Street.

53.4 Turn right (east) on Kingsley Avenue.

53.5 Turn left (north) on River Road.

54.3 Turn left (west) on Campbell Avenue.

54.5 Arrive back at the beginning, the parking lot of Lake Shore Schwinn Cyclery.

Local Information

Clay County Chamber of Commerce, 1734 Kingsley Avenue, Orange Park; www.claychamber.org.

Clay County Sheriff's Department, 901 North Orange Avenue, Green Cove Springs; (904) 264-6512; www.claysheriff.com.

Green Cove Springs, www.greencovesprings.com.

Jacksonville, www.coj.net or www.visitjacksonville.com.

North Florida Bicycle Club, www.nfbc.us.

Local Events/Attractions

Adventure Landing, 1944 Beach Boulevard, Jacksonville Beach; (904) 246-4386. Open all year, the private park offers go-karts, a mega-arcade, laser tag, and miniature golf. Shipwreck Island Water Park is seasonal. Call for hours. www.adventurelanding.com.

Castillo de San Marcos, 1 South Castillo Drive, St. Augustine; (904) 829-6506. The

oldest masonry (coquina) fort and best-preserved example of a Spanish colonial fortification in the continental United States, built 1672–95. Open year-round 9:00 a.m. to 5:00 p.m. Adults 16 and over, $6 admission.
Orange Park Kennel Club, 455 Park Avenue, Orange Park; (904) 646-0001; www.jax kennel.com. A few blocks north of the start/finish of your challenge, this greyhound-racing facility offers betting on the races plus restaurants and a lounge. From June through August, doors open at 11:30 a.m.; from September through May, hours are variable. Closed Tuesday.
Timucuan Preserve/Kingsley Plantation, 11676 Palmetto Avenue, Jacksonville; (904) 251-3537; www.nps.gov/timu. A 46,000-acre national park unit with visitor-use areas located at Fort Caroline National Memorial, Theodore Roosevelt Area, Kingsley Plantation, and Cedar Point. Activities include hiking, photography, fishing, birding, and boating.

Restaurants

Athena Restaurant, 14 Cathedral Place, St. Augustine; (904) 823-9076; www.athena cafe.com. In the heart of old St. Augustine's tourist district with shopping and attractions all around. Serving breakfast, lunch, and dinner daily with Greek specialties.
Ronnie's Wings, Oysters & More, 232 Walnut Street, Green Cove Springs; (904) 284-4728; www.ronnieswingsflorida.com. Relaxed, casual, and located in the downtown area with a menu that is as diverse as customer apparel: fried clams, chicken wings, oysters on the half-shell, burgers, steaks, salads. . . .
Sarnelli's Ristorante, 2023 Park Avenue, Orange Park; (904) 269-1331. Customer reviews generally rate it very high for northern Italian cooking.

Accommodations

Hampton Inn Jacksonville-Orange Park, 6135 Youngerman Circle, Jacksonville; (800) 434-6835; http://hamptoninn.hilton.com. Rooms from $75.
The Inn at Oak Street, 2114 Oak Street, Jacksonville; (904) 379-5525; www.innatoak street.com. An elegant and comfortable inn 2 miles north from downtown Jacksonville and 2 blocks from the St. Johns River.
River Park Inn Bed & Breakfast, 103 South Magnolia Avenue, Green Cove Springs; (904) 284-2994; www.riverparkinn.com. Across the street from the beautiful medicinal spring in Spring Park. Within easy walking distance of antiques shops, restaurants, and movies.
St. George Inn, 2-6 St. George Street, #101, St. Augustine; (904) 827-5740. In the heart of old St. Augustine, plenty of tourist attractions are within walking and easy driving distance, and Florida's world-class beaches are only a mile away.

Bike Shops

Lake Shore Schwinn Cyclery, 947 Park Avenue (US 17), Orange Park; (904) 264-9052. The beginning and end of this loop ride.

Restrooms

0.0 Lake Shore Schwinn Cyclery, 947 Park Avenue (US 17), Orange Park; (904) 264-9052. The beginning and end of this loop ride.
41.5 Spring Park has public restrooms, and this is a beautiful location on the river with a flowing brook for a ride break.

Maps

DeLorme: Florida Atlas & Gazetteer: Pages 57 C-D 2, 67 A 1-2.

20 Poe Springs Challenge

This spirited ride takes in two picturesque towns, Alachua and High Springs. Expect long views of farmland, wide shoulders, and miles of bike lanes on this popular challenge. The final 7-mile stretch beneath enormous live oaks that shade the entire road is one of the most pleasant in the state.

Start: The traditional start for the Gainesville Cycling Club is the parking lot of the Chevron Gas Station on the southeast corner of Millhopper Road (NW 53rd Avenue) and NW 43rd Street in northwest Gainesville. A better starting point now may be the more spacious parking lot of the Public Grocery/strip mall directly across 43rd Street from this gas station.
Length: A 55.7-mile loop.

Terrain: Flat to gently rolling countryside with an occasional easy hill.
Traffic and hazards: Traffic on the county roads is light and cyclists have worked with Alachua County to add paved shoulders and/or bike lanes to about half of the route. U.S. Highway 441 is busy, as is the intersection near the start, and pedaling through crowded small towns always requires a special wariness.

Getting there: Take Interstate 75, which runs roughly northwest-southeast through Alachua County, to the most northerly Gainesville exit at State Road 222/NW 39th Avenue. Exit the interstate and drive due east to the traffic light at NW 43rd Street. Turn left (north) and drive to the traffic light and intersection at NW 53rd Avenue. Parking for the strip mall is directly to your left on the west side of this busy four-lane road.

The love bug can be a problem on this challenge, and no, I am not making this up, nor am I referring to Hollywood's magical Herbie the Volkswagen here.

If you make this ride—or most other rides in Florida—in the months of April/May or September/October, keep your mouth closed and your eyes covered. Love bugs love hot road surfaces, perhaps because the rising air gives their tiny wings lift. After all, they commonly fly in pairs, linked at the rear of the thorax. Thus, one of them—the female—is always flying forward while the other—the male—flies backwards. It is true. As *Miami Herald* columnist Carl Hiaasen wrote, "You couldn't make this stuff up!"

During these spring and fall months in Florida, this dark little tropical invader can be found plastered by the thousands on the windshields of speeding cars and trucks, and more than a few riders—bicyclists and motorcyclists—will practically have a seizure gagging and spitting after they suck one in. This pest has a disgusting flavor (trust me on this). The good news is that they fly slowly and they don't bite!

In spite of *Plecia nearctica* (the love bug, for technically inclined spirits—and it is actually a fly, not a bug), even on days when they swarm by the millions, the Poe Springs Challenge is a fine and memorable ride. The northern half plays tag with crowded U.S. highways and two truly delightful small towns, Alachua and High

Springs. The southern half cuts into the northern edge of Florida horse country and ends with a shaded sprint along a scenic and tightly twisting suburban two-lane.

Although they are quite different, Alachua and High Springs have fought—successfully thus far—to maintain a small-town feeling while still participating in the Sunshine State's growth. Around these towns are new housing developments and growing industrial parks that double their size each census. Nevertheless, you will cycle through the center of each (and you should either pedal slowly or plan to return for a relaxed visit) and they are just dandy for shaded sidewalks, antiques shops, restaurants that are locally owned and operated, often by the chef, and plenty of charming (and I use the word in the kindest, most manly sense) bed-and-breakfast inns.

The attractiveness of this ride and this area is its outdoor nature, its prolific options for enjoying fresh air. Poe Springs lies near the middle of the challenge and it is best to visit it on a very hot day—fortunately we have plenty of those in Florida—because you will be sorely tempted to jump into the crystal clear spring waters. Now an Alachua County Park, Poe Springs pumps an amazing forty-five million gallons of clear, cold water into the tannin-brown Santa Fe River. Poe is one of several dozen wonderful springs available for swimming, tubing, and snorkeling in north-central Florida.

Another trip will also be needed to rent a kayak on the Santa Fe River and either paddle or just lazily drift down that quiet stream. At times, because the river seems so primeval, you can truly imagine that you are a member of Hernando DeSoto's 1534 expedition marching through the area, or perhaps one of the native Timucuans who surely wished the Spaniards a very speedy passage onward.

This ride has several sections of tight roadway with no shoulder, but principally it's wide and welcoming. It would be a rare pedal if you did not encounter at least a few gaggles of speeding cyclists and numerous solos, for this is a popular ride from the city of Gainesville. In fact, riders familiar with the route alternate directions from the starting parking lot, as if seeing the sights from different angles gives them a deeper and more meaningful perspective on the roadway and the countryside.

Assuming you are taking this ride on a weekend other than the five or six fall weekends during which the University of Florida in Gainesville has a home football game—weekends that draw 80,000 enthusiastic Gator fans from out-of-town—you will find only moderate traffic on any portion. The cautions in Alachua and High Springs, of course, are inattentive drivers backing automobiles out of parking spots, for parking along their tree-lined streets is headfirst. Otherwise, bikers are common and local motorists are accustomed to providing extra room for them on the highway.

The bywords on the Poe Springs Challenge are hydrate, respect the power of speeding vehicles, keep your mouth shut, and enjoy!

Poe Springs Challenge

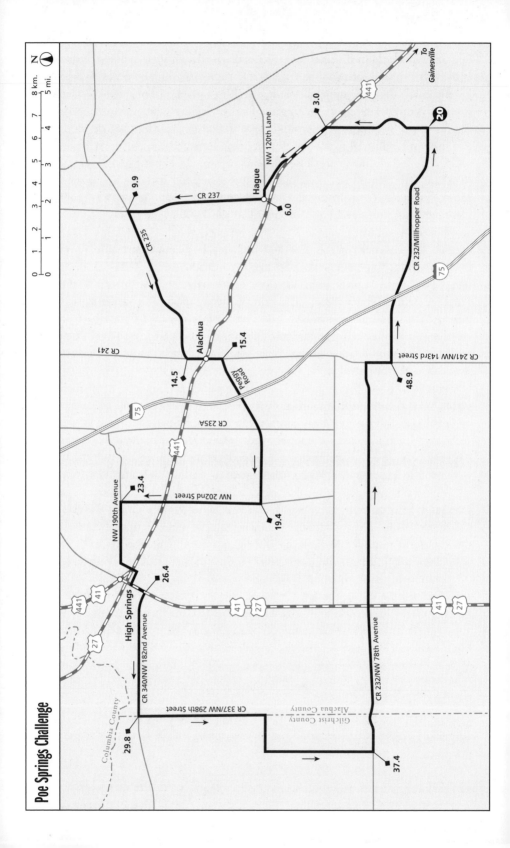

Miles and Directions

0.0 From the parking lot of the strip mall (or perhaps the Chevron Station), cross to the opposite (east) side of NW 43rd Street and then point your bicycle left (north) on NW 43rd Street. Cross 53rd Avenue and your ride begins at this wide but busy intersection.

3.0 Carefully cross US 441 and turn left (northwest) onto US 441. This is a four-lane divided highway with a traffic light.

4.7 Turn right on NW 120th Lane. This is a funky little intersection/detour. Technically you have turned north, but this narrow street immediately swings leftward and parallels the railroad tracks.

5.9 Jog left (west) as NW 120th Lane merges with NW 126th Avenue in the hamlet of Hague. You cannot go straight at this intersection.

6.0 Turn right (north) on County Road 237 and cross the railroad tracks.

9.9 Turn left (southwest) onto County Road 235.

14.5 Merge on this broad, sweeping curve south with NW 140th Street in the town of Alachua.

15.4 Angle right (southwest) on Peggy Road just before the railroad tracks. Pass beneath I-75 after 1.1 miles. At 2.2 miles, you must stop at CR 235A before continuing straight.

19.4 Turn right (north) on NW 202nd Street. After 2.7 miles you again cross US 441.

23.4 Turn left (west) on NW 190th Avenue. It will bend to the left in the town of High Springs and merge into NE 6th Street. Cross US 441 again and travel a half block to the stop sign.

25.4 Turn right (west) on NE 1st Avenue.

25.8 Turn left (south) on U.S. Highway 27/41.

26.4 Turn right (west) on County Road 340/NW 182nd Avenue, or Poe Springs Road.

29.8 Turn left (south) on County Road 337/NW 298th Street just as you pass Poe Springs Park on your right. After 3.5 miles this road makes a sudden, sharp right turn, and at 4.6 miles it makes a sudden, sharp left turn.

37.4 Turn left (east) onto County Road 232/NW 78th Avenue. At 3.4 and 7.6 miles, you'll cross railroad tracks.

48.2 Turn right (south) on County Road 241/NW 143rd Street.

48.9 Turn left (east) on CR 232/Millhopper Road. It is 1.8 miles to I-75. This most beautiful section of the ride is saved for last.

55.7 Arrive at the strip-mall parking lot at the intersection of Millhopper Road/NW 53rd Avenue and NW 43rd Street.

Local Information

Alachua, Florida, www.cityofalachua.com or www.alachua.com.

Alachua County Sheriff's Department, 2621 SE Hawthorne Road, Gainesville; (352) 367-4000; www.alachuasheriff.org.

Gainesville/Alachua County Visitors & Convention Bureau, www.visitgainesville.net.

Gainesville Area Chamber of Commerce, 300 East University Avenue, Suite 100, Gainesville; (352) 334-7100; www.gainesville chamber.com.

Gainesville Cycling Club, www.gainesville cyclingclub.org.

High Springs, Florida, www.highsprings.com.

Local Events/Attractions

Butterfly Rainforest, Florida Museum of Natural History. On the campus of the University of Florida in Gainesville, the screened vivarium houses subtropical and tropical plants and trees to support fifty-five to sixty-five species and hundreds of free-flying butterflies. Take a winding path and relax to the sounds of cascading waterfalls year-round. Monday through Saturday 10:00 a.m. to 5:00 p.m., Sunday 1:00 to 5:00 p.m. Admission $6 adults.

Devil's Millhopper Geological State Park, beside the route a few hundred yards from the start/end. Take the steps down a 120-foot-deep sink to a tropical-jungle viewing platform at the bottom. Open Wednesday through Sunday 9:00 a.m. to 5:00 p.m. $2 per vehicle.

High Springs Pioneer Days, the fourth weekend in April. Parade, petting zoo for children, arts and crafts, food vendors. The theme is fun, family, and heritage for this annual celebration.

Poe Springs Park: More than 200 acres of woodland on the banks of the scenic Santa Fe River and one crystal clear spring pumping forty-five million gallons of cold water a day. Swimming, snorkeling, and kayaking.

Restaurants

Alachua Sports Pub & Grill, 14003 NW 150th Avenue, Alachua; (386) 462-5333. It's on the route. Drop in for a burger and beer.

Conestoga's Restaurant, 14920 Main Street, Alachua; (386) 462-1294. Heavily advertised, heavy fare: steaks and potatoes. Monday through Thursday 11:00 a.m. to 9:30 p.m., Friday and Saturday until 10:00 p.m., closed Sunday.

Floyd's Diner, 615 NW Santa Fe Boulevard, High Springs; (386) 454-5775; www.floydsdiner.com. A new diner in the 1950s style, burgers to pizza to mom's old-fashioned meatloaf. Monday through Thursday 11:00 a.m. to 9:00 p.m., but hours vary.

Ristorante Deneno, 14960 Main Street, Alachua; (386) 418-1066; www.deneno.com.

Intimate or casual dining rooms with a wine list. Original Italian foods plus seafood and steaks. Chef trained in Italy. Reservations requested for dinner.

Accommodations

Grady House Bed & Breakfast, 420 NW 1st Avenue/PO Box 205, High Springs, FL 32655; (386) 454-2206; www.gradyhouse.com. This quiet B&B in downtown High Springs boasts a garden and koi pond, plus nearby antiques shopping, biking, kayaking, and canoeing. Three modern hotels, at intersection of I-75 and US 441, less than a mile north of Alachua: **Quality Inn,** (386) 462-2244, www.qualityinn.com; **Comfort Inn,** (386) 462-2414, www.comfortinn.com; and **Days Inn,** (386) 462-3251, www.daysinn.com. Three old-fashioned 1950s-style motels with 1950s-style rates on US 27 (Santa Fe Boulevard) north of downtown High Springs: **The Alamo Plaza,** (386) 454-1248; **Cadillac Motel,** (386) 454-1701; and **High Springs Country Inn,** (386) 454-1565; http://cyberstudiosinc.com/cinns/.

Bike Shops

Santa Fe Bicycle Outfitters, 10 North Main Street, High Springs; (386) 454-2453. Downtown High Springs next to the railroad tracks.

Restrooms

15.0 City of Alachua: City Park, 1 block north of the route, City Hall (Monday through Friday 8:00 a.m. to 4:30 p.m.), and Public Library (Monday through Thursday 11:00 a.m. to 7:00 p.m., but hours vary).

25.0 City of High Springs: chamber of commerce/visitor center just before the railroad tracks (hours variable through middle of the day; closed Saturday through Monday).

Maps

DeLorme: Florida Atlas & Gazetteer: Pages 65 B-C 1-2, 64 B-C 2-3.

21 Wacahoota Ramble

Among hard-core bikers, Florida is best known for endurance rides because the only constant challenges are the heat and the traffic. You can conquer both on this satisfying loop through the countryside south of Gainesville. Borrowing the nickname of the great Chicago Bears running back Walter Payton, "sweetness" is the best way to describe it.

Start: The spacious parking lot of the Publix shopping center on the northwest corner of SW 34th Street and Williston Road (State Road 121) in southwest Gainesville.
Length: The basic ride is a 30.6-mile loop, but easy-to-find options either shorten it to 17.7 miles or lengthen it to 38.2 miles.
Terrain: Typical of Florida, there are long stretches of flat to gently rolling riding interspersed with a few hills, none of them steep.

Traffic and hazards: Both Williston Road (SR 121) and U.S. Highway 441 have well-marked bike lanes, but both are heavily trafficked, especially on weekday mornings and evenings as people commute to and from Gainesville and the University of Florida. Otherwise, the country roads are narrow with dirt-and-grass shoulders. Traffic in the countryside is light.

Getting there: From the intersection of Interstate 75 and SR 121 (Williston Road), turn northeast (toward Gainesville) on SR 121 and drive 1 block to the traffic light at SW 34th Street. The Publix shopping center and its substantial, paved parking lot are immediately to the left and you only need to circle the block to find the entrance.

The Wacahoota Ramble is typical of many Florida rides: half countryside with sparse traffic and narrow roads, and half with wide lanes, bike paths, and plenty of cars and trucks, all in a great hurry.

This ride begins with a frenetic flurry of traffic and commercial driveways. Within a quarter mile along two-lane Williston Road, however, it settles into a fast, easy glide. Marked bike lanes, not just the shoulder of the road, give you room to maneuver around any of the omnipresent squashed armadillos, and after a gentle hill about a mile out, you settle into a high gear through oaks hung with Spanish moss and mobile homes tucked haphazardly into their shade.

By the time you warm up, you pass SW Wacahoota Road, which splits left for the short, 17.7-mile loop. If you are pressed for time or just out for a quick sprint, Wacahoota Road is ideal. Sure, it is narrow with no bike lane, but it is quite straight—with gentle rolling hills—and little traffic until it intersects US 441, where you turn left to return to the start.

The longer route beneath the intermittent shade of Williston Road soon crosses into Levy County. Trees thin to rolling pastures and the occasional pine plantation as you turn left onto County Road 320, a narrow two-lane without much room for vehicular error, but traffic is light, although usually a little too fast.

In the nineteenth century, a plugged sinkhole caused this 16,000-acre marsh/wet prairie to became a lake. Today you may see alligators, wild horses, deer, bison, and 270 species of birds.

For the next 6.7 miles until you come to a four-way stop, now in Marion County, you may see white-tailed deer, Brahma bulls, thoroughbred horses, migratory sandhill cranes, and some of the loveliest rural countryside remaining in the Sunshine State. Watch for curious farm dogs, who will chase something that appears to run from them, though only for a short distance, and you will quickly leave them behind.

Unless you wish to take the longer, 38.2-mile ride into McIntosh, turn left at the four-way stop onto County Road 329 for more rural scenery. The longer ride continues to the hilly, but otherwise unremarkable, hamlet of McIntosh, which thrived when oranges could still be grown this far north in Florida . . . but that was a century ago.

If you have taken the standard, 30.6-mile ride and turned left onto CR 329, it is only a few miles to I-75. On the east side of that north–south thoroughfare is one of a chain of interstate-based strip joints—you may have noticed their billboards—so watch for squealing pickups, eighteen-wheelers, loose gravel, and men wearing dark glasses.

There is a long mile to US 441. CR 329 became CR 234 when you crossed back into Alachua County before the interstate, and as you turn the curve toward

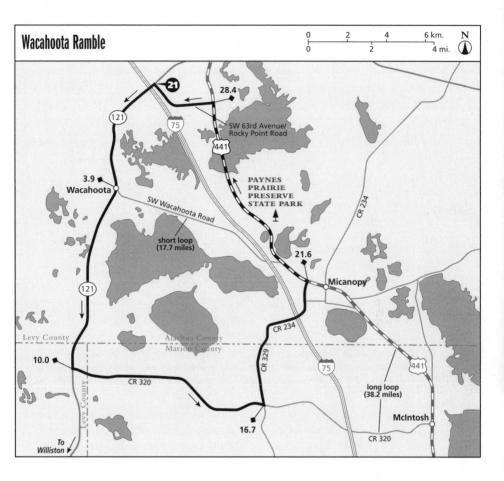

the small town of Micanopy, you have a choice. Continue straight on CR 234 and avoid the choked town with its numerous speed humps or ride into the town for ice cream. (Just 10 miles from the start, you can easily return for antiques shopping.) Because the CR 234 bypass has only been in existence a half-dozen years, older maps may not show it.

Once on US 441 headed north, whether you have taken the short, the standard, or the long loop, you are on a heavily trafficked four-lane divided highway. Your saving grace is a bike lane and the presence of the spacious and magnificent Paynes Prairie. (It is only a mile to the state park entrance, where you may turn off for an easy, mostly shaded glide to the visitor center and its friendly staff.)

A few miles ahead on US 441, the wide prairie itself opens. Halfway across, you ought to stop for the observation point on the right. A sunny, well-kept boardwalk extends a hundred yards into the marsh, and you will see alligators and abundant bird life, perhaps osprey and bald eagles. Unless you are in a hurry, this is a pleasant stop, although the parking area is too small for many visitors. Another spot to watch for gravel.

Back on the bike, it is a short, open ride to the bluff—you won't work up a sweat here if you haven't done so already—and the magnificent 15-foot massaging hands of the Florida School of Massage on the right. They mark your turn.

Turn left onto the eerily beautiful Rocky Point Road, marked as SW 63rd Avenue. You are only 2.2 miles from the start point, but this is no stretch for a slumber. The road is quite narrow and there are no shoulders, paved or otherwise; it is also heavily shaded and thus a bit dark, even in the middle of the day. Then, halfway along, Rocky Point makes a long, sweeping turn to the right and drivers tend to enter this curve a little too fast. You're almost home.

Miles and Directions

0.0 Turn right (southwest) out of the parking lot onto SR 121 toward Williston. The first quarter mile is dangerous with multiple on/off ramps and commercial driveways.

3.9 Continue on SR 121, which has now bent southward. **Option:** Turn left (east) at this shady intersection with SW Wacahoota Road if you wish to take the short, 17.7-mile loop.

10.0 Turn left (east) onto CR 320. The road is almost hidden and not well marked.

16.7 Turn left (north) onto CR 329 at the intersection of CR 320 and CR 329, a four-way stop. CR 329 becomes CR 234 when you cross from Marion County into Alachua County, and dead-ends on US 441, a four-lane divided highway. **Option:** To take the longer, 38.2-mile ride, continue on CR 320 to the hamlet of McIntosh, where you will turn left (north) at the flashing light onto US 441.

21.6 Turn left (north) again. (Just 1.3 miles north on US 441, you'll pass SE Wacahoota Road on the left. This is the point where the short ride enters 441.) Continue on US 441 past Paynes Prairie Preserve State Park on your right and down onto the prairie itself, passing the overlook on the right and being wary of traffic entering and leaving the highway from its parking lot. Up the bluff, look for the unmistakable healing hands of the Florida School of Massage on the right.

28.4 Turn left (west) onto SW 63rd Avenue (Rocky Point Road). A very narrow two-lane, watch for speeding vehicles, especially on the long right-hand turn.

30.6 Arrive at the start of the ride.

Local Information

Alachua County Sheriff's Department, 2621 SE Hawthorne Road, Gainesville; (352) 367-4000; www.alachuasheriff.org. Although this ride begins in Alachua County, it also circles through Levy and Marion Counties.

Alachua County Visitors and Convention Bureau, 39 East University Avenue, Gainesville; (866) 778-5002; www.visit gainesville.net.

Gainesville Area Chamber of Commerce, 300 East University Avenue, Suite 100, Gainesville; (352) 334-7100; www.gainesville chamber.com.

Gainesville Cycling Club, www.gainesville cyclingclub.org.

Local Events/Attractions

Micanopy, Florida, http://welcometomicanopy .com. This small town near your bike trail is known for its charm and its antiques shops. Their fall festival attracts thousands.

Paynes Prairie Preserve State Park, 100 Savannah Boulevard, Micanopy; (352) 466-3397; www.floridastateparks.org/

paynesprairie/default.cfm. Magnificent ecological systems in and around a vast prairie—a former lake—Paynes connects to the paved 17-mile Gainesville-Hawthorne Trail on the north side of the prairie. The park hosts the spring Knap-In and Primitive Arts Festival. **University of Florida Homecoming,** www.ufhomecoming.org. This weekend in fall attracts 100,000 visitors to Gainesville for a parade, football game, and party. Date in October varies.

Restaurants

43rd Street Deli & Breakfast House South, 3483 SW Williston Road, Gainesville; (352) 373-5656. One block from the start of the ride, west on Williston Road. Serves breakfast and lunch. On weekends get in line for breakfast. **Harvest Village Grill,** (352) 591-9623. One mile north of McIntosh on the west side of US 441. Closes at 3:00 p.m. except Friday and Saturday nights when it is open until 8:00 p.m. A separate building includes an antiques shop. **Ivey's Grill,** 3303 West University Avenue, Gainesville; (352) 371-4839. You will pass more than fifty restaurants serving every fast and semi-fast food in the 3 miles from the start due north to the next Publix shopping center, in which Ivey's Grill is located. Nothing is prepackaged here.

Accommodations

Cabot Lodge, 3726 SW 40th Boulevard, Gainesville; (352) 375-2400; www.cabot lodge.com. One of a dozen motels along I-75 within a few miles of the start of this ride. **Herlong Mansion,** PO Box 667/402 NE Cholokka Boulevard, Micanopy, FL 32667; (352) 466-3322; www.herlong.com. The rooms have names and are advertised as "elegant." This enormous brick bed-and-breakfast has wide verandas and inlaid mahogany floors. Built almost one hundred years ago.

Bike Shops

Gator Cycle, 3321 SW Archer Road, Gainesville; (352) 373-3962; www.gator cycle.com. Just 1.5 miles north of the start on 34th Street.

Restrooms

29.6 Turn into Paynes Prairie Preserve State Park. The visitor center is about a mile along narrow, twisting park road. Clean, air-conditioned restrooms from 8:00 a.m. to sundown.

Maps

DeLorme: Florida Atlas & Gazetteer: Pages 65 D 3-4, 71 A 2-4.

22 Cedar Key Cruise

Along the majority of this wonderful ride through the country, there is very little traffic. The delightful fishing village of Cedar Key sits smack-dab in the middle of Florida's "Nature Coast." It leads by the ruins of Native American villages and old-style trailer parks on the Suwannee, through farm and ranch country, low flatwoods, and pine plantations, and across long island causeways.

Start: Any one of the central parking areas in the small town of Cedar Key.

Length: A 52-mile loop.

Terrain: Flat, flatter, and flattest.

Traffic and hazards: The only competition on the road will be in the village of Cedar Key itself and along State Road 24. Heat and thirst could be an unprepared rider's biggest problem outside town as this is wide-open country with only one country store (the intersection of County Roads 347 and 345) along the remainder of the route.

Getting there: From the intersection of Interstate 75 and SR 24 in Gainesville, take SR 24 southwest through the small towns of Archer and Bronson, and the intersection called Otter Creek, straight to the coastal village of Cedar Key. There are no turns and the drive will take about one and one-quarter hours.

Cedar Key has recently become a destination for people looking to include a little grassroots magic in their lives. Depending upon what kind of activity or event, what kind of meaning they are seeking, this small coastal island may very well provide that sparkle.

For outdoors people, this is a wonderful and rich area because there are plenty of uncrowded country roads for biking; tidal waterways and streams to canoe, kayak, and fish; plenty of hiking and boating (including air boats, and if you have not tried this, you must!), and hunting and bird watching. If these are the kinds of activities that help you discover magic, you are in awesome luck . . . and in the right place!

I have never seen a sunrise in Cedar Key—the island is, after all, on Florida's west coast—but with the bicycle locked in the car rack and parked somewhere on Dock Street, I have seen my share of sunsets over the Gulf while I ate seafood and drank iced tea: "Sweet with extra lemon, please." And every time, I find magic. No matter how tired I am or how thirsty I've become, when splashy riots of color burst high on the western horizon and god's own cumulus casts pinks and oranges over the water, I realize that I am a rich and lucky man.

This ride begins in Cedar Key. It is not much more than a hamlet, although it is building into quite the small town. Parts of the town are scruffy and cute, while other parts have acquired some smallish condominiums and a veneer of bright paint. It is a perfect getaway location, especially if you have your pilot's license, because the island has an airport, a single runway that angles northeast–southwest, and, if no planes are landing or taking off, you can do wheelies right in the middle of the cement slab.

A public memorial to cyclists killed by vehicles has been erected on Depot Avenue in nearby Gainesville, Florida. It is close to the western hub of the 17-mile Gainesville-Hawthorne Trail.

The first day of your visit, take the 52-mile cruise. It introduces Florida's Big Bend, or Nature Coast, once called the Mud Coast. The more I enjoy this area, the more I believe it should be called the Magic Coast because the muddy nature of the coastline with its marshes and swamps preserves, an extraordinary area thriving with life that unaccountably affords enormous outdoor entertainments.

The only way in or out of Cedar Key by land is via the two-lane causeway, SR 24, to the mainland—all roads here are two-lane, and few have paved shoulders—and you must ride across several tiny islets, called "keys" (pronounced "keys" or "cays"), over Back Bayou and the canal, then over Number 3 Channel and Number 4 Channel to the mainland.

Your first half hour is the most scenic part of the ride, and you will want to come back later and take pictures. Eat conch fritters and drink sweet tea at one of the small, family-owned establishments that have sprung up recently along the causeway.

In spite of the condos, Cedar Key has remained small and quiet and comfortable, which from my way of thinking is a good thing. There is still plenty of parking for trucks and trailers for anglers and superior launching sites downtown.

And so the ride. Once you swing north on Levy County 347, you are in for a great deal of pedaling pleasure. For the first half of this ride, there are plenty of

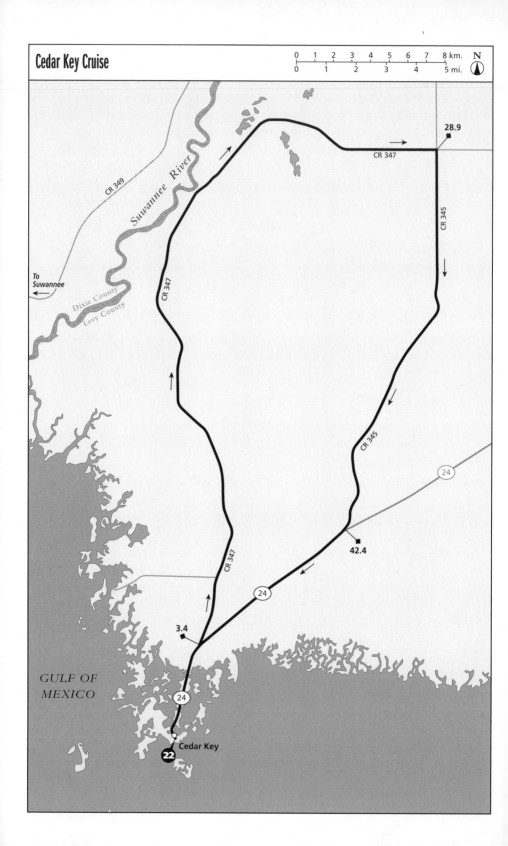

0   1   2   3   4   5   6   7   8 km.   N

0   1   2   3   4   5 mi.

28.9

CR 347

CR 349

Suwannee River

CR 345

To
Suwannee

CR 347

Dixie County
Levy County

CR 347

CR 345

24

42.4

CR 347

24

3.4

24

GULF OF
MEXICO

24

Cedar Key

22

woods and you may see deer and fox and alligators, and have osprey and bald eagles overhead plus the occasional owl swooping at helmet height across the road. Snakes will wiggle across the road, and nine-banded armadillos waddle toward the opposite side. The chance of seeing a black bear is slim, but they show up in these parts on rare occasions: "Just checking, thank you."

You will ride past Shell Mound, now a county park, and a prehistoric site where Native American inhabitants feasted on clams, oysters, and fish—and according to the archaeological record, during poor fishing years, on each other! So over a few thousand years, they built quite a pile of trash and this is one dump you ought not miss. There is camping nearby and a super spot to launch a kayak. (It is possible to become bewildered out in the marsh, so take a map and compass or GPS, sunscreen, and plenty of water. Depending on the season, you will also want insect repellent to keep the mosquitoes, flies, and a biting midge called a "no-see-um" at bay.)

Along the left of CR 347 is the 53,000-acre Lower Suwannee National Wildlife Refuge. Most of it is wet swamp and mixed pine flatwoods, and there could be wildcats and even an endangered cougar watching from the deep shade. This is a wonderful route, especially if you bike early, at dawn even, because then there is no predicting your wildlife encounters.

Before you turn south on CR 345, stop at the little convenience store at the intersection because it will be your only indoor toilet stop in the middle of this trip and the managers are friendly. The second half of your ride cuts between farms and ranches with cows for dairy and cows for hamburger, and a surprising number of— I use this word in its biological sense only—jackasses. (In an era of mechanized farming, what is their function?)

There is little traffic, except in Cedar Key and on SR 24, and there are many other county roads and biking options in the Nature or Magic Coast area. In spite of its history of being a poor but proud area of self-sufficient farming and small-time fishing, this country is filled with enchantment and your bicycle will help you find it.

Miles and Directions

0.0 Swing out of the parking area along 1st Street in Cedar Key to D Street, which becomes SR 24 on the causeway to the Florida mainland. On some maps this may be labeled SW 155th Court. All of the roads on this ride are two-lane and have no or narrow paved shoulders. On weekends or holidays, traffic can be heavy on SR 24; otherwise, traffic on this ride is light.

3.4 Turn left (north) on CR 347. (It is only 2.4 miles along this road to the left turn to Shell Mound. This is a 3.3-mile rough-paved road with another mile or so of twisting gravel, sand, and shell road to the mound and boat ramp, but it is one you will want to take at some point at your leisure.) CR 347 is designated a cycling club "preferred route."

28.9 Turn right (south) on CR 345.

42.4 Turn right (southwest) on SR 24.

52.0 Arrive at the start of the ride in Cedar Key.

Local Information

Cedar Key Area Chamber of Commerce, 618 2nd Street, Cedar Key; (352) 543-5600; www.cedarkey.org.
Levy County Sheriff's Department, 9150 NE 80th Avenue, Bronson; (352) 486-5111; in Florida, toll-free (800) LEVY-SOS; www.levyso.com.
Gainesville Cycling Club, www.gainesville cyclingclub.org.

Local Events/Attractions

Cedar Key, Florida, www.cedarkey.org, www.cedarkey.net, www.visitcedarkey.com, or www.purewaterwilderness.com. Barely a small town, Cedar Key is a fishing village that is rapidly becoming quite a tourist center on Florida's Nature Coast.
Old Florida Celebration of the Arts, www.cedarkeyartsfestival.com. Held annually on a late April weekend. Booths of fine arts and crafts line both sides of Cedar Key's main street while the school and civic and church groups serve seafood in City Park. Musical entertainment, too. A juried show, and prizes will be awarded.
Paddling, www.fws.gov/cedarkeys or www.visitcedarkey.com/cedar_key_kayak.html. The Cedar Key area is a paddler's paradise, with locations for every taste from open Gulf waters to grass flats. There are numerous islands, the largest one being the town of Cedar Key; the smaller ones are managed by the Cedar Keys National Wildlife Refuge.
Rosewood, Florida, www.rosewoodflorida.com or www.displaysforschools.com/history.html. Now little more than a hamlet with a small marker and scattered farms and homesteads, this is the site of the infamous race riots of 1923.
Shell Mound Park: This park is adjacent to a prehistoric Indian mound and nature trail off CR 347 and CR 326 outside Cedar Key. Camping, boat ramp, and picnic facilities (352-543-6153).

Restaurants

Dock Street Restaurants. This street bends out into the Gulf and is lined with restaurants such as the Dock Street Depot, Seabreeze, Frog's Landing, and the Captain's Table. Just walk in. Reservations are not required and dress is Bermuda shorts and flip-flops.
Island Hotel & Restaurant, 373 2nd Street, Cedar Key; (352) 543-5111; www.islandhotel-cedarkey.com. Try their hearts-of-palm salad!
The Island Room Restaurant at Cedar Cove, 192 East 2nd Street, Cedar Key; (352) 543-6520; www.islandroom.com. Dining in Cedar Key is casual. Menus are listed online.

Accommodations

While there are no chain hotels and motels, Cedar Key's variety of lodging choices is good. From small housekeeping cottages, motels, and efficiencies to private vacation homes and condos to historic B&Bs, there is something to fit every taste and budget. Visit www.cedarkey.org/lodging.php for a complete overview, addresses, prices, and Web sites.
Island Hotel & Restaurant, 373 2nd Street, Cedar Key; (352) 543-5111; www.islandhotel-cedarkey.com. This is the old standby and is right in village center.

Bike Shops

At one and a quarter hours from Cedar Key, these are the nearest full-service bicycle shops to your ride:
The Bike Route, 3429 West University Avenue, Gainesville; (352) 374-4550.
Chain Reaction Bicycles, 1630 West University Avenue, Gainesville; (352) 373-4052.
Gator Cycle, 3321 SW Archer Road, Gainesville; (352) 373-3962; www.gatorcycle.com.

Restrooms

Toilet facilities are located in the small city park near the "beach," and you can't miss them in Cedar Key. Otherwise, there will probably not be any public facilities open for toilet stops during your bike outing in Cedar Key and Levy County. Still, this hamlet has become a tourist mecca, and restaurants, gift shops, and convenience stores are all accustomed to visitors needing an outlet. On popular weekends the town sets up porta-potties, and along the route you will need to avail yourself of the many miles of partially fenced wildlife refuge and woods!

Maps

DeLorme: *Florida Atlas & Gazetteer:* Pages 69 C-B-A 3, 70 A-B-C 1.

23 Atlantic Beach Cruise

This is a wonderfully scenic ride on Highway A1A along the Atlantic coast of north Florida, beginning in Flagler Beach and riding north to Crescent Beach (and perhaps to St. Augustine Beach if you wish to keep pedaling).

Start: Begin in the municipal parking lot at the intersection of Highway A1A and State Road 100.
Length: A 44-mile in-line loop.
Terrain: Flat.
Traffic and hazards: Highway A1A is a two-lane highway and can be crowded, but recent improvements have resurfaced the road and increased the width of the shoulders. The hazard on this ride may be keeping your eyes on the road rather than on formations of pelicans cruising overhead and yachts sailing the Intracoastal Waterway.

Getting there: The town of Flagler Beach sits between the Atlantic Ocean and the Intracoastal Waterway, only 4 miles east of Interstate 95 exit 285 on SR 100/Moody Boulevard.

Living on the beach sounds like a dream. Jogging along the shore at sunrise. Everyone strutting their stuff amid days filled with sunshine and salty sea breezes. Sailboats offshore. Dolphin sightings. Margaritas at sunset. If there is a downside, it is perhaps that the Atlantic beaches offer too much of a good thing—okay, you'll get a little sand between your sheets, but count your many blessings.

This ride, however, offers the absolute best of everything. There is just no downside on a bicycle here, and a smooth road with fine bike lanes negates even the traffic on two-lane Highway A1A, heavy on holidays like Memorial Day and July 4. Plus, the view of white sand and sparkling water as you pedal is virtually continuous.

So this is an island ride. On your east is the Atlantic Ocean and on the west is the Intracoastal Waterway. The islands vary in length and width, as you will discover. They are "barrier islands," a chain of islands stretching along the coast that act as a buffer to hurricanes and northeasters, those out-of-season storms that originate in the North Atlantic rather than in the tropics. Aside from their picturesque white sand beaches and sand dunes topped with blowing sea oats, they always have intriguing histories.

This is the view east across the Intracoastal Waterway from old Fort Matanzas on Rattlesnake Island. This underappreciated Spanish fortress on the west side of the route is part of Fort Matanzas National Monument.

Spanish explorers sailed to Florida in numbers in the 1500s and built both the massive Castillo de San Marcos (in downtown St. Augustine and definitely worth a visit) and the diminutive coquina fortress Fort Matanzas (now a National Monument) at the south end of Anastasia on the adjacent, landward Rattlesnake Island. This little fortress, including the National Park Service boat ride, is enormously inviting and lightly visited. Unless you are careful, you might bike right past the entrance and that would deprive you of the opportunity to use this beautiful little park as a rest stop and stretch your legs with a cool, shady walk beneath the low but dense canopy of seaside oaks.

You must stop and enjoy the scenery when you cross Matanzas Inlet, which separates Anastasia Island from the islands to the south. This is one of the finest views of waves and surfers, white beach, blue water and sky, white puffy clouds, anglers, and wide tidal marsh that you will see in Florida. This single, revealing spot makes the cruise memorable and worthwhile.

Cycling north and south, you will pass one of Florida's earliest tourist destinations, Marineland, the "World's First Oceanarium." Indeed, it opened in 1938 fea-

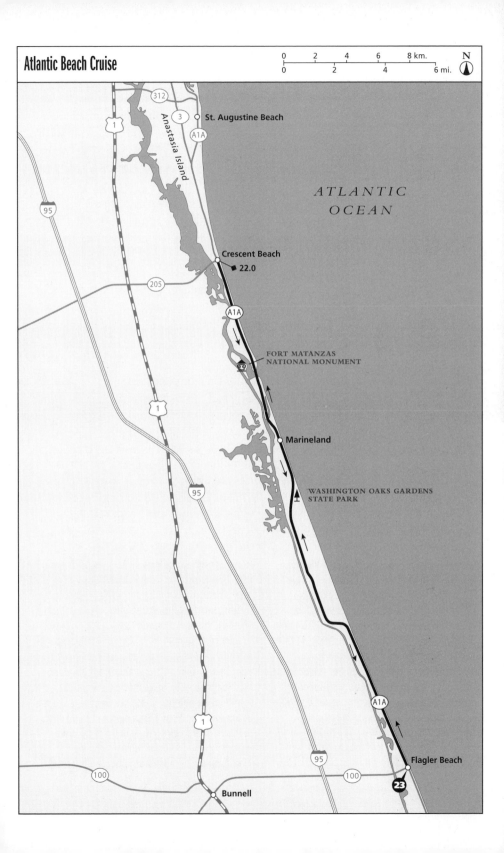

Atlantic Beach Cruise

0   2   4   6   8 km.

0   2   4   6 mi.

N

St. Augustine Beach

Anastasia Island

ATLANTIC
OCEAN

Crescent Beach

22.0

FORT MATANZAS
NATIONAL MONUMENT

Marineland

WASHINGTON OAKS GARDENS
STATE PARK

Flagler Beach

23

Bunnell

turing dolphins and sea turtles. Today, it is being revitalized with a new oceano-graphic institute, affiliated with the University of Florida.

An excellent place to turn around and head back south is Crescent Beach Park. With a sheriff's department sub-station and cop cruisers on the premises, this is as safe as it gets. In addition, except on holidays, parking is generous and there are shady pavilions for lunch. One could turn around farther north in St. Augustine Beach, where there is also excellent parking, but the north end of the island is hectic with driveways and traffic.

A wide multi-use trail runs between Flagler Beach and Marineland. It winds back and forth through the dunes and across Highway A1A. I believe you should opt off the road and take this trail because it gives you so much in the way of sights of the beach and the sound of the surf, views of kites flying overhead and . . . well, the whole-cloth flavor of Atlantic Florida.

Along this ride, you will pass a number of fine parks that are worth a visit, especially the charming Washington Oaks Gardens State Park with formal gardens and one of Florida's rare naturally rocky coastlines. It isn't Maine, but it is especially beautiful and quite tranquil early or late in the day.

Miles and Directions

0.0 Begin by turning north from the parking area in Flagler Beach at the intersection of Highway A1A and SR 100.

22.0 Pull into Crescent Beach Park, which is on the Atlantic Ocean side of the road, and stop for a rest break under the pavilions before turning back south to return on the route in the west bicycle lane, the lane closest to the Intracoastal Waterway. **Option:** You may proceed north toward St. Augustine Beach and St. Augustine on Highway A1A as far as you desire.

44.0 Arrive at the beginning/end of the ride in the parking area at the intersection of Highway A1A and SR 100 in Flagler Beach.

Local Information

Daytona Beach Area Convention & Visitors Bureau, 126 East Orange Avenue, Daytona Beach; (386) 255-4138; http://daytonabeachcvb.org or www.daytonabeach.com.

Flagler Beach Police Department, 204 South Flagler Avenue, Flagler Beach; (386) 517-2020; www.fbpd.org.

St. Augustine, Ponte Vedra & the Beaches Visitors and Convention Bureau, 88 Riberia Street, Suite 400, St. Augustine; (800) 653-2489; www.getaway4florida.com.

St. Johns County Sheriff's Department, 4015 Lewis Speedway, St. Augustine; (904) 824-8304; www.co.st-johns.fl.us.

Local Events/Attractions

Castillo de San Marcos, downtown St. Augustine, www.nps.gov/casa. You can't miss the fort because it is the center of St. Augustine's historic district. The oldest masonry structure in the continental United States, the Spanish began construction in 1672. Later, the British, Spanish, and Americans all made changes to the Castillo before it was finally retired as an active fortification in 1900. Proclaimed a National Monument in 1924.

Richard Petty Driving Experience, 1801 West International Speedway Boulevard, Daytona Beach; (386) 947-6530; www.daytonausa.com. Reservations are not required. Just show up at the track for ride-alongs or—after instruction—you can take the wheel yourself on the speedway's 31-degree banked track.

The **Atlantic Ocean** is the star attraction of this bike ride, and there are dozens of places you can access the beach for free if you are walking or for a small fee if you are driving. This is one of the few places in the nation where you can drive your vehicle on the beach!

Restaurants

Barrier Island Inn & Restaurant, 7601 A1A South, St. Augustine; (904) 461-4288; www.barrierislandbb.com. Open to the public and on the route, right next to the Intracoastal at Channel Marker 71B. Looks very interesting.

Gypsy Cab Co. Restaurant, 828 Anastasia Boulevard, St. Augustine; (904) 824-8244; www.gypsycab.com. Funky, urbane, and several miles north of the ride near the historic lighthouse, on the right side of Highway A1A.

Salt Water Cowboys, 299 Dondanville Road, St. Augustine; (904) 471-2332; www.salt watercowboys.com. Good seafood and authentic ambience.

Accommodations

Casa Monica Hotel, 95 Cordova Street, St. Augustine; (904) 827-1888; www.casa monica.com. This is a beautiful old place in the heart of downtown St. Augustine.

Daytona Beach: "There are hundreds of hotels, condominiums, cottages and bed & breakfast inns listed in our directory, many with online booking functions," according to www.daytona beach.com/where.cfm.

Whale Watch Motel, 2448 South Oceanshore Boulevard, Flagler Beach; (386) 439-2545 or (877) 635-5535; www.whalewatchmotel.com. Not a chain and one of literally thousands of places to spend the night along the beach.

Bike Shops

Bike Fitters at Bike America, 3936 A1A South, St. Augustine; (904) 461-5557; www.bikefitters.com. A complete bike shop a couple miles north of Crescent Beach Park.

PC Bike, 132 Palm Coast Parkway, Palm Coast; (386) 447-2453; www.pcbike.com. This bike shop considers itself Flagler County's "only full-service bike shop." On the route, but closed Sunday.

Restrooms

Mile 5.0/39.0: Varn Park is on the east, Atlantic Ocean side.

Mile 10.6/33.4: Bings Landing Park is on the east, Atlantic Ocean side.

Mile 18.4/25.6: Southeast Intracoastal Waterway Park is on the west, Intracoastal side.

Maps

DeLorme: Florida Atlas & Gazetteer: Pages 68 B-C-D 3, 74 A 3, 75 A 1.

24 Atlantic Beach Ramble

A fine ride south from Flagler Beach to Ormond Beach, a suburb of Daytona. The views of the ocean are bright and fresh, and one gets a sense of old beach property . . . and the future as well.

Start: Begin in the municipal parking lot at the intersection of Highway A1A and State Road 100.
Length: A 29 mile in-line loop.

Terrain: Flat.
Traffic and hazards: This beachfront ride on beautiful Highway A1A is a little more crowded with traffic than the Flagler ride north.

Getting there: Flagler Beach sits between the Atlantic Ocean and the Intracoastal Waterway, only 4 miles east of Interstate 95 exit 285 on SR 100/Moody Boulevard. It is just north of Ormond Beach and Daytona Beach.

The ride south from Flagler Beach toward Daytona along coastal highway A1A is unusual because it combines sweeping vistas of beach and ocean, preserved areas of native beauty, roads filled with busy day-to-day traffic, and interesting views of both old and new Florida.

If you are not in a hurry—and hurry is one mental strain that you ought to avoid on a bicycle—slip a block west and ride Central Avenue or 2 blocks onto South Daytona Avenue. These two residential streets are straight, and you may ride them for about 3 miles until they end, at which point you can swing to the left toward the ocean and rejoin A1A. Although they are lined with homes, driveways, and shrubbery that sometimes overflows into the roadway, they pass through a 1950s vision of living near the beach—Ozzie and Harriet are here and Fred and Wilma wish they were. This is a neighborhood of small and unpretentious single-story homes, many with flat roofs, and carports and sandy yards rather than rich green lawns. There is normally plenty of "mess," the complete stuff of life, as well: bicycles and beach balls and old cars, clothes on the line, and occasionally 1950s-style jalousie windows cranked open from the inside to take advantage of ocean breezes.

State and local governments have worked in harmony to establish or preserve a number of small plots of land as parks in this area and all are worthy of a visit. The Gamble Rogers Memorial State Recreation Area just 3.5 miles south of the ride's start is such a park, as is the North Peninsula State Recreation Area at 4.5 miles south, the even smaller Bicentennial Cross-Island Park at 11 miles south, and the tiny, ocean-side Tom Renick Park at 11.5 miles south. All are user-friendly and have something unique to teach or some unique way to enjoy Florida.

Imagine what this ride would have been like when moms and dads took the family on Sunday drives. The road was narrower (and unlike today there were certainly no helmeted cyclists), but automobiles were smaller and they were not air-

Julie Keen, a resident of Brighton, England, waved and then stopped to chat up the photographer as yachts passed in the Intracoastal Waterway/Matanzas River.

conditioned, so the kids in the backseats took out their frustrations about being cooped up in the car on their siblings. Ahh, life was good!

Miles and Directions

0.0 Begin by turning south from the parking area in downtown Flagler Beach at the intersection of Highway A1A and SR 100. (Actually, there are interesting alternate routes riding the parallel Central and South Daytona Avenues, 1 and 2 blocks to the west of A1A—the island is narrow here—south to about South 28th Street.)

14.5 Turn around 180 degrees to make this ride a loop at the intersection of A1A and State Road 40 in Ormond Beach. (Riding farther south on this road, one encounters continuously high volumes of traffic and it is not recommended.)

29.0 Arrive at the beginning/end of the ride in the parking area at the intersection of Highway A1A and SR 100 in Flagler Beach.

Local Information

Daytona Beach Area Convention & Visitors Bureau, 126 East Orange Avenue, Daytona Beach; (386) 255-4138; http://daytona beachcvb.org or www.daytonabeach.com. **Daytona Beach Police Department,** 990 Orange Avenue, Daytona Beach; (386) 671-5100; http://dbpd.us/.

Flagler Beach, www.flaglercounty.com, www.floridavacations.com/fv/Flagler-Beach-Florida.html, or www.cityofflaglerbeach.com. **Flagler Beach Police Department,** 204 South Flagler Avenue, Flagler Beach; (386) 517-2020; www.fbpd.org.

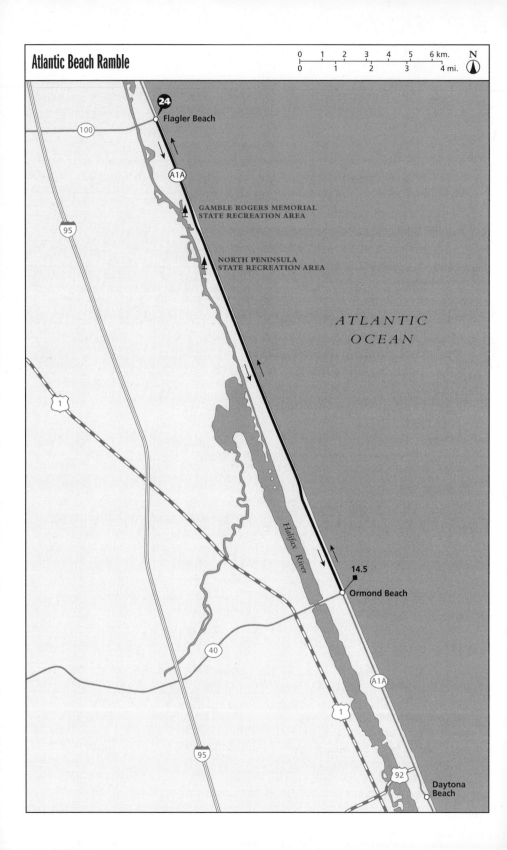

0   1   2   3   4   5   6 km.   N

0   1   2   3   4 mi.

24

○ Flagler Beach

100

A1A

GAMBLE ROGERS MEMORIAL
STATE RECREATION AREA

NORTH PENINSULA
STATE RECREATION AREA

95

*ATLANTIC
OCEAN*

1

Halifax River

14.5

○ Ormond Beach

40

A1A

1

95

92

Daytona
Beach

St. Augustine, Ponte Vedra & the Beaches Visitors and Convention Bureau, 88 Riberia Street, Suite 400, St. Augustine; (800) 653-2489; www.getaway4florida.com.
St. Johns County Sheriff's Department, 4015 Lewis Speedway, St. Augustine; (904) 824-8304; www.co.st-johns.fl.us.

Local Events/Attractions

The beach: Beaches in the Daytona Beach area are always open and free to pedestrians. Cars are allowed on the beach from sunrise to sunset when tidal conditions permit. During December and January the $5 beach access fee for vehicles is waived.

Daytona Bike Week (www.officialbikeweek.com) takes place in mid-October each year. Sorry, they don't mean "Bicycle" Week. Best avoided by cyclists, but if you are a motorhead, this event is all about you!

Daytona International Speedway, 1801 West International Speedway Boulevard, Daytona Beach; (386) 254-2700; www.daytona internationalspeedway.com. Fast, loud, and furious. The best time to truly feel what speed is all about is the mid-February running of the "Daytona 500" automobile race.

Gamble Rogers Folk Festival, 6713 Hidden Creek Boulevard, St. Augustine; (904) 208-5210; www.gamblefest.com. Music and story-telling in the best tradition of old-time Florida. Held annually in May, this festival is the antithesis of speed!

Restaurants

You can't walk a hundred yards along the popular east-coast beaches of Florida without stumbling onto a couple of good restaurants.

Athena Restaurant, 14 Cathedral Place, St. Augustine; (904) 823-9076; www.athenacafe .com. Greek restaurant serves all meals. One of the author's favorites.

Columbia Restaurant, 95 St. George Street, St. Augustine; (904) 824-3341; www.columbia restaurant.com. In the historic district of St. Augustine.

Fisherman's Net, 500 South Oceanshore Boulevard, Flagler Beach; (386) 439-1818.
The Golden Lion Cafe, 500 North US A1A,

Flagler Beach; (386) 439-3004; www.goldenlioncafe.com.
Julian's Dining Room & Lounge, 88 South Atlantic Avenue, Ormond Beach; (386) 677-6767; www.juliansrest.com. No matter who writes the review, the atmosphere is definitely '70s and upbeat in this A-frame building.

Accommodations

Anastasia Inn, 218 Anastasia Boulevard, St. Augustine; (904) 825-2879 or (888) 226-6181; www.anastasiainn.com. Just over the Bridge of Lions from the St. Augustine historic district. North of the ride, but clean, convenient, and available.

Lillian Place Bed & Breakfast Inn, 111 Silver Beach Avenue, Daytona Beach; (877) 893-7579; www.discoverourtown.com. B&B prices and plenty of rooms. The only waterfront inn in Daytona Beach. Author Stephen Crane (The Red Badge of Courage, The Open Boat) stayed here after being rescued from a sinking boat in the 1800s.

White Orchid Inn & Spa, 1104 South Oceanshore Boulevard, Flagler Beach; (386) 439-4944 or (800) 423-1477; www.whiteorchid inn.com. On the ocean and on your route. Pricey but well recommended.

Bike Shops

PC Bike, 132 Palm Coast Parkway, Palm Coast; (386) 447-2453; www.pcbike.com. This bike shop considers itself Flagler County's "only full-service bike shop." Just north of Flagler Beach. Closed Sunday.

Xtreme Cycles, 39 South Yonge Street, Ormond Beach; (386) 677-3480. A few blocks from the turnaround at the midpoint of this ride.

Restrooms

3.5/25.5 Gamble Rogers Memorial State Recreation Area at Flagler Beach.
11.0/18.0 Bicentennial Park: a "cross-island" park situated on the west side of A1A.
11.5/17.5 Tom Renick Park: a small, crowded beach-side urban park.

Maps

DeLorme: Florida Atlas & Gazetteer: Pages 74 A 3, 75 A-B 1.

25 The Great Florida Ranch Cruise

When you have reached a limit of dodging traffic and looking at the sights, it is time to glue your eyes to the road and pump. This is cattle country and commercial nursery country. It is all two-lane and there is not much to look at, but plenty to see!

Start: The Pierson Town Park, approximately 16 miles north of the city of DeLand on U.S. Highway 17.
Length: A 37-mile loop.
Terrain: Flatmus!
Traffic and hazards: Half of this ride is quiet country and half is . . . well, quite busy. Traffic

along US 17, roughly north and south through Florida, can be difficult at times, and State Road 40 between Ocala and Ormond/ Daytona is often busy. On the other hand, this ride is all about stretching and training, so you will be going as fast as they are!

Getting there: Pierson is a small town. Before I found it on the map, I had never heard of it. So, from Interstate 95, which lies just a couple of miles west of Ormond/Daytona Beach, take exit 268 off SR 40 west toward Ocala and the Ocala National Forest. It is about 20 miles to US 17 and then about 4 miles north to Pierson.

There is little "typical Florida" scenery on this ride. It is two-lane with no generous allowances for bicycles. On the other hand, this is the perfect place to burn calories and stretch those tight muscles.

No, there are no ocean waves crashing on the shore and no long vistas over submerged coral reefs. But there is not much frantic traffic, either, although on popular holidays SR 40, which runs from Ormond Beach on the Atlantic Ocean through the Ocala National Forest and Ocala to Yankeetown and Pumpkin Island on the Gulf of Mexico, effectively drawing a line across state maps, can be hectic as people surge to and from the beach. And US 17 always has a full share of vehicles. The other half of the ride is authentically "traffic-lite."

This is farm and ranch country. Cows everywhere. No towns or cities to speak of. No historic sites. A sprinkling of horses and goats. More cows. And vistas of wholesale nurseries growing acres and acres of ferns and exotic plants . . . all hidden beneath miles of lightweight black shade cloth. At today's prices, just that cloth is worth a fortune.

So with little to look at, this ride is all about muscle tone and burning toxins. Wanting to learn some technical "good stuff" about caloric expenditures, I Googled "bicycle exercise." What I found, of course, was the exercise where you lie on your back (good so far!), then lace your fingers behind your head, lift the head, lift the legs, and pump "as if" you were on a bicycle. Without promoting a special brand of beer that should be imbibed with this exercise, I figured I could do better on my real bike, an old street-wise Peugeot. But I tried twenty of the floor exercises any-

Can you identify this breed of cow? Cracker? Longhorn? Brahma? In a recent test, Florida agricultural experts guessed incorrectly . . . and it is imported to Florida ranches. It is an Ankole-Watusi from East Africa: productive on low-quality forage, and heat and drought resistant. And look at those horns!

way and all I could think of was cows looking up as I pumped by their pastures. Thanks Paige Waehner, you cute devil. Now, get a real bike!

To be more specific with my Google quest, I typed "bicycle riding exercise." This directed me to real information, or sort-of-real information. Sharyl Calhoun's article "Bike Riding for Weight Loss" at www.ezinearticles.com says that as you push your distance and speed, you are bound to feel pain in miscellaneous internal and external body parts. By the time you turn left off US 17 onto SR 40 at Barberville—which isn't really a town, just a spot on the map—you can already feel that pain, although it could just be last night's burritos. Anyway, if you can't feel the strain, it is time to turn up the power.

Then came the good stuff at DavidHolt.bigstep.com. Holt says riding a bicycle is excellent cross training for running marathons and, of course, for triathlons in which cycling is required. Riding a bicycle, he says, helps improve 10k running times by 9 percent and boosts "VO2-max."

Figuring that was a misprint, I went to my favorite free encyclopedia,

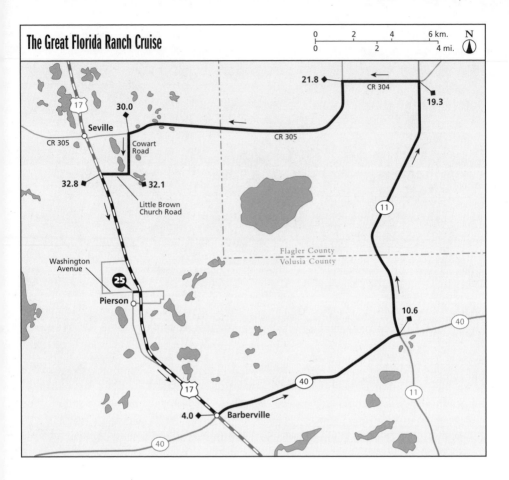

Wikipedia.com, and discovered that there really is such a thing as "VO2-max": the maximum capacity to transport and utilize oxygen during incremental exercise expressed as liters of oxygen per minute (l/min). Tour de France winners Lance Armstrong and Greg LeMond, for instance, have very high VO2-maxes whereas I, apparently, have a relatively high beer-max. It is a relative world. Einstein said so and I believe it. Even cows along this route know it. They are contentedly munching sweet alfalfa and enjoying the sunshine while waiting to be turned into hamburger. *Cest la vie,* eh.

While going on about how biking outdoors fosters a sense of "freedom and exhilaration" at Lifetimetv.com/reallife/health, Daryn Eller used the "C" words. Crotch clearance. Daryn says you need an inch of space between your crotch and the top bar of the bike's body for a road bike, 2.5 inches for a mountain or hybrid bike. That makes me question the skinny tires on this old bike.

Bonjour, mes amis la vache. But these lovely cows are too clever to be torn away from contented munching to pass the time with a common cyclist, so I check traffic and speed left off State Road 11 onto another two-laner, County Road 304, at the general store at Cody's Corner, and suddenly the sun is on my back, but out of nowhere love bugs are in my face and eyes and mouth, and it isn't only the legs and lungs that feel the burn. . . .

From CR 304, turn left onto CR 305 and in just a few miles, take another left onto Cowart. The road is rough, but this little jog—about 3 miles—lets you avoid the busy intersection with US 17 and gives you a chance to see a quiet corner of the roadway.

Turn right at Cowart and Little Brown Church Road (I couldn't locate the church) . . . because there is no other way. Left is a dirt road between small homes and black shade cloth and straight ahead is a dead end. Now feel the burn as you are close to the end of this ride. Pump to US 17 and back to Pierson. After all, there is a nudist resort in Pierson—actually, there are several around Lake George just to the west, and you need a break after a long, hot ride. Jokes aside, I suspect that an hour at one of these resorts—the one near Pierson is pleasantly titled "Sunny Sands Florida"— will be more than enough to put your butt back on the road . . . and with gusto.

Miles and Directions

0.0 From the parking area of the Pierson Town Park, turn left (east) on West Washington Avenue and pedal 1 block to US 17. Turn right (south).

4.0 Turn left (east) in Barberville onto SR 40.

10.6 Turn left (north) at the SR 40 intersection with SR 11.

19.3 Turn left (west) at the intersection with CR 304.

21.8 Turn left (south) at the intersection with CR 305. This road will shortly make a broad, sweeping 90-degree turn to the west.

30.0 Turn left (south) at the intersection with Cowart Road, unmarked except for a small street sign.

32.1 Turn right (west) at the intersection with Little Brown Church Road.

32.8 Turn left (south) at the intersection with US 17.

37.0 Turn into West Washington Avenue and travel the block to the parking area.

Local Information

Daytona Beach Area Convention & Visitors Bureau, 126 East Orange Avenue, Daytona Beach; (386) 255-4138; http://daytona beachcvb.org or www.daytonabeach.com.

DeLand Chamber of Commerce, 336 North Woodland Boulevard, DeLand; (386) 734-4331; www.delandchamber.org.

Ocala National Forest, www.fs.fed.us/r8 /florida/recreation/index_oca.shtml.

Tourist information, www.visitflorida.com.

Volusia County Sheriff's Department, PO Box 569, DeLand, FL 32721; http://volusia.org /sheriff/. For emergencies anywhere in Florida, dial 911.

Local Events/Attractions

Daytona International Speedway, 1801 West International Speedway Boulevard, Daytona Beach; (386) 254-2700; www.daytona internationalspeedway.com. Home of the famous mid-February running of the "Daytona 500" automobile race. Jammed motels and restaurants for 100 miles in every direction.

Stetson University, 421 North Woodland Boulevard, DeLand; www.stetson.edu/home/. Highly regarded private university with 2,200 undergraduates and 195 instructors.

St. Johns River, www.riveroflakesheritage corridor.com. One of two significant rivers in the world that flows north. The other is the Nile. Festivals, boating, fishing, antiquing, swimming, scuba diving, and snorkeling.

Sunny Sands Florida, 502 Central Boulevard, Pierson; (386) 749-2233; www.sunnysands .com. For those days when you really have to get away from it all, try this "clothing optional" resort. And there is a restaurant.

Volusia Speedway Park, 1500 SR 40, De Leon Springs; (386) 985-4402; www.volusia speedwaypark.com. Dirt track raceway calls all motorheads!

Restaurants

Artisan Inn, 215 South Woodland Boulevard, DeLand; (386) 734-6550; www.deland artisaninn.com. Cleverly remodeled with accommodations, restaurant, and lounge.

Carter's Country Kitchen, 105 North Center Street, Pierson; (386) 749-4983. On the route, and you don't have to call ahead for reservations.

Old Spanish Sugar Mill, 601 Ponce DeLeon Boulevard, De Leon Springs; (386) 985-5644. A way-cool rustic eatery in De Leon Springs State Park!

Accommodations

Camping: Ocala National Forest, www.fs.fed .us/r8/florida/recreation/index_oca.shtml.

Eastwood Terrace Inn, 442 East New York Avenue, DeLand; (386) 736-9902; www .eastwoodinn.com. Built as a hotel eighty years ago.

Hotel Pierson, 107 South Volusia Avenue, Pierson; (386) 749-1577; www.hotelpierson.com. Right "downtown" and nearly 90 years old.

Victorian Lace-Bed & Breakfast Inn, 5444 US 17, De Leon Springs; (386) 985-5223; www.victorian lacebedandbreakfast.com. Five rooms filled with antiques and comfort.

Bike Shops

Big Bike, 1081 North U.S. Highway 1, Ormond Beach; (386) 672-0309.

DeLand Cyclery, 111 West Indiana, DeLand; (386) 822-9422; www.volusia.com/deland /index.htm.

JC's Bikes & Boards, 1520 South Woodland Boulevard, DeLand; (386) 736-3620.

Restrooms

Mile 0.0/37.0: Pierson Town Park.

Mile 19.3: In case of a personal emergency, there is a general convenience store at Cody's Corner at the intersection of SR 11 and CR 304.

Maps

DeLorme: Florida Atlas & Gazetteer: Pages 74 B-C 1-2.

26 Ocala National Forest Classic

This classic ride offers an excellent day in the woods with quick trips through several hamlets, the largest of which is Salt Springs, and dozens of ponds and lakes. The forest scenery is not dramatic, often having been cut over or carefully burned, but the traffic is not too bad, either—except for construction trucks traveling over the speed limit on State Road 19. Several long uphill stretches will test your endurance.

Start: Begin in the lime-rocked parking lot of the Ocklawaha Visitor Center a block north of State Road 40 on County Road 315 due east of the city of Ocala. There are restrooms here and friendly staff who sell books, mugs, and T-shirts and hand out free literature.
Length: A 74-mile figure-eight loop.
Terrain: Flat to moderately rolling with several long but low-grade uphill stretches.

Traffic and hazards: This ride takes place entirely on two-lane roads divided half and half between those with no shoulder and those with a paved yard of asphalt. Although this is a great ride, most bikers in the national forest are busy with mud and dirt off-road, so thin-tire riders are rare. SR 40 can be very busy as can SR 19 to a lesser extent.

Getting there: From Interstate 75 west of Ocala in north-central Florida, take SR 40 east through the city for 10 miles to CR 315 (on the left). This road, four lanes through the city, is also known as Silver Springs Boulevard because it passes that still-sparkling 1950s attraction Silver Springs, east of Ocala and just west of the start of this ride.

The good news: Since 1908 the Ocala National Forest (ONF) classic ride has presented long stretches of road uncrowded with gawking tourists looking at the views and only moderately thronged with traffic. Today most of Ocala's business commuters and churchgoers live to the west, and only a couple of spots on this long ride require extra caution—the stretch along SR 40 to County Road 314A, for example—but it is otherwise a zone for letting it all hang out, breathing deeply, and feeling the fat turn into raw, stringy muscle.

This forest is one part of a national treasure of resources administered by the U.S. Forest Service. Aside from its timber, most of which has long been cut over, leaving scrub oak barrens in its place, the ONF offers hundreds of campsites from well tended with hookups to primitive. In addition, it offers year-round recreational activities from swimming and snorkeling in its several pristine springs to off-road biking trails; canoeing and kayaking the rivers; hiking the 61-mile Florida National Scenic Trail (www.florida-trail.org); and hunting, fishing, nature photography, and birding. It truly is a great place to spend the day or visit for a week.

Any time of year or time of day is fine for this ride, but summer afternoons have a tendency to "come up a boil" of thunderstorms, as old-timers say. Although they do not last long, these storms can be violent, with strong wind, hail, lightning, and

Horses, hikers, deer, bear . . . Now that is a multiuse-trail sign. But where are the bikers? Bikers in the Ocala National Forest have typically worn boots and chains.

thunderous rain. If you are caught on the road during a thunderstorm, look for immediate shelter, even if it is only under a low scrub oak away from the side of the road. Cut a couple of palmetto fronds to hold over your head and make the best of it. Think of the cold soaking and the steaming humidity afterwards as *an experience!*

Depending upon your interest in the forest, you may discover two animals that could provide a lifetime of memories. The alligator is ubiquitous now in the Sunshine State and they are always ready to wrestle a target of opportunity. In recent years, they have eaten several Floridians and are indicted in more attacks than sharks. Except during their mating season in May, alligators do not roam far from water and although the springs and swimming holes are well protected, you will spot gators along the streams and riverbanks. Shine a spotlight across an area lake at night and you will probably see their eyes reflecting, reptilian and merciless, on the dark surface.

The other animal of special interest is the black bear. Bears, like their scaly neighbors, are always hungry. This may cause some anxiety for campers who are careless with their food or take candy into their tent, especially at night, but the black bear is both rare and rarely aggressive. (That noise outside is probably a raccoon or an armadillo . . . probably, but not always.) Attacked by a grizzly in Montana, the best avail-

Ocala National Forest Classic

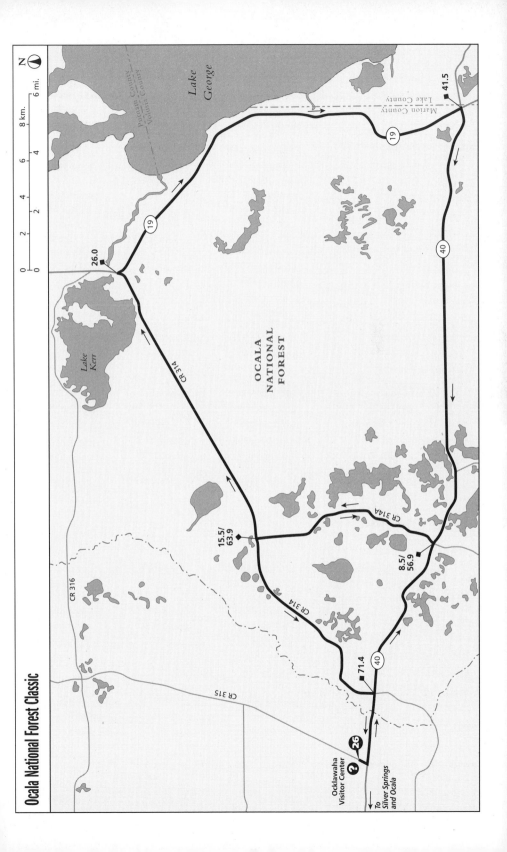

able advice is to play dead and let it chew on you awhile. The opposite is true with black bears. Of course, these bears are accustomed to people and handouts (strictly forbidden, however, and for good reason) and may have lost their shyness, so keep a clean camp and do not even think about approaching them for a "grip-and-grin" photo.

You will see plenty of gators, but if you see a black bear, your sighting will be brief—a dark shape ambling suddenly across a road and disappearing into the scrub. Unlike bears begging along Skyline Drive in the Great Smoky Mountains, these mammals are a bit introverted and the population faces enormous competition from human pressure. BEAR CROSSING signs may outnumber actual bears.

Ride scenery is unspectacular and that, in a way, reflects the poor sandy soils, the isolated pockets of water and longleaf pine—called "islands"—and the harsh realities of scratching out an eighteenth-century living as a small farmer, hunter, fisherman, moonshiner, or trapper. Marjorie Kinnan Rawlings documented this way of life and its hardy pioneer people in her 1938 book *The Yearling*. In fact, in 1933 she lived for a month with the last two residents of "Pine Island" in the ONF, Calvin and Mary Long, and collected stories and information for her novel. (She also lived for a time in Cross Creek, about thirty minutes north between Ocala and Gainesville, where she owned a small orange grove. Her semiautobiographical book *Cross Creek* was written about her life there in the 1930s.)

So the ONF Classic is a ride unlike many in Florida. No spectacular scenery. No beach. No wild and crazy theme parks nearby. And yet in many ways, this endurance pedal embodies (apologies if this sounds melodramatic) the soul of the state. The wonders of the forest are small and delicate; you have to search for them. The aquamarine springs. Blowing moss over the streams. A cool breeze on a hot day. This is exactly the kind of place and exactly the kind of ride that will bring you back to central Florida.

Bon voyage.

Miles and Directions

0.0 Begin in the parking lot of the Ocklawaha Visitor Center a block north of SR 40 on CR 315 due east of the city of Ocala. Turn left (south) out of the parking lot of the visitor center and go 1 block to SR 40.

0.1 Turn left (east) onto SR 40 at the flashing red light.

8.5 Turn left (north) at the traffic light onto CR 314A.

15.5 Turn right (northeast) at the stop sign onto CR 314.

26.0 Turn right (south) at the stop sign onto SR 19.

41.5 Turn right (west) at the speed bumps, flashing light, and stop sign onto SR 40.

56.9 Turn right (north) onto CR 314A.

63.9 Turn left (southwest) onto CR 314.

71.4 Turn right (west) on SR 40.

73.9 Turn right (north) on CR 315.

74.0 Arrive at the parking lot of the Ocklawaha Visitor Center.

Local Information

Marion County Sheriff's Department, 692 NW 30th Avenue, Ocala; (352) 732-8181; www.marionso.com.

Ocala/Marion County Chamber of Commerce, 110 East Silver Springs Boulevard, Ocala; (352) 629-8051; www.ocalacc.com.

Ocala National Forest, www.fs.fed.us/r8/ florida/recreation/index_oca.shtml.

Tourist information: www.visitflorida.com.

Local Events/Attractions

Appleton Museum of Art, 4333 East Silver Springs Boulevard, Ocala; (352) 291-4455; www.appletonmuseum.org. Tuesday through Saturday 10:00 a.m. to 5:00 p.m., Sunday noon to 5:00 p.m.

Don Garlits Museum of Drag Racing, 13700 SW 16th Avenue, Ocala; (352) 245-8661; www.garlits.com. Everything you ever wanted to know about drag racing from Big Daddy himself. Situated next to the interstate, one exit south of Ocala.

Silver Springs, 5656 East Silver Springs Boulevard, Silver Springs; (352) 236-2121; www.silversprings.com. A petting zoo, giraffes, glass-bottom-boat rides on the Silver River, and musical entertainment year-round.

Restaurants

Amrit Palace Indian Restaurant, 2635 SW College Road, Ocala; (352) 873-8500. So good, the smell of the food makes your mouth water just thinking about it.

Bella Luna Cafe, 3425 SW College Road, Ocala; (352) 237-9155. This is not a chain restaurant and the food is memorable.

The Melting Pot, 10 South Magnolia Avenue, Ocala; (352) 622-9968; www.meltingpot.com. Fondue seems so '60s. Takes time, but it is a fun experience. Call for reservations.

Accommodations

Holiday Inn Express, 1212 South Pine Avenue, Ocala; (352) 629-7300 or (888) 400-9714; www.hiexpress.com. You will have to ask for a nonsmoking room.

Ocala National Forest offers many **camping** and **cabin-rental** opportunities. Reservations through (877) 444-6777 or online at reservations.nps.gov or www.recreation.gov.

Seven Sisters Inn Bed & Breakfast, 820 SE Fort King Street, Ocala; (352) 867-1170 or (800) 250-3496; www.sevensistersinn.com. Ornate and a bit pricey.

Shamrock Thistle & Crown Bed & Breakfast, PO Box 624/12971 SE CR 42, Weirsdale, FL 32195; (352) 821-1887 or (800) 425-2763; www.shamrockbb.com. If you are visiting your folks in the popular retirement area of Lady Lake, this is an option. Reasonable rates.

Bike Shops

Ocala Bicycle Center, 2801 SW 20th Street, Ocala; (352) 291-5268; www.ocalabicycle center.com. Closed Sunday.

Santos Trailhead Bicycle Shop, 8900 South U.S. Highway 441, Ocala; (352) 307-BIKE; www.santosbikeshop.com.

Restrooms

Mile 0.0: Ocklawaha Visitor Center, USDA Forest Service, 3199 NE CR 315—the start and end of this ride. Restrooms are open every day from 9:00 a.m. to 5:00 p.m. and accessible from inside.

Numerous designated and well-marked camping areas along the ride offer toilet facilities.

Maps

DeLorme: Florida Atlas & Gazetteer: Pages 72 B-C 3, 73 B-C 1-2.

27 Lake Rousseau Cruise

Another of Florida's spectacular rides, it begins in a parking lot in the Gulf of Mexico and swings through environmentally delicate land. Looping around a perfectly straight and quite artificial stretch of the Withlacoochee River, it returns to the Gulf via shady lanes along "Follow That Dream Parkway."

Start: The parking lot of the Levy County Park at the west end of County Road 40, which is literally on an islet in the Gulf of Mexico. The gate to this park is locked at sunset, so if you might be late returning, you should park in the marked rows that are usually reserved for trucks pulling trailers for recreational fishing boats.

Length: A 44.4-mile loop.

Terrain: Flat.

Traffic and hazards: Traffic will be light but fast on the narrow parts of the ride.

Getting there: . . . is only half the fun: Just a little formatting joke, bikers. From Interstate 75 north, take the State Road 121 exit in south Gainesville and continue southwest for about forty-five minutes until SR 121 intersects with U.S. Highway 19/98. Turn left (south) and continue to Inglis, where you turn right (west) on CR 40 for the trip to the end of the road. From I-75 south, exit the interstate at County Road 44, the Wildwood exit just north of the intersection of 75 and the Sunshine Parkway. Continue west about an hour on CR 44 to Crystal River and turn right (north) on US 19/98. It will be about twenty minutes to Inglis and CR 40.

The first part of this ride qualifies as one of the downright prettiest spots in the world. From the Gulf of Mexico along the two-lane and admittedly narrow CR 40 through Yankeetown on Riverside Drive and back on 40 through "Crackertown" to US 19/98, the scenery is picturesque.

For the first 3 miles, you will bike from an islet, which is half a mile or more out in the Gulf, to the mainland, and the beauty—with no rooftops or condominiums to spoil the view—breathtaking. There are wide expanses of salt marsh, and the shimmering Gulf itself is dotted with dozens of tiny coastal islands. Birds are everywhere. Heck, why ride? Why not just lay the bike down in the shade, slide down beside it, and let your eyes relax into the distance and the shimmer of heat waves? As you might guess, sunsets here are spectacular.

To the south you can see the cooling towers of the Crystal River power plant. According to www.progress-energy.com it is a single-unit, 838-MW nuclear facility located on a site that also includes four coal-fired generating units that, fed properly, give us a steady 2,313 MW . . . for those easily impressed by big numbers!

In Yankeetown itself, Riverside Drive is one line of homes—some quite old, some new—away from the Withlacoochee River. Open your nose and you can smell the cool flowing water. And by smell I do not mean anything other than freshwater. This water still carries a natural odor of sweetness—cypress knees, tannic acid,

Lake Rousseau Cruise

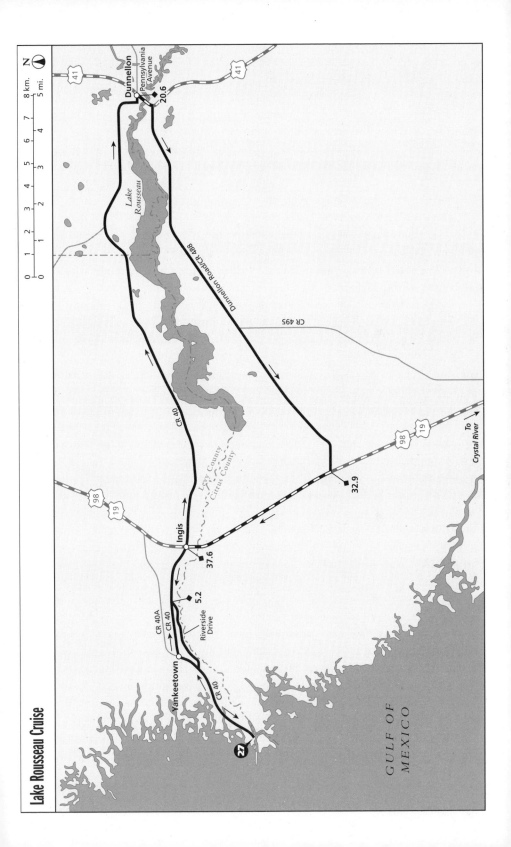

sunfish near the surface, and perhaps a touch of tidal marsh. It's pure and wild and cool all at once, the breath of the river itself.

The one caution on this road is pickup trucks pulling fishing boats. Give them as much room as you are able to because the trailer is a foot wider on either side than the truck bed. I like plenty of room when I'm riding and I know that many drivers out here are either in a hurry to put their boats in the water or in a hurry to get home and clean fish. (Boaters subconsciously rate one another by the size of their boats and motors. So don't expect that they will give your tricked-out, but comparatively tiny, Cannondale more than a passing glance.)

When you leave Riverside Drive coming out of Yankeetown, you will see small BIKE TRAIL signs along CR 40 or Follow That Dream Parkway, but they are something of an illusion. This bike trail is only the sidewalk on the north side of the road. I would avoid it, because it was probably a well-meaning gesture to remind the local kids to stay off the highway.

The road between Inglis and Dunnellon is a bit lonely and thus perfect for biking. Two lanes and no shoulders—like the return road on the opposite side of Lake Rousseau. To the left, on the north side of CR 40, is the Goethe State Forest. Sand, scrub oaks, stands of pines, mockingbirds, blue jays, crows, gopher tortoise, and . . . sand. You will not see the lake that is on your right, however, unless you turn into the Inglis Lock Recreation Area, which is 4.9 miles from US 19/98. It is worth a quick side trip, however.

The return on County Road 488 rolls with the undulating terrain. There is more development here, but not much to see. Throughout this ride you will be only a few hundred yards from Lake Rousseau, but will rarely glimpse it.

The lake itself was formed when a dam was built across the Withlacoochee River near Inglis in the 1920s. It was subsequently fitted with a barge-type lock and designated as part of an interesting, but environmentally insensitive, scheme called the Cross-Florida Barge Canal. Fortunately, political pressure and a belated but realistic economic assessment halted it in the 1970s and that left Lake Rousseau as one of the few large, man-made bodies of water in the state . . . and the bass and bluegill fishing is very good.

You will see remnants of the barge canal when you pedal over the high bridge on US 19/98. Running in both directions should be a picturesque meandering river overhung by cypress and moss-laden oaks. Instead what you will observe is a ruler straight ditch designed by the U.S. Army Corps of Engineers. Be very careful on this bridge, as it is steep, with only two narrow lanes. Once you are over the top, traffic briefly cannot see you and vehicles on this highway move along smartly.

Over the bridge, however, you cruise into Inglis and turn left again on CR 40. Heading for the Gulf and a picnic or a bucket of fried chicken or the All-South Favorite snack—RC Cola and Moon Pie, which you can purchase at any convenience store—you could even kick back and toss a bobber in the water. Catch your own dinner. There's no better place for it in Florida.

Miles and Directions

0.0 From the parking lot of the Levy County Park at the west end of CR 40 in the Gulf of Mexico (literally!), ride east.

3.0 Turn right (southeast) on Riverside Drive and follow it as it winds through Yankeetown.

5.2 Turn right (east) again on CR 40, which becomes Follow That Dream Parkway. Stay on CR 40 through Inglis and across US 98. CR 40 becomes Cedar Street as it enters Dunnellon on a sweeping right turn.

20.4 Turn left (east) at the stop sign on West Pennsylvania Avenue in Dunnellon.

20.6 Turn right (south) at the traffic signal onto U.S. Highway 41, a four-lane divided highway.

21.1 Turn right (west) at the traffic signal on West Dunnellon Road/CR 488.

32.9 Turn right (north) at the stop sign on US 19/98, a four-lane divided highway. The highway narrows to two lanes a half mile before the narrow high bridge over the Cross-Florida Barge Canal, and expands to four lanes once you are on the opposite side.

37.6 Turn left (west) at the traffic signal onto CR 40.

44.4 Arrive at the start/end of the ride, the Levy County Park at the west end of CR 40. (The slight detour on Riverside Drive through Yankeetown is always an option. It will be a slower ride, but it is shady and more scenic.)

Local Information

Levy County Sheriff's Department, 91 NE 80th Avenue, Bronson; (352) 486-5111; www.levyso.com.

Nature Coast Florida, (888) 732-2692; www.naturecoastcoalition.com, www.swimwithamanatee.com, or http://goflorida.about.com/cs/tampawestcoast/a/coast_nature.htm.

Local Events/Attractions

Birding: Florida is home to an immense crowd of migrating and resident species. Contact the Nature Coast Birding & Wildlife Experience, (352) 543-5600; www.ncbwe.com. A resource for festivals, flocks, and flights is www.nbbd.com/fly/festivals.html.

Kayaking: This area is known for its marvelous kayaking. Here are a few Web sites to check: www.wild-florida.com: In Williston, (877) 945-3928. www.adirondackexposure.com: In Tampa December through April, (315) 335-1681. www.manateetours.com/kayak/: In Citrus County, (866) 352-7946.

Swimming, snorkeling, diving: Almost too much to choose from without moving here. Visit www.purewaterwilderness.com, an excellent guide for activities in the water plus birding and nature activities.

Restaurants

December's Waterway Lounge, 141 Highway 19 South, Inglis; (352) 447-3451; www.inglisdining.com. Casual dining on the banks of the Withlacoochee River. All meals every day, but closing hour varies. "Steak night" is every Thursday.

Snappy Tomato Pizza Co., 12149 South Williams Street, Dunnellon; (352) 522-0533; www.snappytomato.com. This is a chain pizza restaurant, which is news to me, and I like pizza.

Accommodations

Pine Lodge Bed & Breakfast Inn, 649 Highway 40 West, Inglis; (352) 447-7463; www.pinelodgefla.com. In the center of Crackertown/Old Inglis. Gets great reviews and has a covered pool, too. Nonsmoking. Standard B&B rates: $85 to $125 per night.

Rod-N-Nod: A Waterfront Fishing Camp Bed & Breakfast, 10234 West Grotto Court, Homosassa; (352) 628-5986; www.rodnnod.com. Not fancy or old and decorated with faux-colonial froufrou, and you can fish or kayak right from your back door! Rates: $125/night single bedroom, $800/week.

Withlacoochee Motel, 66 Highway 19 South, Inglis; (352) 447-2211; www.withlacoochee motel.com. Family-owned. Rates start at $45/night!

Bike Shops

Lenco Bicycles, 800 North Suncoast Boulevard (US 19/98), Crystal River; (352) 795-8688.

Seven Rivers Bicycle Club, www.srbikeclub.com.

Suncoast Bicycles Plus, 322 North Pine Avenue, Inverness; (352) 637-5757; www.suncoastbicycles.com. Only a couple blocks from the start of this ride and next to the Withlacoochee State Trail, Suncoast caters to the serious cyclist.

Restrooms

Mile 0.0: The Levy County Park at the west end of CR 40, the beginning and end of the ride.

Mile 10.0: Porta-potties at Inglis Loc Recreation Area on the south side of CR 40.

Mile 20.8: Dunnellon City Park west of US 41 and on the north bank of the Withlacoochee River in Dunnellon. Open sunrise to sunset.

Mile 35.0: Marjorie Harris Carr Cross Florida Greenway Recreational Trail–Felburn Trailhead on the east side of US 19/98 prior to the high bridge over the Cross Florida Barge Canal. The ride to the restrooms (open sunrise to sunset) is at least a mile and you must exit US 19/98 on the right almost a mile before the bridge.

Maps

DeLorme: Florida Atlas & Gazetteer, Pages 70 D 3, 71 D 1-2, 76 A 3, 77 A 1.

28 Inverness–Lake Henderson Ramble

For cyclists who are accustomed to endurance sprints and marathons, this will be a beginner ride. Relax! Have fun. Take it easy, ride it in both directions, and enjoy spinning around Lake Henderson.

Start: Wallace Brooks City Park on Lake Henderson in downtown Inverness is one link in a chain of pit stops on the rapidly developing Withlacoochee State Trail. It also has a small swimming area, restrooms, and a generous parking area only a block from city hall and the police department.

Length: 9 miles.

Terrain: Flat to gently rolling.

Traffic and hazards: You will notice traffic on County Road 470 around the lake (a little more than half the ride), but only because the road is narrow. I actually recommend that you

take the sidewalk (horrors!) around part of Lake Henderson: from the point that Dr. Martin Luther King Jr. Avenue intersects U.S. Highway 41 and you turn left, until you turn left again paralleling County Road 44 onto CR 470/Gospel Island Road. For much of the distance, the sidewalk has a metal railing on both sides, so ride controlled. If you would prefer the pure road route, watching out for speeding vehicles in heavy traffic and never getting a glimpse of this beautiful lake, go ahead and get out on the street, but don't say I didn't warn you. . . .

Getting there: From Interstate 75, take the Wildwood exit, CR 44. It is the first exit after I-75 and Florida's Turnpike join about an hour north of Tampa and a half hour south of Ocala. Inverness and Wallace Brooks City Park are 20 miles west on CR 44.

As if it is surfing, this Florida alligator takes the sun on a fallen log. Gators can run as fast as racehorses, out-swim a fast-moving kayak . . . and only ate two human residents in 2006. Watch where you step!

There is so much waiting for you outdoors in this slice of Florida's Nature Coast that a little bike ramble may only be an excuse to go and do and learn. Nature Coast is a pretty good name for the Big Bend area of the Gulf of Mexico. From the Suwannee River south to Chassahowitzka. Homosassa. Crystal River. And maybe as far north as Steinhatchee or even Panacea.

Not long ago, this was the "Forgotten Florida." Everybody knew the Keys and the Everglades. The Gold Coast (Miami, Lauderdale, Palm Beach). The Space Port and the lovingly, if humorously, named "Redneck Riviera" around Panama City. They knew Tallahassee because for the capital of a state, it has a funky name, a fine college football team, and has ended up in several songs. They knew Jacksonville because it incorporated the entire county of Duval. Gainesville for the Gators and Pensacola as the home of the Navy's Blue Angels flying team.

People thought they knew the Suwannee area from "Old Folks at Home," but Stephen Foster fooled them, having failed to ever set foot in Florida. At first it was "Way down upon the PeeDee River," but that South Carolina name just didn't seem

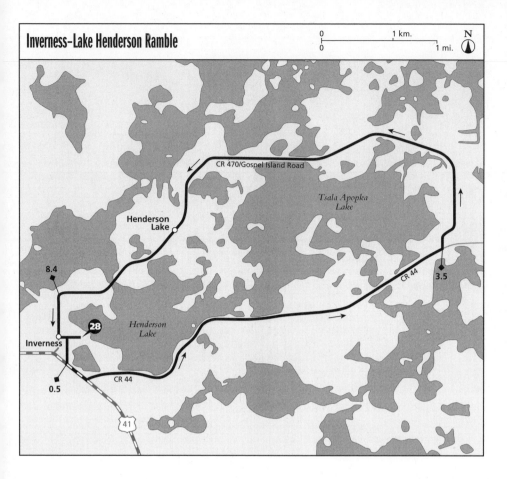

0   1 km.
0   1 mi.

N

CR 470/Gospel Island Road

Tsala Apopka Lake

Henderson Lake

8.4

CR 44

3.5

Inverness

28

Henderson Lake

0.5

CR 44

41

right and so, seeing "Swanee" on a map, he made the fortunate substitution, spelling being fluid in the 1850s. Well, it worked and the rest is history.

At some time in the affluent, happening 1980s, people woke to ecotourism. That meant more camping and kayaking, snorkeling and biking. Sustainable use. Leave no footprint. Etcetera. That decade began watering the seeds of Florida's rapidly expanding multiuse trail system, a branch of which, the Withlacoochee State Trail, passes by the beginning of this little ramble around Inverness. That asphalt trail, the longest in Florida by the way, is 46 miles long and 12 feet wide.

So Inverness is in the Nature Coast, the Fresh Water Coast region, and there are lakes aplenty. Lakes for riding tubes behind speedboats. Lakes for fishing and swimming. Lakes clear and deep and beautiful.

Citrus County is often thought of in connection with mermaids. Current thinking is that early sailors—even a thousand years ago they couldn't really have been this nearsighted, could they?—saw the manatee and thought they were gorgeous women who lived in the sea, complete with flippers instead of legs. But manatees are fat and ugly and bearded. Hook up on a blind date with someone that resembles a manatee and you'll spend a lot of time in the restroom staring at your watch. Modern entrepreneurs attempted to re-create this myth with real, honest-to-goodness live mermaids—sort of—at Weeki Wachee Springs, about forty-five minutes west and south of Inverness on U.S. highway 19/98 (www.weekiwachee.com). Today, former mermaids have reunions . . . at hotels, on land.

Still, the manatee is an endangered species. The trouble is basically the propeller on motorboats. This big, slow, gentle vegetarian just can't seem to get out of the way. If you want to see manatees, Citrus County is the place. Try Captain Mike's Sunshine River Tours (www.sunshinerivertours.com) or any number of other tour operators, and remember that these are endangered animals. It is not only motorboats that kill them, by the way, but also the Gulf's peculiar "red tide," an algae bloom that is particularly hazardous to manatees and many fish species as well.

Henderson Lake, around which the ride revolves, offers a little of everything and this ramble is only a teaser. A tune-up. A sample of the Fresh Water Coast.

In your ramble, you may notice individual orange and grapefruit trees in yards of private homes. Most years, these will bear fruit. While citrus was once strong in the area between Lake Panasoffkee and the Gulf, the "great freeze" of 1894–95 effectively ended citrus production in the county. Mining was also strong once, and today the economy is strong in tourism, and the nuclear/coal electric power plant near Crystal River is a dominant employer.

So, speaking of rambling . . .

Miles and Directions

0.0 From the parking lot of Wallace Brooks City Park, turn right onto Dampier Street.

0.1 Turn left (south) onto Dr. Martin Luther King Jr. Avenue and continue to the stop sign.

0.5 Take an immediate left (southeast) onto the near, or inside, sidewalk and follow it in a counterclockwise manner, bending east between the lake and US 41 and then CR 44.

3.5 Turn left (north) on CR 470/Gospel Island Road.

8.4 Turn left (south) on North Apopka Avenue.

8.8 Turn left (east) on Dampier Street.

9.0 Arrive at the start/end of the ride.

Local Information

Citrus County Chamber of Commerce, PO Box 5085, Inverness, FL 34450; (352) 726-2801; www.citruscountychamber.com.

Citrus County Visitors & Convention Bureau, www.visitcitrus.com.

Inverness Police Department, 401 North Apopka Avenue, Inverness; (352) 726-2121.

Local Events/Attractions

Crystal River Archaeological State Park, 3400 North Museum Point, Crystal River; (352) 795-3817; www.floridastateparks.org/crystal river/default.cfm. Burial and temple mounds, shell middens, and upright stone stelae near walking tours and museum.

Crystal River National Wildlife Refuge, 1502 SE King's Bay Drive, Crystal River; (352) 563-2088; www.fws.gov/crystalriver/. Home to endangered manatees.

Homosassa Springs Wildlife Park, 4150 South Suncoast Boulevard, Homosassa; (352) 628-5343; www.manateecam.com. View black bears, cougars, deer, and alligators and see the unique "Fishbowl" with manatees and schools of fish.

Restaurants

Cockadoodle's Restaurant, 206 Tompkins Street, Inverness; (352) 637-0335. Well, the girls at www.judysbook.com like the decor and the food.

Little Italy of Inverness Deli, 124 North Apopka Avenue, Inverness; (352) 726-5044. Italian food with good reviews. **Heidi's Italian** at 901 Highway 41 North (352-637-1355) also gets excellent reviews.

Stumpknockers on the Square, 110 West Main Street, Inverness; (352) 726-2212. Generally good reviews for its steaks and seafood. Definitely not a chain!

Accommodations

Central Motel, 721 US 41 South, Inverness; (352) 726-4515; www.centralmotel.com. Along the Withlacoochee Trail 1 mile south of the ride's start. Offers secure bicycle storage. Reasonable rates.

Lake House Bed & Breakfast Inn, 8604 East Gospel Island Road, Inverness; (352) 344-3586. Right on the route.

Magnolia Glen Bed & Breakfast Inn, 7702 East Allen Drive, Inverness; (352) 726-1832 or (800) 881-4366; www.magnoliaglen.com. A beautiful inn with reasonable rates that is just 1.25 miles from the Withlacoochee State Trail.

Bike Shops and Clubs

Seven Rivers Bicycle Club, www.srbikeclub.com.

Suncoast Bicycles Plus, 322 North Pine Avenue, Inverness; (352) 637-5757; www.suncoastbicycles.com. Only a couple blocks from the start of this ride and next to the Withlacoochee State Trail, Suncoast caters to the serious cycling enthusiast.

Restrooms

Mile 0.0: Public restrooms are available in Wallace Brooks City Park, which is also a part of the Withlacoochee State Trail.

Maps

DeLorme: Florida Atlas & Gazetteer: Page 77 B 3.

29 Bakery Heart-of-Florida Challenge

Just when you thought a challenge ride in Florida simply meant long—and hot—and sunscreen, along come hills, serious hills! If you like to push yourself, this ride has it all: scenery, length, heat . . . and super hills.

Start: Killarney Station, the western terminus of the West Orange Trail and the eastern terminus of the connecting Lake Minneola Scenic Trail.
Length: A 58.1-mile loop.
Terrain: Hills, lakes, and more hills!

Traffic and hazards: Typical of Florida rides, there is some traffic and few of the roads along the route have paved shoulders. There is a magnificent multiuse trail for part of the ride, however.

Getting there: From Orlando, take Highway 50 west to the intersection with Old Lake County 50 at the Orange County–Lake County line between Winter Garden and Clermont.

This is the heart-of-Florida ride. Center of the peninsula. Pedaling through the middle of the very things that make the Sunshine State famous: oranges, retirement communities, and golf courses. Then—drum roll, please—on this unique ride, you get to climb hills, real hills . . . and not just any old hills but the highest hill on the peninsula, the 312-foot Sugarloaf Mountain.

Begin your tour in the spacious parking lot of Killarney Station, the west end of the paved, multiuse West Orange Trail and the east end of the Lake Minneola Scenic Trail. These linked trails spin off in opposite directions, and although you will only ride a small portion on this challenge, Florida's multiuse trail system will eventually allow you to enjoy hundreds of scenic miles from coast to coast.

Such paved trails are excellent for riders of all ages and ability levels and they are being laid across the United States. This movement is spearheaded by America's millions of cyclists, but it is given structure and legitimacy by the nonprofit Rails-to-Trails Conservancy (www.railtrails.org). That organization began operation in 1986 and now, with 100,000 members and 13,600 miles of rail-trails, has an office in Washington, District of Columbia, thank you!

Although a rail-trail is a wonderful paved path through town and country, smooth and safe, it does not have the flexibility or the element of surprise of road riding. Thus, this challenge begins on a rail-trail, but 90 percent is open road.

Study a map of the ride area such as the one found in the *DeLorme Florida Atlas & Gazetteer,* and all you will see are lakes, "orchards," and a sprinkling of small towns. This is scenic, busy Florida at its finest.

The first half of the Bakery Challenge rolls gently like a roller coaster warming to its lung-bursting climax. It even has a couple of extended uphill sections on County Road 33 that will wear you out—in a good way—if the day is hot and bright.

Like other rides in Florida, heat and brilliant sun are reminders to lather on the sunscreen and either carry plenty of water or expect to stop at a few convenience stores. If you were to stop at only one store, the old store in Okahumpka at the intersection of County Roads 33 and 48 (where you will turn right/east) would be the one. This family-owned business gives you the flavor of Florida in the first half of the twentieth century when all you would be able to see from the top of the 226-foot Citrus Tower in nearby Clermont (built in 1956) would be the round tops of trees filled with oranges, grapefruit, lemons, limes, clementines, satsumas, tangelos, and tangerines.

This ride is special because of its relative difficulty. Signs of that difficulty are the twisting up- and downhill curves of County Roads 48 and 455. As county roads, these were built to follow the landscape between the villages of Montverde and Howey in the Hills, and the hamlets of Yalaha and Okahumpka. A state road or U.S. highway would have paved a straighter, flatter path.

No stretch of pavement in Florida will be more strenuous, and few will be more scenic, than the "back nine," the second half of the Bakery Challenge. The star of the show is Sugarloaf Mountain. At 312-feet above sea level, it is the highest spot on the Florida peninsula, and CR 455 takes you right over the top.

So okay. You bikers from Knoxville and Denver and Calgary have "real" mountains with snow and bears, glaciers and Yeti, but possibly by the time this book is in your bookstore, we Floridians will have a golf course on top of the highest point on the peninsula. You can bike this route one day and then return the next and hit eighteen holes with multiple views over lakes, groves, and small, scenic towns.

From the top of Sugarloaf, you see an area of lakes and hills that is unique in citrus productivity in the world. The lakes are filled with largemouth bass and sunfish, and if you do not play golf, you can at least swim or take sailing lessons or sit in the shade and drink piña coladas.

Central Lake County is a charming area and the towns of Mount Dora, Winter Garden, Leesburg, and Tavares all have unique festivals and parades. Virtually everything that can be done for the visitor is done except relaxing and enjoying the sights and the sounds—that's left up to you.

Alaska and Minnesota may have more lakes than Florida, which counts 7,700 larger than ten acres and a remarkable twenty-seven first-magnitude springs. The lakes in Florida are never solid in the winter, however, and I do believe that if you stop to catch your breath on top of Sugarloaf Mountain, you can see a whole lot of them. That, in itself, is worth the effort.

◀ *The Bakery Challenge begins at Killarney Station, and the first 6.4 miles are ridden on a multiuse trail.*

Bakery Heart-of-Florida Challenge

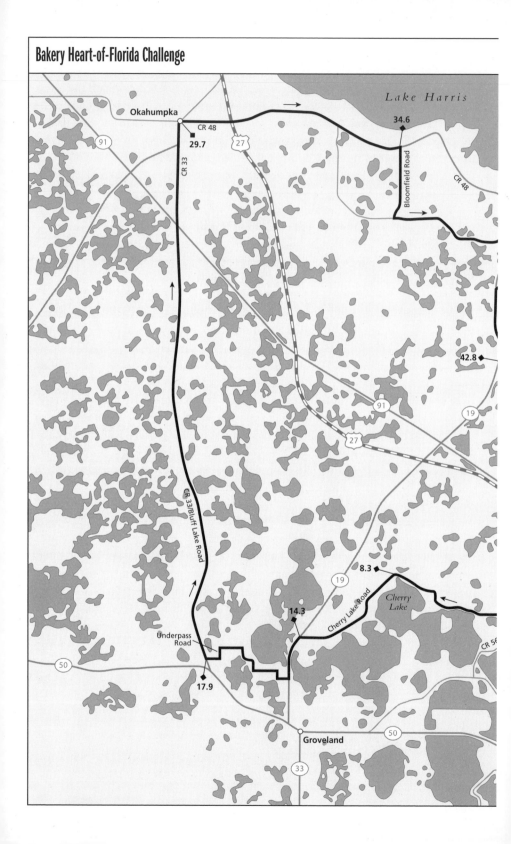

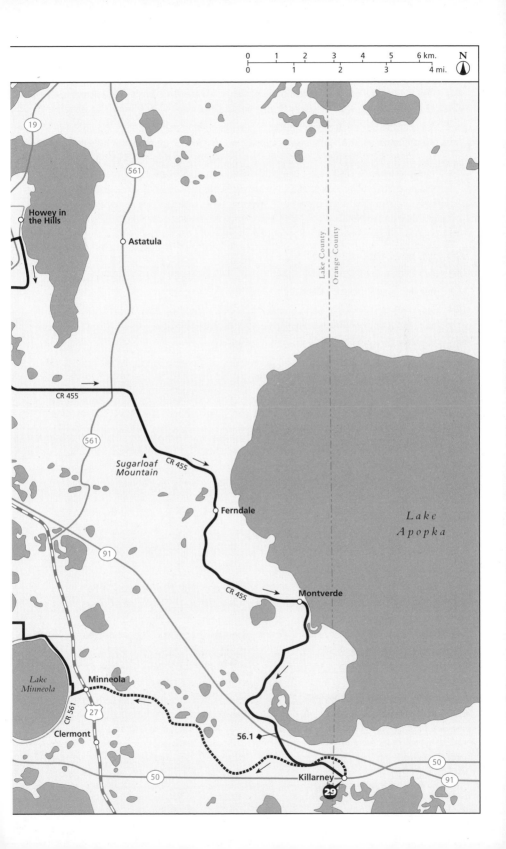

19

561

Howey in
the Hills

Astatula

Lake County
Orange County

CR 455

561

Sugarloaf
Mountain

CR 455

Ferndale

Lake
Apopka

91

CR 455

Montverde

Lake
Minneola

Minneola

CR 561

27

Clermont

56.1

50

Killarney

29

50

91

Miles and Directions

0.0 Take the trail out of the entrance to the parking lot of the West Orange Trail Killarney Station west onto the Lake Minneola Scenic Trail.

5.5 Arrive at the City of Minneola Trailhead Park (do not continue to Clermont), ride out the entrance, and turn left (west) on East Madison. Ride 2 blocks and turn right (north) on South Bloxam Avenue. Ride 2 more blocks and turn left (west) on East Washington Street/Old Lake County 50. Ride across U.S. Highway 27 onto West Washington Street, which ends facing Lake Minneola but bends about 90 degrees to the right and curves north and west on Lakeshore Drive, with the lake, to the intersection of County Road 561.

7.5 Turn left (west) on CR 561.

7.9 Turn right (north) on Jalarmy Road.

8.3 Turn left (west) on Cherry Lake Road.

14.3 Turn left (south) on State Road 19.

15.4 Turn right (west) on Bible Camp Road and follow it around as it bends, first a 90-degree turn right (north) and then a 90-degree turn left (west).

16.1 Turn right (north) on Villa City Road.

16.8 Turn left (west) on Underpass Road, which takes a 90-degree turn to the left (south) and another 90-degree turn to the right (west).

17.9 Turn right (north) on CR 33, Bluff Lake Road.

29.7 Turn right (east) on CR 48 in Okahumpka, and in about a mile cross US 27 again.

34.6 Turn right (south) on Bloomfield Road.

36.1 Turn left (east) on Number Two Road, which becomes West Central Avenue and, after crossing SR 19, East Central Avenue.

39.2 Turn right (south) on Lakeshore Boulevard, which becomes East Revels Road as it bends west.

41.2 Turn left (south) on SR 19.

42.8 Turn left on CR 455, angling briefly southeast before straightening out east. Stay on CR 455 as it bends around the lakes east and south through the town of Montverde.

56.1 Turn left on Old Lake County 50.

58.1 Arrive at the beginning, the entrance to the parking area of West Orange Trail Killarney Station on Old Lake County 50.

Local Information

Lake County Sheriff's Department, 360 West Ruby Street, Tavares; (352) 343-9500; www .lcso.org.

Leesburg Area Chamber of Commerce, 103 South 6th Street, Leesburg; (352) 787-2131; www.leesburgchamber.com.

Orlando Racing Club, www.orcracing.com. I found the map to this ride on this fine site.

Local Events/Attractions

Citrus Tower, 141 North US 27, Clermont; (352) 394-4061; www.citrustower.com. One of the attractions that made Florida famous fifty years ago.

Gatorland, 14501 South Orange Blossom Trail (US 441), Orlando; (407) 855-5496 or 800-393-JAWS; www.gatorland.com. A 110-acre theme park and wildlife preserve that opened in 1949 and now features thousands of alligators, crocodiles, reptiles, and birds, plus a splash park and petting zoo.

Lake County events and attractions, www.lakegovernment.com/enjoying_lake _county/attractions.aspx. Visit this site for a complete list of things to do in Lake County.

Orlando-area attractions: Here are links to the largest and most publicized theme parks in the Orlando area, from Disney World to Universal Studios: www.orlandofunparks.com (866-281-8643), www.orlandoattractions.com (352-241-8539), and www.orlandoinfo.com (Orlando–Orange County Convention & Visitors Bureau, 407-363-5872 or 800-972-3304).

Restaurants

Angelo's Italian Restaurant, 2270 Vindale Road, Tavares; (352) 343-2757; www .angelositalianrestaurant.net. Family-owned and very Italian.

Bistro by Glynne, 335 South Highland Street, Mt. Dora; (352) 735-5499; www.bistroby glynne.com. Formerly Laura's Bistro. Open for breakfast and lunch.

Sugarboo's BBQ, 1305 North Grandview Avenue, Mt. Dora; (352) 735-PORK; www .sugarboo.com. You want small, family-owned, and unique? You got it.

A Third Place Pub & Cafe, 12 East Magnolia Avenue, Eustis; (352) 357-9595; www.athird placepubcafe.com. Serving "healthy comfort food," plus an espresso bar, a full bar for lunch and dinner, and Sunday brunch.

Accommodations

The Duncan House Bed & Breakfast Plantation, 426 Lake Dora Drive, Tavares; (407) 401-2692 or (877) 477-0739; www.the duncanhouse.com. Beautiful but expensive. It

is easy to visit the Lake Ridge Winery (www.lakeridgewinery.com) from this B&B, so make the trip and discover the taste of our native muscadine grapes.

The Old Bicycle Inn, 931 West Montrose Street, Clermont; (352) 394-6944; www.the oldbicycleinn.com. Not fancy, moderately priced—just right to have fun at the annual Clermont Pig-on-the-Pond barbecue event in March (www.pigonthepond.org).

Wekiva Falls Park, 30700 Wekiva River Road, Sorrento; (352) 383-8055. Tent camping with laundry and showers; allows pets; full hookups; canoe rentals. North of Lake Apopka and thirty to forty-five minutes from the start of this ride.

Bike Shops

Orange Cycle, 2204 Edgewater Drive, Orlando; (407) 422-5552; www.orangecycleorlando .com. About 15 miles east of the beginning of the ride in Orlando's College Park neighborhood.

South Lake Bicycles, 121 West Washington Street, Minneola; (352) 394-3848; www.southlakebicycles.com. This shop is right on the challenge.

Restrooms

Mile 0.0: West Orange Trail Killarney Station— the beginning and end of this ride.

Mile 5.5: The trailhead for the Lake Minneola Scenic Trail in Minneola.

Maps

DeLorme: Florida Atlas & Gazetteer: Pages 79 D-C 1-2, 78 C-D 3.

30 Astatula Hills Ramble

This is a busy ride, twisting up- and downhill and winding among a half-dozen sparkling lakes. It is central Florida at its best, with one of everything—cattle and horse and goat ranches, trailer parks, exclusive gated communities, industrial parks, quaint downtowns—and plenty of orange groves. Be careful about the traffic and enjoy the views . . . and the hills!

Start: The parking lot of Gilbert Park on the east side of Lake Dora in Mt. Dora.
Length: A 29-mile loop.
Terrain: And you thought there were no hills in Florida! Not intimidating, but not flat, either; some of the hills on this lake-country ride are a biking joy!

Traffic and hazards: Almost the entire ride is on two-lane roads with no bike lanes. Depending on the day, traffic can be hectic. An antiques festival in Mt. Dora will generate more cars than bees in a hive.

Getting there: From Orlando, drive north on U.S. Highway 441/Orange Blossom Trail to Mt. Dora. North of the towns of Apopka and Zellwood, swing left (west) on Old US 441 (State Road 500A). After about a mile, turn left (west) on Liberty Avenue. It is 3 blocks to the start at Gilbert Park.

So, you don't believe there are hills in Florida? Okay, the highest point in the state is in the Panhandle, close to the Alabama state line. There, an astonishing altitude of 345 feet above mean sea level can be found at Britton Hill, north of Eglin Air Force Base and Interstate 10 (reached via the Highest Ride Ramble), and bikers from Colorado to West Virginia and Vermont are giggling already. On the other hand, bikers from Iowa and Texas and Maryland will understand and gear up for a little up-and-down activity.

Mt. Dora, the beginning and end of this ramble, rises to a breathtaking 184 feet above sea level and curiously, with its sister city Tavares, the county seat of Lake County, to the west, is situated in the very heart of Florida's lake country. While you probably will not be trailering a boat into Florida for your biking vacation, this ride is all about lakes and hills.

Actually, the ride is about a lot more than that, because from the seat of your bicycle, you can see practically everything that central Florida offers on this 29-mile loop, not just lakes and hills. One rambles beside a score of orange groves; wends around half a dozen lakes; passes exclusive resorts and expensive gated communities; and then, only minutes later, bumps along on pavement next to a mobile-home community occupied by vigorous snowbirds from Ohio, Ontario, and Michigan. They never had it so good! There are long flat stretches through small towns where all you need to watch for is sand on the highway, because it could cause a nasty spill; and there are intensely hilly sections through boutique

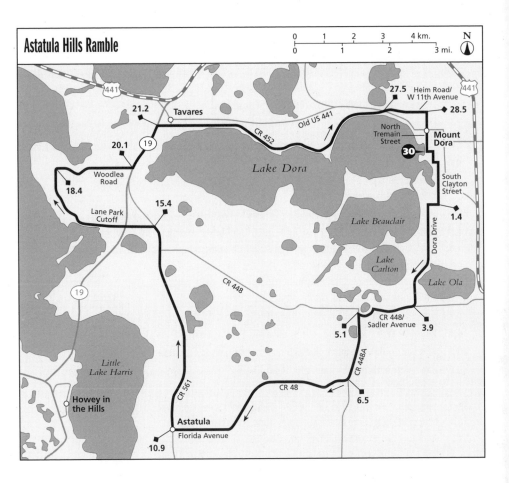

communities where a vehicle coming to a "rolling stop" at an intersection or a suddenly opened car door could leave you pining for a bicycle air bag.

This lake region—Florida has more than 7,700 lakes with at least ten acres of
surface area—you can look it up—is the northern fringe of the state's citrus and
highly publicized attractions.

The attraction industry has undergone a huge transformation during the last
generation. It used to be that mom-and-pop places like Silver Springs in Ocala (an
hour north of this ride) or the Mermaid Show at Weeki Wachee Springs (about an
hour and a half west) or even "Spook Hill" in Lake Wales (where your automobile
appears to back *up* an incline; an hour and a half south and *free*—no mom or pop
required) were the highlight of a tourist's visit to the Sunshine State. And yes, my
dad actually drove the family to all of those venerable spots. This was the same dad
who unloaded everyone at roadside stops where you "used to be" able to drink all
the orange juice you wanted for one thin dime. Those places are, of course, long
gone, which is too bad because I could drink a gallon or two of OJ right this minute.

This bike ride is great fun, especially after you have taken a few of our horizontal tours—Florida is, after all, mostly horizontal. There is plenty to see and landscape that changes with every mile. Do it backwards and you'll think you have never seen the place before.

Y'all come back now, y'hear!

Miles and Directions

0.0 Begin by pedaling east and uphill from Gilbert Park in Mt. Dora. It is 1 block to South Grandview Street. Turn right (south) and go 3 blocks, turning east with the road, which now becomes East Johns Avenue.

0.5 Turn right on South Clayton Street after just 2 blocks on East Johns Avenue.

1.4 Clayton takes a 90-degree turn right (west) and becomes Beauclair Drive.

1.5 Beauclair takes a 90-degree turn left (south) and becomes Dora Drive, which rambles around the west side of Lake Ola.

3.9 Bear right (west) on Sadler Avenue (County Road 448), which will bend around the very small Lake Jem (or Lake Gem—maps vary in spelling).

5.1 Turn left (south) on CR 448A. After 0.3 mile cross the railroad tracks.

6.5 Turn right (west) on CR 48, which becomes Florida Avenue in Astatula.

10.9 Turn right (north) at this traffic light in Astatula onto County Road 561, a busy street.

15.4 Turn left (west) on the Lane Park Cutoff. There is no signal or sign, so be aware of your location and of traffic.

18.4 Turn right (east) as Lane Park Cutoff merges with Woodlea Road.

20.1 Left (north) on State Road 19, a four-lane divided highway.

21.2 Turn right (east) on West Main Street in Tavares. (The official Daytona Bike Club ride zig-zags on small streets—County Drive, Mansfield Road, Wells Street, and Lake Avenue—east of SR 19, between 19 and Lake Dora. This section winds through mobile-home parks and is a bit confusing without a guide. Plus, there is often construction and hence, detours.) At 21.9 miles you will cross double railroad tracks and at 26.5 miles another single track on Lake Dora Drive (County Road 452).

27.5 After crossing Old US 441, pedal another block and merge right (east) on West Heim Road/West 11th Avenue.

28.5 Turn right (south) on North Tremain Street. (Traffic is often rerouted during local festivals so mileages are only approximate in the town of Mt. Dora.)

29.0 Arrive at Gilbert Park, the start and end of the Astatula Ramble.

Local Information

Lake County BCC, 315 West Main Street/PO Box 7800, Tavares, FL 32778; (352) 429-4040; www.lakegovernment.com.

Lake County Sheriff's Office, 360 West Ruby Street, Tavares; (352) 343-2101/9500; www.lcso.org.

Mt. Dora Chamber of Commerce, PO Box 196, Mt. Dora, FL 32757; (352) 383-2165; www.mountdora.com.

Local Events/Attractions

Mt. Dora is the center for a number of festivals of the arts, antiques, music, sailing, and dining. The **38th Annual Arts Festival,** for example, takes place the first weekend in February every year. The **34th Annual Bicycle Festival** features dozens of rides at all skill levels and will take place on an early weekend in October 2008 (352) 383-2165. Check www .mountdora.com/festivals.php for a complete listing of events and festivals.

Disney World, Sea World, Universal Islands of Adventure, and many other family-oriented tourist attractions are less than an hour south of the Mt. Dora/Tavares area in Orlando. **The Kennedy Space Center** is only an hour and a half east on the Atlantic coast. Check them out individually on the Internet or go to www.touristflorida.com.

Restaurants

The Goblin Market Restaurant, 331b North Donnelly Street, Mt. Dora; (352) 735-0059; www.goblinmarketrestaurant.com. Housed in a refurbished warehouse, this small, quirky restaurant is excellent for lunch or dinner. Open Tuesday through Saturday for lunch and dinner, Sunday for lunch only.

O'Keefe's Irish Pub and Restaurant, 115 South Rockingham Avenue, Tavares; (352) 343-2157. Beer, burgers, steaks, seafood, pasta. You can't go wrong with this kind of menu.

Pisces Rising, 239 West 4th Avenue, Mt. Dora; (352) 385-2669; www.piscesrisingdining.com. Seafood and steaks with a great view of Lake Dora.

Accommodations

Holiday Inn Express, 3601 West Burleigh Boulevard, Tavares; (352) 742-1600; hiexpress.com. Affordable and convenient to the ride.

Inn on the Green, 700 East Burleigh Boulevard, Tavares; (352) 343-6373 or (800) 935-2935; www.innonthegreen.net. Pool, boating, and golf. A beautiful resort on the lake. Very affordable and they have efficiencies.

Lakeside Inn, 100 North Alexander Street, Mt. Dora; (352) 383-4101 or (800) 556-5016; www.lakeside-inn.com. A hundred years of history plus a fine dining room and tavern.

Bike Shops

Bicycle Store of Eustis, 1321 South Bay Street, Eustis; (352) 357-1617. North of the route, but it gets good reviews.

Cycle Shoppe of Mt. Dora, 301 North Baker Street, Mt. Dora; (352) 385-4346.

Sun Cycle, 100 West Burleigh Boulevard, Tavares; (352) 343-4181; www.suncycle center.com. Open all day Monday through Saturday and Sunday afternoon.

Restrooms

Mt. Dora has built several facilities as public restrooms and erected signs downtown indicating their locations. Restrooms are also available at the start/finish of the ride in Gilbert Park.

On Main Street in Tavares, a variety of public buildings offer public restrooms, including Tavares City Hall and Lake County Courthouse.

Maps

DeLorme: Florida Atlas & Gazetteer: Page 79 2 B.

31 Lake Mary Ramble

Citrus once grew as far north as the Georgia border, but since the great freeze of 1898, earlier and earlier frosts—in an era of global warming!—have driven cold-sensitive oranges south. This ride takes you through the northern fringe of orange groves and along the shore of Lake Monroe in Sanford. There is something here for everyone.

Start: The parking lot of Lake Mary Shopping Center, 3801 West Lake Mary Boulevard (south side) in Sanford, just east of Interstate 4.
Length: The basic ride is a 39.2-mile loop, but a shorter 30.9-mile variation can also be done.
Terrain: This is a flat route with a very special stretch on the south bank of Lake Monroe.

Traffic and hazards: Don't look for bike lanes on this ride. Even paved shoulders are a luxury. During peak traffic hours, this ramble is not recommended; pedal during off-peak hours, however, and you will find vehicular traffic to be manageable.

Getting there: From Orlando, take I-4 (State Road 400) north and east toward Daytona Beach. Then exit east on West Lake Mary Boulevard in Lake Mary/Sanford. (The exit is about halfway between downtown Orlando and the I-4 intersection with Interstate 95, which runs north–south.) The Lake Mary Shopping Center is one-quarter mile east on the south side of the road just after Lake Emma Road.

This ride is called the Lake Mary Ramble, perhaps because it starts at the Lake Mary Shopping Center, which is named after quite a small puddle a couple miles to the east. You will actually ride for miles along the bigger lake, Lake Monroe. So, why wasn't this ride named the Lake Monroe Ramble and who was Mary, anyway?

The city of Lake Mary was only incorporated in 1973, 150 years after the final battles here with the Seminoles. Its official Web site says that it was named "after the wife of a minister who settled on the northern shores of the lake. Lake Mary started as a village of two tiny settlements called Bent's Station and Belle Fontaine. They were located along the railroad that ran between Sanford and Orlando." Lake Bent didn't seem right, I suppose, and Lake Belle probably sounded foreign, so we may never know.

In truth, however, this nifty ride has the heart of Florida tied up in knots. It begins at a shopping center; twists through a community college; passes an obscure international airport; winds through Florida's northernmost citrus fringe; zips along a terrific bass lake and through a sector of light industry; and then goes past both mobile homes and fancy gated communities. Early Saturday mornings, roads will be relatively deserted.

Traffic varies tremendously. On the eastern half of the ride, traffic will be light; on the western half, it will be moderate—mostly residential; in the center along

"He's from the newspaper," a rider said in passing. Not exactly, but a friendly wave makes a nice picture anyway.

Lake Mary Boulevard, vehicle clutter will be as thick as mosquitoes after a summer hatch. Still, I found that drivers were courteous and gave me plenty of room. That was a good thing because there are no bike lanes and paved shoulders are practically nonexistent. On the most scenic stretch of road, that along Lake Monroe, you can pedal with the cars and trucks on Seminole Boulevard or on a wide, multiuse path with joggers, dogs on leashes, and lovers strolling hand in hand along the lakefront.

If this is your first ride in citrus country, pay special attention to the orange groves. They won't be here for long. At one time citrus grew as far north as the Georgia state line, but historians mark the great freeze of 1898 as the date from which citrus began declining southward into the peninsula. It is recorded—somewhere—that cold was so intense that winter that smoke rising out of chimneys would freeze, fall over, and pile up alongside the homes of residents. When spring came, all that smoke thawed and thousands of people suffocated.

There is no indication that global warming has reversed the trend of freezes and frosts that are gradually pushing citrus south. It decimates polar bear habitat; opens the Northwest Passage to shipping; allows the Russians to plant their flag on or under the North Pole . . . and still, it can't help our oranges! What's the problem, here?

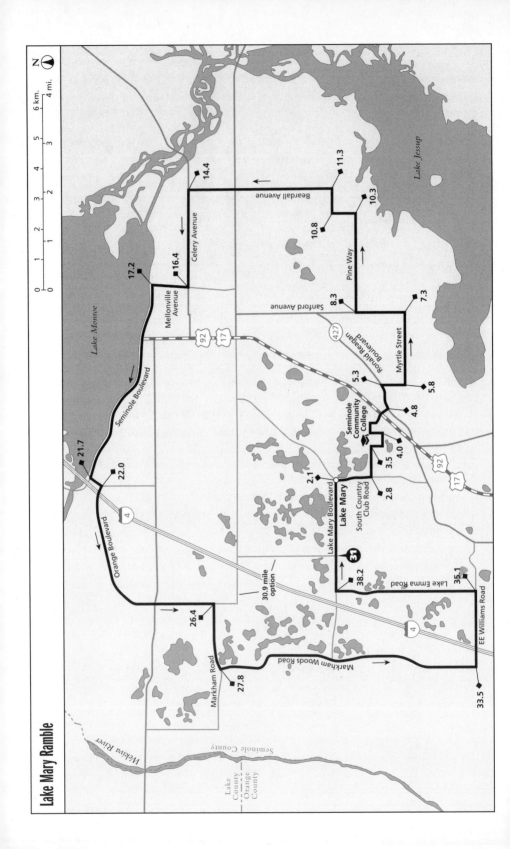

Lake Mary Ramble

An interesting option for shortening the basic ride allows you to cut south from Orange Boulevard to Lake Mary Boulevard. This trims 7.2 miles of twisting road along Markham Woods, EE Williams, and Lake Emma Roads that are thick with subdivision walls and gated communities, by substituting 2.3 miles of rather pleasant ride along International Parkway. The International is a gently curving, well-manicured roadway with large, glass-sided office buildings behind lawns, fountains, and man-made ponds.

Amidst all the urban bustle, it will surprise you to see signs noting deer crossing and, if you are lucky (as I was), you may spot a flock of wild turkeys along Beardall Avenue in the east.

Watch for flowering bougainvillea cascading in bright red and purple, but never take your eyes off the road because western stretches can be pretty rough.

As you pedal, you will pass a dozen nurseries and greenhouses. This is a significant and diversified industry in Florida, which as citrus unfortunately declines due to a variety of climate changes and the introduction of exotic pests, has become a mainstay of the state's economy.

Miles and Directions

0.0   Turn right (east) out of the parking lot of the Lake Mary Shopping Center onto Lake Mary Boulevard, a heavily trafficked six-lane highway.

2.1   Turn right (south) onto South Country Club Road. Within blocks you cross railroad tracks.

2.8   Turn left (east) onto Broadmoor Road, which becomes Broadmoor Drive.

3.5   Turn right (south) at the dead end—with Seminole Community College ahead—onto First Road. It bends left (east), becoming Main Road, and dead-ends on Weldon Boulevard.

4.0   Turn left (north) and follow Weldon as it bends right through the college campus and dead-ends on College Drive/West County Home Road.

4.4   Turn right (southeast) and cross U.S. Highway 17/92/State Road 600/South Orlando Drive.

4.8   Turn left (roughly east) on Ronald Reagan Boulevard/State Road 427.

5.3   Turn right (south) on Hester Avenue.

5.8   Turn left (east) on Myrtle Street.

7.3   Turn left (north) on Sanford Avenue.

8.3   Turn right (east) on Pine Way (also marked Pineway).

10.3   Turn left (north) on Sipes Avenue.

10.8   Turn right (east) on Kentucky Street.

11.3   Turn left (north) on Beardall Avenue.

14.4   Turn left (west) on Celery Avenue.

16.4   Turn right (north) on Mellonville Avenue.

17.2   The road bends left (west) onto Seminole Boulevard for a ramble along the south shore of Lake Monroe.

21.7   Turn left (south) immediately before I-4. (Some maps refer to this street as Upsala Avenue while others refer to it as Monroe Road.)

22.0 Turn right (west) immediately after crossing rough railroad tracks onto Orange Boulevard and cross beneath I-4. Orange Boulevard curves south. **Option:** For a shorter, 30.9-mile route, continue south 0.9 mile on Orange Boulevard past Markham Road and turn left (east) on HE Thomas Jr. Parkway/25th Street. After 0.7 mile turn right (south) on International Parkway. After 2.3 miles turn left on Lake Mary Boulevard, and after 0.6 mile turn into the Lake Mary Shopping Center where the ride begins and ends.

26.4 Turn right (west) on Markham Road, which is not well marked.

27.8 Turn left (south) on Markham Woods Road.

33.5 Turn left (east) on EE Williams Road, which becomes Longwood Hills Road a few blocks before you turn north on Lake Emma Road.

35.1 Turn left (north) on Lake Emma Road.

38.2 Turn right (east) onto Lake Mary Boulevard.

39.2 Turn right (south) into the parking lot of the Lake Mary Shopping Center.

Local Information

Florida Freewheelers, www.floridafreewheelers.com.

Orlando Road Club, www.orcracing.com.

Sanford Chamber of Commerce, 400 East 1st Street, Sanford; (407) 322-2212; www.sanfordchamber.com.

Seminole County Convention and Visitor's Bureau, 1101 East 1st Street, Sanford; (407) 665-0311; www.visitseminole.com.

Seminole County Sheriff's Department, 100 North Bush Boulevard, Sanford; (407) 665-6600; www.seminolesheriff.org. This ride is entirely in Seminole County.

Local Events/Attractions

Central Florida Zoological Park, 3755 NW US 17/92, Sanford; (407) 323-4450; www.centralfloridazoo.org. Hundreds of animals, reptiles, and birds with special animal activities/programs.

Helen Stairs Theatre for the Performing Arts, 201 South Magnolia Avenue, Sanford; (407) 321-8111; www.helenstairstheatre.com. Restored vaudeville theater hosts a variety of plays, performances, and activities.

Little Big Econ State Forest, 1350 Snow Hill Road, Geneva; (407) 971-3500; www.fl-dof .com/state%5Fforests/little_big_econ.html. Canoeing, hiking, off-road biking, and bird watching.

Restaurants

Hollerbach's Willow Tree Café, 205 East 1st Street C-D, Sanford; (407) 321-2204; www.willowtreecafe.com. Gemütlichkeit happens! Family-owned restaurant specializing in German foods.

Joe's Crab Shack, 4659 West State Road 46, Sanford; (407) 323-0934; www.joescrab shack.com. A chain restaurant, but it doesn't feel like one.

Rivership Romance, 433 North Palmetto Avenue, Sanford; (407) 321-5091 or (800) 423-7401; www.rivershipromance.com. Offers a variety of lunch and dinner cruises on Lake Monroe and the St. Johns River.

Accommodations

Higgins House Bed & Breakfast Victorian Inn, 420 South Oak Avenue, Sanford; (407) 324-9238; www.higginshouse.com. Situated in downtown Sanford only blocks from the lake. A beautiful and restful inn with owners who are intimately acquainted with area events and activities.

The Palms Island Resort & Marina, 530 North Palmetto Avenue, Sanford; (407) 323-1910; www.palms-resort.com. In the middle of the ride on Lake Monroe in Sanford, it has ninety-five uniquely furnished rooms and great views of manatees and alligators. Cross between a bed-and-breakfast and a conventional motel, of which there are many within a few miles.

Bike Shops

Outspoken Bike Shop, 4279 West Lake Mary Boulevard, Lake Mary; (407) 688-1959; http://outspokenbikes.com/index.cfm. Just 2 blocks east of the start of the ride.

Restrooms

Mile 17.6: Restrooms are available in the spacious Fort Mellon Park on the shore of Lake Monroe in downtown Sanford.

Maps

DeLorme: Florida Atlas & Gazetteer: Page 80 B 2-3.

32 Cape Canaveral Seashore Cruise

This ride through the Merritt Island National Wildlife Refuge and Canaveral National Seashore on the north end of Merritt Island will put you in harmony with the wind and water, with a natural condition of life that still exists in Florida. You will see alligators, snakes of various varieties, osprey, gulls, feral hogs, rabbits, and if you are very lucky, a bobcat. It is a marvelous ride and you can picnic and splash in the waves, as well.

Start: Begin in the parking area of Sand Point Park on the Intracoastal Waterway/Indian River in downtown Titusville, Florida.
Length: A 34.7-mile loop.
Terrain: Flat.
Traffic and hazards: Except for the brief time it takes to get out of the public park in Titusville and across the causeway to Merritt Island, traffic should not be a problem. Unless, however, you choose to ride on a holiday when traffic on the beach road on the national seashore is busy.

Getting there: Take exit 220 on Interstate 95 and drive east on State Road 406/Garden Street. At the intersection with U.S. Highway 1, turn left (north) and proceed to the entrance to Sand Point Park, which will be almost immediately on your right. The park is approximately 3.5 miles from the interstate.

When cyclists enter "the zone," the bike becomes a natural extension of their body. And this must be true. At times. Otherwise, how would you explain Captain Lance winning the "French thing" an amazing seven times? For most humans, pedaling the 2,241-mile, three-week Tour de France would begin as a lark, quickly become a grind, and eventually perhaps, for the very few who did not turn aside, meld into that mind-body-bike thing that we call "the zone."

Becoming "one with your bike" does happen. It is a point where the effort of moving the pedals becomes unconscious, effortless. It is a time when the pounding of a hard seat up through your coccyx is almost bearable. Well, if that happens on this ride, and its length is barely 1.5 percent of the Great Tour, you are going to miss something; save it for the long, challenging tours—the Okefenokee or Okeechobee

Classics. Your pedal through the Merritt Island National Wildlife Refuge and the Canaveral National Seashore is much more than just another chance to get out on your bike. It is an opportunity to see Florida's distant past while riding alongside its future, the Kennedy Space Center.

The ride begins in a small park at a busy intersection on US 1. At one time, before there were interstates, Route 1 was the highway that brought people down the East Coast and into Florida. It was the route of dreams and, because it paralleled the coast, entrepreneurs built motels and restaurants by the thousands for the newly affluent and motoring public after World War II ended. Many of those motels or "motor-inns," practically all of them being refinished, still stand, many having been revitalized for nostalgic or budget-conscious travelers. These places have passed through many hands since the earliest days of the astronaut-training program when America's best and brightest partied there.

Going and returning, this ride wheels over the Indian River. As much intra-coastal as actual "river," the Indian River is a peculiar piece of geologic engineering. Your map shows considerable opportunity for inflow from the land side, but outflow possibilities are quite limited. Thus, residents and governmental bodies have redou-bled their efforts to keep this body of water in good shape.

You will have a chance to watch alligators nosing innocently along in the shal-lows; spindly-legged wading birds, head down, swishing their bills from side to side; osprey hauling their catch to nearby nests. Nature, it seems, is eternally hungry.

On my ride, I stopped to watch an osprey struggle with a fish that may have been a tad too large. After several unsuccessful takeoffs, both the bird and its wiggling aqueous vertebrate made it into the air, whereas I, scrambling to retrieve my camera and ride within range, observed very little of that life and death struggle. You can either participate or record, it seems, but rarely both.

This ride is different from many others recorded here, those where we recom-mend that people rise early and take in the sunrise on a weekend morning. For this ride, it may be best to take it on a weekday, a bit later than normal, although that will make the day warmer. Evenings may be best. First, most of the refuge lies within space center boundaries and on early mornings thousands of individuals commute to work via the Kennedy Parkway. Thus, overlapping federal jurisdictions, which we might otherwise contest, afford in this case multiple opportunities to preserve a pre-cious swatch of natural environment.

Roads through the refuge and the national seashore were practically empty when I visited on a Sunday evening in midsummer 2007. The marsh and lagoon, the distant launch towers, and an opportunity to climb stairs over the dunes to meditate at the beach are worth almost any effort. I saw dozens of stern-faced osprey or sea eagles, alligators, snakes, roseate spoonbills, cranes and herons, pipers and gulls, feral hogs, and one brief, startling view of a bobcat. Bobcats are extraor-dinarily shy, rarely seen anywhere, and this one may have been surprised by the

Cape Canaveral Seashore Cruise

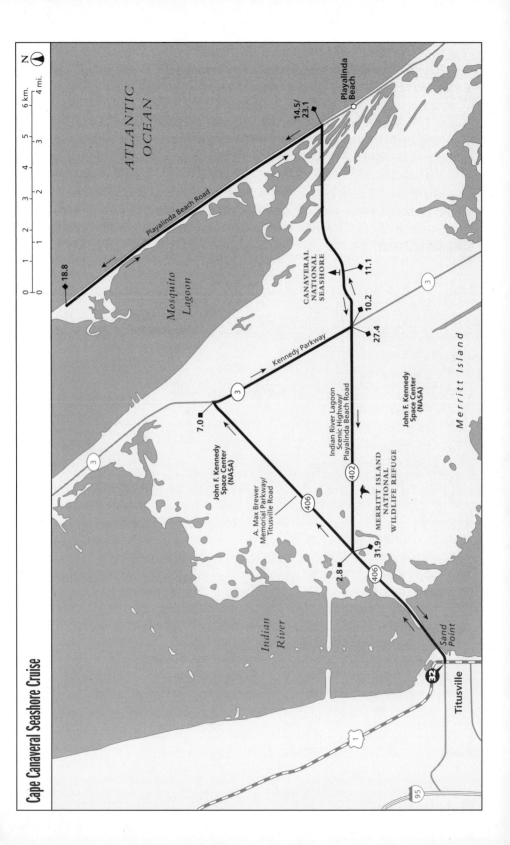

silence of my approach even though it disappeared immediately into the thick tangle, probably unconcerned with my bike and more interested in catching one of the local brown dune rabbits for its supper.

Because it was windy and slightly overcast, my ride was superb and absolutely traffic-free. The beach was empty and the day was as quiet as one could possibly wish for. I stopped often to take pictures and just to look, to try to see the things in the way of a Zen master who would teach how to look beyond the forest or even the trees; not at the branch, or even at the bird, but at the wiggling worm in the bird's beak. And so while I am self-conscious about becoming "one with my bike," it is the point for which I always aim and somehow, on this ride, in spite of myself, achieved.

Miles and Directions

0.0 Turn left (south) out of the parking area of Sand Point Park onto US 1.

0.1 Turn left (northeast) to the A. Max Brewer Memorial Parkway/*Indian River Lagoon Scenic Highway*/SR 406.

2.8 Veer left (northeast) onto SR 406 as the A. Max Brewer Memorial Parkway/Titusville Road/SR 406 separates from the Indian River Lagoon Scenic Highway/Playalinda Beach Road/State Route 402.

3.3 Cross the railroad tracks.

7.0 Turn right (south) on Kennedy Parkway North/State Road 3.

10.1 Cross the railroad tracks.

10.2 Turn left (east) at the lights on Playalinda Beach Road/SR 402.

10.3 Cross the railroad tracks.

11.0 Cross more railroad tracks.

11.1 Stop and pay entrance fee to Canaveral National Seashore: $3/bicycle.

14.5 Turn left (north) on Playalinda Beach Road.

18.8 Turn around at the end of Playalinda Beach Road and return south.

23.1 Turn right (west) on Playalinda Beach Road.

26.6 Cross the railroad tracks.

27.3 Cross more railroad tracks.

27.4 Cross Kennedy Parkway/SR 3.

31.9 Veer left on A. Max Brewer Memorial Parkway/Titusville Road/SR 406.

34.6 Turn right (north) on US 1.

34.7 Turn right (east) into Sand Point Park and the end of the ride.

Local Information

Brevard County Sheriff's Department, 700 Park Avenue, Titusville; (321) 264-5308; www.sheriff.co.brevard.fl.us/.

Space Coast Office of Tourism, 430 Brevard Avenue, Suite 150, Cocoa Village; (321) 433-4470 or (877) 572-3224; www.spacecoast.com.

Titusville Area Chamber of Commerce, 2000 South Washington Avenue, Titusville; (321) 267-3036; www.titusville.org.

Local Events/Attractions

Canaveral National Seashore, (321) 267-1110; www.nps.gov/cana/.

Kennedy Space Center Visitor Complex, SR 405, Kennedy Space Center; (321) 449-4444; www.kennedyspacecenter.com. It is open every day from 9:00 a.m. to 6:00 p.m. except Christmas and certain launch days.

Merritt Island National Wildlife Refuge, PO Box 6504, Titusville, FL 32782; (321) 861-0667; www.fws.gov/merrittisland/index.html. Wonderful spaces only lightly touched by man.

U.S. Astronaut Hall of Fame, 6225 Vector-space Boulevard, Titusville; (321) 269-6100; www.kennedyspacecenter.com. Open from 10:00 a.m. to 6:00 p.m. Fun and educational. This proves that you can have both.

Restaurants

Black Tulip, 207 Brevard Avenue, Cocoa; (321) 631-1133. A reputation for fancy.

Cafe Margaux, 220 Brevard Avenue, Cocoa; (321) 639-8343; www.margaux.com. Offers "creative French and European cuisine" indoors or in an outdoor courtyard.

Dogs R Us, 4200 South Washington Avenue, Titusville; (321) 269-9050. No Web site but gets pretty good reviews for its dogs-on-a-bun online.

Paul's Smokehouse, 3665 South Washington Avenue, Titusville; (321) 267-3663; www.nbbd.com/pauls/index.html. Grease and salt—count me in. Boo-ya!

Uno's Chicago Grill, 795 East Merritt Island Causeway, Merritt Island; (321) 452-4345; www.unos.com. Deep-dish pizza and more.

Accommodations

Aloha Motel Apartments, 6700 Turtle Mound Road, New Smyrna Beach; (386) 428-3386; www.thealoha.com.

Dickens Inn Bed and Breakfast, 2398 Singleton Avenue, Mims; (321) 269-4595; www.dickens-inn.com.

Hampton Inn, 4760 Helen Hauser Boulevard, Titusville; (321) 383-9191; http://hamptoninn.hilton.com.

Super 8 Motel, 3480 Garden Street, Titusville; (321) 269-9310; www.super8.com.

Bike Shops

Ten Speed Drive Bicycle Center, 3428 South Hopkins Avenue, Titusville; (321) 269-3325.

Restrooms

Facilities with porta-potties are located in multiple locations on the beach along Playalinda Beach Road and at the visitor center at about mile 30.3.

Maps

DeLorme: Florida Atlas & Gazetteer: Pages 81 C-D 3, 82 C 1.

33 Kennedy Space Center Ramble

This ride gives us a unique opportunity to ramble close to the grounds of America's Spaceport, and if we are lucky and time our ride properly, we may even see a rocket launch.

Start: Begin the ride in the parking lot of the U.S. Astronaut Hall of Fame on the south side of State Road 405, south of Titusville, Florida.
Length: 15.6 miles.
Terrain: Flat.

Traffic and hazards: Columbia Boulevard is a busy four-lane divided highway during peak rush hours at the Cape or leading up to a rocket launch. The long causeway over the Indian River Lagoon may be thronged with sightseers. Caution is advised.

Getting there: From Interstate 95 just west of Titusville, take exit 215 and turn east on State Road 50/Cheney Highway. After a quarter mile, turn right onto SR 405/Columbia Boulevard. Proceed about 4 miles to the start of the ride at the U.S. Astronaut Hall of Fame, which will be on the right (south) side of the road and immediately across the street from the American Police Hall of Fame and Museum.

As citizens of the United States, our civics books tell us that we own some portion of our national parks, of the White House, of the interstate highway system, and perhaps a small part of the space shuttle as well. Nevertheless, it costs money to visit these things that we own. A tour of the space center including the IMAX theater, the Astronaut Hall of Fame, and flight simulators is $38, but it is good for two days. Throw in lunch with an astronaut for $22.99 (the pictures look good when you're hungry) and perhaps a day for the Astronaut Training Experience at $250 and . . . well, I truly think it's an unforgettable bargain!

This ride is only an excuse to get you to the space center. Maybe see—or "experience" might be a better word—the launch of a spacecraft. What we called a "rocket ship" in the glory days of Arthur C. Clark *(2001: A Space Odyssey)*, Isaac Asimov *(The Foundation Series)*, and Robert Heinlein *(Starship Troopers)*, the "big three" masters of science fiction. Although I never learned enough science and math to become an astronaut, I grew up reading plenty of science fiction—the distant future when anyone can get a rocket driver's license like we get an automobile driver's license now. So this is all still great fun.

I have had the good fortune to experience a couple of launches, both here at Kennedy and at Vandenberg Air Force Base on the Pacific coast. I don't mind saying—I realize I'm beginning to sound like a PR guy for the space program—that making the effort to see a launch is definitely worth the effort, even considering the inevitable countdown delays and occasional cancellations. Even if you have run marathons, made love, traveled around the world, and experienced a spiritual conversion, the blast of a rocket taking off is overwhelming and magnificent.

The author (behind the camera) and his daughter, Morgan, parked their bikes and toured the Mad Mission to Mars 2025 exhibit at Kennedy Space Center.

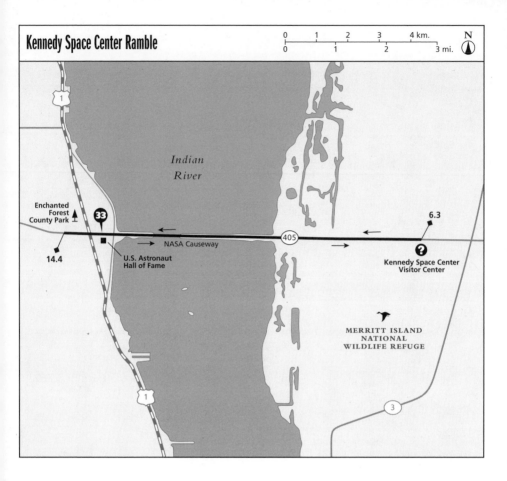

From your bicycle, you can see a great deal of the space complex here in the Cape Canaveral area and it begins in the U.S. Astronaut Hall of Fame ($17), just across the causeway from Merritt Island. We Floridians didn't mind the federal government changing the name of the cape to Cape Kennedy for ten years after President Kennedy was shot on November 22, 1963, but we were by and large happy when they allowed the cape itself to become "Canaveral" again and reserved "Kennedy" for the space complex. The name "Canaveral" has deep roots in Florida soil.

The area is more than the space center complex and related air force base, even though those are its technological "claims to fame." Still, Spanish explorers named the protruding geographical feature of the cape "Canaveral," or cape of reeds (or canes), more than 400 years ago. The narrow, outer barrier island buffers the Banana River from the Atlantic Ocean, and the river separates Canaveral proper from Merritt Island. In turn, Merritt Island is distinct from the mainland because the Indian River Lagoon serves as the east coast Intracoastal Waterway segment here.

Consequently, the region is geographically complex and ecologically exotic.

According to one brochure, "Cape Canaveral was chosen for rocket launches because it could take advantage of the earth's rotation. The linear velocity of the Earth's surface is greatest towards the equator and thus, the relatively southerly location of the Cape allows rockets to take advantage of this by launching eastward, in the same direction as the earth's rotation. It is also highly desirable [as we occasionally are reminded when rockets explode, the most spectacular example being the Space Shuttle Challenger on January 28, 1986] to have the downrange area sparsely populated, in case of accidents; an ocean is ideal for this. Although the United States has sites closer to the equator with expanses of ocean to the east of them (for example, Hawaii, Puerto Rico), the east coast of Florida has substantial logistical advantages over these distant island locations."

When you ride across the Indian River, stop and watch alligators cruising in the lagoon and shorebirds feeding through the shallows. Schools of minnows rustle through the water, perhaps chased by bigger minnows. Overhead, eagles and osprey scan the water for larger dining opportunities.

Brevard County's Enchanted Forest Nature Sanctuary, purchased as part of its Environmentally Endangered Lands program, anchors the opposite end of the ride from America's space center. This area is home to the gopher tortoise, indigo snakes, swallow-tailed kites, bald eagles, painted buntings, wild turkeys, white-tailed deer, and many other creatures and plants (native orchids, for instance) that call both its dry upland scrub and its low, cool hammocks home.

Farther to the south on Cape Canaveral (insiders just say "the Cape") is Port Canaveral, home to the Southeast's cruise liner industry. In 2006 more than 4.5 million paying tourists took ships from this port for jaunts around the Caribbean or even more distant locations with Carnival, Disney, or Royal Caribbean cruise lines.

My recommendation is to make the ride an excuse to see the space center. After all, some small part of the moon and Mars and the International Space Station belongs to you. Maybe it's time to go find it.

Miles and Directions

0.0 Turn right (north) from the parking lot of the U.S. Astronaut Hall of Fame onto Vectorspace Boulevard and immediately turn right (east) on NASA Parkway. (This stretch of road may also be called Columbia Boulevard or even the Indian River Lagoon Scenic Highway.)

6.3 Turn around at the Kennedy Space Center Visitor Center and ride back west on NASA Parkway.

13.8 Turn right (north) into the parking area for the Enchanted Forest County Park.

14.1 Turn around in the forest sanctuary parking area.

14.4 Turn left (east) on Columbia Boulevard.

15.6 Turn right (south) onto Vectorspace Boulevard and take an immediate turn left (east) into the parking area for the U.S. Astronaut Hall of Fame.

Local Information

Brevard County Sheriff's Department, 700 Park Avenue, Titusville; (321) 264-5308; www.sheriff.co.brevard.fl.us/.

Space Coast Office of Tourism, 430 Brevard Avenue, Suite 150, Cocoa Village; (321) 433-4470 or (877) 572-3224; www.space-coast.com.

Titusville Area Chamber of Commerce, 2000 South Washington Avenue, Titusville; (321) 267-3036; www.titusville.org.

Local Events/Attractions

Enchanted Forest Sanctuary, 444 Columbia Boulevard, Titusville; (321) 264-5185; www .eelbrevard.com/eel/enchforest/index.htm. Brevard County purchased this beautiful natural area under its environmentally endangered lands program. Open daily from 9:00 a.m. to 5:00 p.m. and operated with help from Friends of the Enchanted Forest (www.nbbd .com/godo/ef/index.html).

Kennedy Space Center Visitor Complex, SR 405, Kennedy Space Center; (321) 449-4444; www.kennedyspacecenter.com. If you have even the smallest interest in the exploration of space, you will be thrilled. Open every day from 9:00 a.m. to 6:00 p.m. except Christmas and certain launch days.

U.S. Astronaut Hall of Fame, 6225 Vectorspace Boulevard, Titusville; (321) 269-6100; www.kennedyspacecenter.com. Open from 10:00 a.m. to 6:00 p.m. Interesting and fun.

Restaurants

Dixie Crossroads Seafood Restaurant, 1475 Garden Street, Titusville; (321) 268-5000; www.dixiecrossroads.com. "We only serve domestic wild ocean shrimp. . . ." I want a couple dozen right now!

El Leoncito, 4280 South Washington Avenue, Titusville; (321) 267-1159. No Web site, but the reviews for this Mexican restaurant are good.

Majestic Restaurant, 702 Cheney Highway, Titusville; (321) 383-4882; www.majestic restaurantinc.com. Chinese . . .

Pumpernickel's Delicatessen, 2850 South Hopkins Avenue, Titusville; (321) 268-5160.

Accommodations

There are a lot of old 1950s-style motels in this area and especially on the US 1 route north-to-south through Titusville. Some of them have been refurbished and are truly fun in a quaint and funky kind of way. When our family traveled, half a century ago, and looked for a motel room in the $13-per-night range—with a television set and a pool—my folks checked out the room first. I suggest you do the same today.

Apollo Inn Motel, 4125 North Cocoa Boulevard, Cocoa; (321) 636-8511. When this place was built, the Internet was science fiction. Old and cheap, but clean and quiet.

Best Western Space Shuttle Inn, 3455 Cheney Highway, Titusville; (321) 269-9100; www.best westernflorida.com/hotels/best-western-space-shuttle-inn/.

Casa Coquina Bed & Breakfast, 4010 Coquina Avenue, Titusville; (321) 268-4653; www.casacoquina.com. A "European-style eclectic mansion built during the Roaring '20s." Complimentary breakfast, happy hour, and wireless Internet. Space-launch watching from second-floor balcony. Exotic building paint and reasonable prices.

Bike Shops

Ten Speed Drive Bicycle Center, 3428 South Hopkins Avenue, Titusville; (321) 269-3325.

Restrooms

Mile 0.0: The U.S. Astronaut Hall of Fame.
Mile 6.3: Kennedy Space Center Visitor Center.
Mile 13.8: The Enchanted Forest County Park.

Maps

DeLorme: Florida Atlas & Gazetteer: Pages 81 D 3, 82 D 1.

South Florida

34 DeSoto Best Ride Ramble

This is, without a doubt, the finest ride in Florida! It ought to be 100 miles long. Congratulations to the activists, environmentalists, and political leaders who made this wonderful park happen. Ride on!

Start: The Fort DeSoto Park, a Pinellas County park on the west side of Pinellas Parkway/County Road 679, on Mullet Key south of St. Petersburg.
Length: 23.1 miles.
Terrain: Flat.
Traffic and hazards: Between the parking area and either end of Mullet Key, traffic will be light and bikers will be plentiful—except on national holidays when traffic will be heavy. There is also a multiuse path bordering the ride on Mullet Key. Traffic becomes more intense on Cabbage and Pine Keys on the northernmost leg (between Fort DeSoto Park and the U-turn at County Road 682), where the road is bordered with condominiums and large homes.

Getting there: From Interstate 275, which runs north–south through St. Petersburg, take exit 12 onto CR 682 and proceed west on Pinellas Bayway. Turn left (south) on CR 679, Pinellas Parkway, and proceed to the entrance of the park, which will be on the right (west) side of the road. (While it may be easy to get lost in St. Petersburg, this should be an easy ride to find because a mile after exiting the interstate, water hems the road on both sides.)

This is, in my estimation, the finest ride in Florida. The scenery is thrilling. Parking, restroom, and snack options are many. It is easy to reach from the urban and tourist areas. Plus, park attendants love bikers and if you wish, you can ride the multiuse trail that parallels the road.

Here are the simple facts about Fort DeSoto Park: It is the largest park within the Pinellas County Park System, 1,136 acres that make up five interconnected islands. First opened on December 21, 1962, when the state toll road, the Pinellas Bayway, was completed, Fort DeSoto Park was dedicated on May 11, 1963, in perpetuity as a public park. Annual park attendance averages more than 2.7 million visitors, and the toll on the Bayway into the park is only 35 cents per vehicle.

From the parking area, turn right toward Mullet Key and ride through the toll booth—no charge for cyclists—but be sure to wave to the attendant, who, except on holidays, will be bored out of his or her skull. (No radios, books, games, or other distractions are allowed inside the booth.) When I rode through, Chuck-the-attendant was friendly and invited me to meet the rabbits and raccoons that kept him company and amused late in the day—perhaps because he fed them Life Savers candies. Such a sweet to a wild and relatively small animal must have about the same effect as a hit of cocaine. It is not mandatory to stop and chat, however; most cyclists breeze past without so much as a wave.

In the park, you must turn left or right at the intersection marked by the giant U.S. flag with park headquarters dead ahead. Either is excellent. Swing to the right

With the cruise ship Inspiration *departing the Port of Tampa in the background, cyclists stop to make a quick repair. A multiuse path borders CR 679 the length of Mullet Key on the DeSoto Ramble.*

and it takes you to the loop turnaround of "North Beach"; to the left the road takes you to the loop turnaround of "East Beach."

With multiple views of the Gulf of Mexico on either side, you quickly realize that you are on a very narrow island. The Gulf of Mexico is to the west, and Tampa Bay is to the south and east. Pirates were here in the days before settlement, as were Native Americans and Spanish explorers. In the 1800s the U.S. Army built Fort De Soto at the southernmost elbow to protect the harbor, and today you can tour it. There are kayak rentals, nature trails, picnic pavilions with grills, a 500-foot pier and a ferry to Egmont Key (a nice day trip, but no bicycles allowed), bait shops for fishing, and restroom facilities with showers. And, of course, cherish the miles of white-sand beach with oceangoing freighters and cruise liners passing so close you will think you can swim out to them and hitchhike. (Go to www.pinellascounty.org /park/maps/color/location/ft_desoto.pdf for a map.)

Once you are on Mullet Key, the roads are straight and, in the summer, open and hot. On this ride the wide multiuse path will be an enjoyable and relaxing option, perhaps for a second ride, even though the path is used by joggers, walkers, folks with dogs on leashes, in-line skaters, and around-the-block recreational riders.

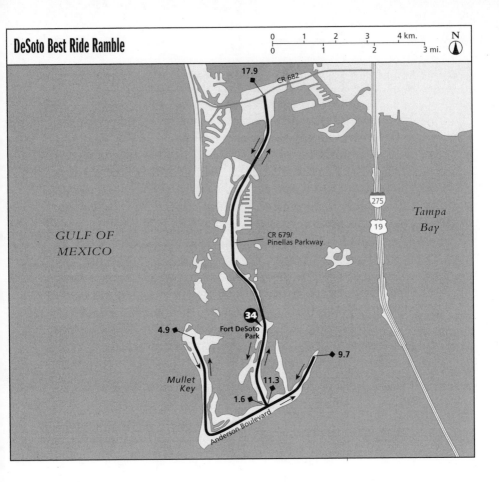

DeSoto Best Ride Ramble

GULF OF
MEXICO

CR 679/
Pinellas Parkway

Fort DeSoto
Park

Mullet
Key

Anderson Boulevard

Tampa
Bay

17.9

4.9

9.7

11.3

1.6

All in all, it is a wonderful place to ride and you will want to visit this area more than once.

Miles and Directions

0.0 Begin in the initial parking area of Fort DeSoto Park, a Pinellas County park, on the west side of Pinellas Parkway (CR 679) on Madelaine Key, south of St. Petersburg.

0.1 From the stop sign at the entrance to the parking area, turn right (south).

1.6 From the stop sign at the T intersection with the giant U.S. flag marking the park headquarters in front of you, turn right (southwest) on Anderson Boulevard.

4.9 CR 679 curves radically north and here, at the end of the road, turn back (south) in the cul-de-sac and ride in the opposite direction.

9.7 CR 679 has curved northeast and here, at the opposite end of Mullet Key, at the end of the road, turn back (southwest) and ride in the opposite direction.

11.3 With the giant U.S. flag and park headquarters on your left, turn right (north) on CR 679.

12.9 Continue straight north on CR 679. **Option:** This point is the entrance to your parking area and you can turn left here and end your ride.

17.9 Make a U-turn at the T intersection of CR 679 at CR 682/Pinellas Bayway and return south.

23.0 Arrive at the entrance to Fort DeSoto Park and turn right (west) into the park.

23.1 Arrive back at the start.

Local Information

Fort DeSoto Park, 3500 Pinellas Bayway South, Tierra Verde: Park Office (727) 582-2267, Campground Office (727) 582-2267; www .pinellascounty.org/park/05_Ft_DeSoto.htm.

St. Petersburg/Clearwater Area Convention & Visitors Bureau, 13805 58th Street North, Suite 2-200, Clearwater; (727) 464-7200 or (877) 352-3224; www.floridasbeach.com.

St. Petersburg Police Department, 1300 First Avenue North, St. Petersburg; (727) 893-7780 (nonemergency); www.stpete.org/police/.

Tampa Bay Convention & Visitors Bureau, 401 East Jackson Street, Suite 2100, Tampa; (813) 223-1111; www.visittampabay.com.

Local Events/Attractions

The beaches of the Gulf of Mexico. These white-sand beaches are the number-one attraction on the entire coastline from Clearwater to Key West.

Egmont Key State Park, 4905 34th Street South, #5000, St. Petersburg; (727) 893-2627; www.floridastateparks.org/egmontkey/. Take the ferry from Mullet Key and combine a great bike ride with the most beautiful beach in Florida—and it is all in the public domain, 365 days a year with no admission charge.

Tampa Bay Buccaneers, www.buccaneers.com. Professional football at its best.

Tampa Bay Devil Rays, www.devilrays.com. Major league baseball is played just a few miles from the ride in this geographically complex and fascinating area.

Restaurants

Blue Moon Cafe, 6101 Gulf Boulevard, St. Petersburg Beach; (727) 360-1820. Tried it. Liked it. Small and funky. Moderately priced. Tropical salad!

Shells Seafood Restaurant, 6300 Gulf Boulevard, St. Petersburg Beach; (727) 360-0889; www.shellsseafood.com.

Wharf Restaurant, 2001 Pass A Grille Way, St. Petersburg Beach; (727) 367-9469. Great views, over the water.

Accommodations

Pasa Tiempo, 7141 Bay Street, St. Petersburg Beach; (727) 367-9907; www.pasa-tiempo .com. All reviews excellent. Pricey, but it's a resort: $185/night January through April and $155/night May through December.

Plaza Beach Resort, 4506 Gulf Boulevard, St. Petersburg Beach; (727) 367-2791; www .plazabeach.com. Rates vary by month and type of room from $85 to $199 per night.

Sea Breeze Manor B&B Inn, 5701 Shore Boulevard, St. Petersburg; (727) 343-4445 or (888) 343-4445; www.seabreezemanor.com. Across Boca Ciega Bay from Pinellas Bayway.

Bike Shops

ABC Bicycles, 6633 Central Avenue, St. Petersburg; (727) 345-5391; www.abc bicycles.com. Due north of the ride in the Pasadena neighborhood. The city's oldest and largest bicycle shop.

J&R Bicycles, 10555 66th Street #A1, Pinellas Park; (727) 544-7076 or (800) 455-9353; www.jrbicycles.com. BMX superstore—just for fun.

Trail Sport Bicycles, 6572 Seminole Boulevard, Seminole; (727) 395-0905; www.trail sportbicycles.com/index.htm. Located on the Pinellas multiuse trail. Closed Wednesday.

Restrooms

From the beginning (and end) of this ride, public restrooms are available throughout Fort DeSoto Park.

Maps

DeLorme: Florida Atlas & Gazetteer: Page 90 C 3.

35 Tampa Interbay Ramble

This ride is all about learning to negotiate a bicycle successfully (is there any other way?) in traffic with about 8 miles of scenic view included. Looking at the scenery and riding a bike, however, won't mix well here, so make this ride early in the day, preferably on a national holiday, and you will enjoy the mix of residential styles and the wonderfully sweeping sight of Hillsborough Bay along Bayshore Boulevard.

Start: The spacious Lowe's parking lot at 4210 South Dale Mabry Highway, just a couple of miles north of MacDill Air Force Base on the Interbay Peninsula, in Tampa.

Length: My Internet chum, William, who originally suggested this route, said it was 23.5 miles, but I clocked it at 22.7. What's a few tenths of a mile among friends?

Terrain: Flat.

Traffic and hazards: There is hurrying city traffic along this entire route, and although the separated bridge lanes to and from Davis Island are one-way, they are a bit narrow for my cycling taste.

Getting there: Take an immediate left (east) upon leaving Tampa International Airport onto West Spruce Street/State Road 589, which curves and becomes West Boy Scout Boulevard. Turn right (south) about 2.25 miles from the airport entrance onto Dale Mabry Highway and continue a little over 4.25 miles to the Lowe's at 4210 South Dale Mabry Highway. From Orlando and the theme park neighborhood, take Interstate 4 west to the intersection with Interstate 275. Continue west on I-275 toward St. Petersburg and watch for the exit to Dale Mabry Highway. The Lowe's parking lot will be about 3.25 miles on the left side of the road. (The drive from southwest Orlando, where the theme parks are located, to Tampa will usually take one and a half hours.)

The casual visitor to Tampa, someone just passing through or attending a convention, might not pause in the neighborhoods on the Interbay Peninsula unless they were lost. These quarters are older, out of fashion . . . and highly livable. Many of them were probably never fashionable, and today that makes them interesting. Yards with unusual do-it-yourself sculptures, homes with exotic paint schemes, differing architectural styles, barking dogs, stray cats, kids on skateboards, and the occasional crowing rooster. Everything that makes a place comfortable, secure, home.

The narrow roads that wind and twist along in the interior of the Interbay are packed with traffic and all of the cars and trucks seem to be in a hurry. Of course, MacDill Air Force Base occupies the lower third of the peninsula, and I-275 and U.S. Highway 92 hurry tourists and commuters to the high bridges connecting Tampa and St. Petersburg. Yet in the interstices, the crowded little strip of land that hangs down in Tampa Bay like a uvula is a delightfully mixed and well-established area that will give you plenty of practice riding your two-wheeler patiently and cautiously in urban traffic. But let's face it: Traffic is part of the thrill of urban riding.

South Florida begins in Tampa-St. Petersburg-Clearwater. The land, air, water, plants, and animals all begin to change to subtropical.

Although half of this ramble takes you through quaint neighborhoods and along roads teeming with small, independently owned businesses, another half gives you wide, scenic views of Hillsborough Bay. The west side of Bayshore Boulevard is lined with parks that have passed their prime, large older homes on spacious lots with shaded lawns, resort hotels built almost a century ago, and—it wouldn't be Florida without a few of these—a sprinkling of high-rise condominiums.

This ride does not specifically take you there, but at the roundabout that signals the southern turn from West Davis Boulevard to South Davis Boulevard, it will be an interesting side ride to speed off directly south on Severn Avenue. Severn twists around the Peter O. Knight Airport—for private planes—and the private marina strategically located at the tip of the island, but open vistas across the bay make this a delightful mile out to the end of Severn . . . and, of course, a mile back.

Not as widely publicized as the Orlando theme park area, Tampa–St. Petersburg–Clearwater is abundantly rich in places to go and things to do once you climb off your bike. There are the white-sand beaches of the Gulf of Mexico to the west and too many attractions to talk about, including a few relatively low-budget and magnificently old-fashioned places that you *can't miss.* I'm thinking of:

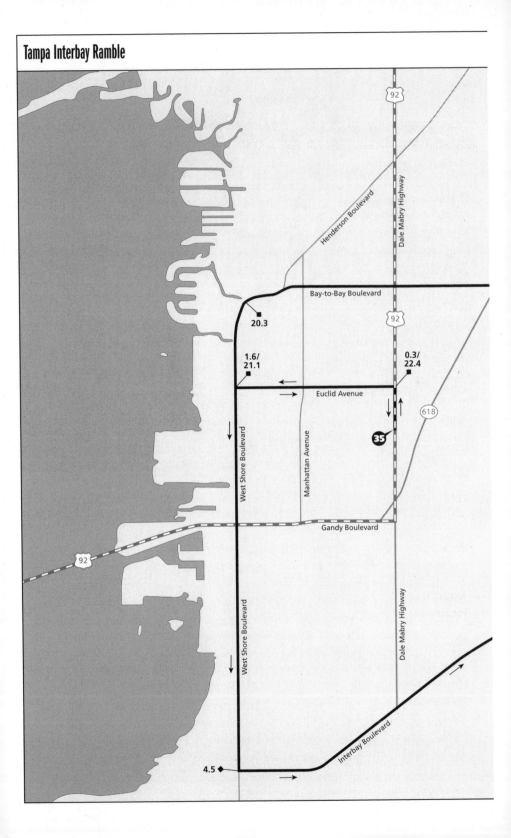

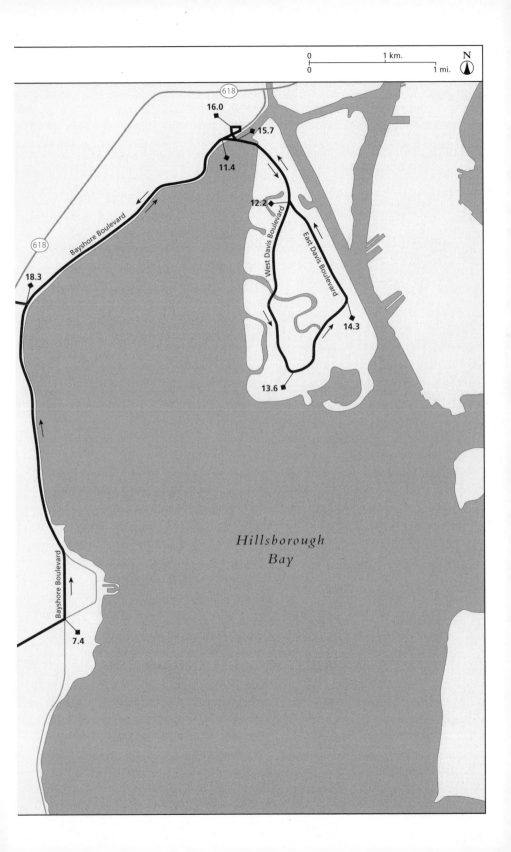

618

16.0

15.7

11.4

618

Bayshore Boulevard

18.3

12.2

West Davis Boulevard

East Davis Boulevard

14.3

13.6

Bayshore Boulevard

7.4

Hillsborough
Bay

0   1 km.

0   1 mi.

N

- **Dinosaur World** in Plant City (www.dinoworld.net) to the east next to I-4. Just $12.75 for an adult to hang out with 150 life-size dino models—and less for kids and seniors. What's not to like!

- Clermont's 226-foot **Citrus Tower** (www.citrustower.com) is an hour and a half east on I-4, then north on U.S. Highway 27. Built in 1956 on one of the highest hills in central Florida, a five-million-pound pile of concrete, all one could see from the top was an endless green grove of citrus. Today you absolutely must take your chances in the tower's rickety elevator to see what has become of Florida's oranges.

- Straight north for an hour on Dale Mabry Highway takes you to **Weeki Wachee Springs** (www.weekiwachee.com). Famous for its "spring of live mermaids," Weeki Wachee was built in 1947 and reflects the taste of the era. After sixty years, Weeki Wachee has fallen on hard times, so check out this exotic little park soon.

The very best time to make this inner-city ramble is early. Catch the sun coming up over the bay and you will surely be enchanted. Sunrise is, after all, the hour when songbirds are out in abundance. It is that time of day when the air is cool, the bay is calm, the neighbors are yawning over coffee, traffic is sparse, and you are pedaling this route like one possessed. The perfect beginning to another beautiful day in the sunshine.

Miles and Directions

0.0   Turn right out of the expansive Lowe's parking lot at 4210 South Dale Mabry Highway. Dale Mabry is a busy four-lane highway.

0.3   Turn left (west) on Euclid Avenue, a two-lane street. Like many of the streets on the Interbay Peninsula, the dividing line between residential and commercial districts is not sharply drawn.

1.6   Turn left (south) on South West Shore Boulevard, a narrow two-lane. About 1.5 miles along on West Shore, you cross railroad tracks that are not marked on many maps. (Google Maps missed it, for instance.)

4.5   Turn left (east) on Interbay Boulevard, which continues this peninsula's tradition of tight two-lanes. Interbay angles left twice along the way.

7.4   Turn left (north) at the stop sign onto Bayshore Boulevard. (Because many drivers are distracted by the view and because this is a rough road with much traffic, you may want to take the multiuse path that parallels the road.)

11.4 Swing right (south) over the Davis Island Bridge, which is narrow but begins as one-way.

12.2 Angle right onto West Davis Boulevard as the road forks around the DAVIS ISLAND sign.

13.6 Circle the roundabout and go left (east) on South Davis Boulevard.

14.3 Take the gradual left (north) onto East Davis Boulevard.

15.7 Arriving back at the Davis Island Bridge, you are confronted with a quick choice of exits. Take the Plant Avenue/Bayshore Boulevard exit rather than the immediate left for Bayshore Boulevard. (If you mistakenly swing hard right onto Bayshore, you can simply bike an extra block and turn around 180 degrees at the small Gasparilla ship parking lot.)

16.0 Immediately over the one-way bridge, turn right on West Verne Street; it loops clockwise back into the six-lane Bayshore Boulevard heading west and then south. (You have a choice of staying in the road and riding hard or crossing to the bay multiuse lane for a more relaxed ride and view of this section.)

18.3 Turn right (west) on Bay-to-Bay Boulevard.

20.3 Take the left fork and cross onto South West Shore Boulevard heading south. (If, because of traffic here, you should take the right fork, simply cross West Shore and turn south.)

21.1 Turn left (east) on West Euclid Avenue.

22.4 Turn right (south) on South Dale Mabry Highway.

22.7 Arrive at the start of the ride, the Lowe's parking lot on the east side of Dale Mabry.

Local Information

Tampa Chamber of Commerce, 615 Channel-side Drive, #108, Tampa; (813) 228-7777; www.tampachamber.com.

Tampa Bay Convention & Visitor Bureau Information Center, 401 East Jackson Street, Suite 2100, Tampa; (813) 223-2752/1111; www.visittampabay.com.

Tampa Bay Freewheelers, (813) 238-2464 or (813) 404-5721; www.tbfreewheelers.com /Main/home.html. "TBF is a touring club that promotes safe cycling through planned rides, bike repair clinics, effective cycling classes, and communication with local and statewide agencies regarding bicycle awareness and advocacy."

Tampa Police Department, 411 North Franklin Street, Tampa; (813) 276-3704; www.tampa gov.net/dept_Police/.

Local Events/Attractions

Attractions: Busch Gardens, www.busch gardens.com; Adventure Island, www.adventure island.com; Dinosaur World, www.dinoworld .net; Discovery Cove, www.discoverycove .com; Florida Aquarium, www.flaquarium.org; Sea World, www.seaworld.com; and Lowry Park Zoo, www.lowryparkzoo.com.

Museums: MOSI—Museum of Science and Industry, www.mosi.org; Salvador Dali Museum, www.salvadordalimuseum.org; The John and Mable Ringling Museum of Art, www.ringling.org.

Professional sports: Tampa Bay Buccaneers, www.buccaneers.com; Tampa Bay Devil Rays, www.devilrays.com; and Tampa Bay Lightning, www.tampabaylightning.com.

The beach: It is only a few miles west or south to some of the Gulf of Mexico's public white-sand beaches. Open 24/7, with seashell collecting, swimming, and sunsets that will cause you to gasp in pleasure, and all at no charge!

Restaurants

Bern's Steak House, 1208 South Howard Avenue, Tampa; (813) 251-2421; www.bernssteakhouse.com. A great reputation. People travel for hours. Moderately expensive depending upon what you order. Reservations needed.

Ceviche Tapas Bar & Restaurant, 2109 Bayshore Boulevard, Tampa; (813) 250-0203; www.ceviche.com. Moderately pricey and upscale.

Mad Dogs & Englishman, 4115 South MacDill Avenue, Tampa; (813) 832-3037; www.mad dogs.com. Better than average with a bar and an outdoor patio. Moderately priced.

Accommodations

Comfort Inn & Suites, 445 South Gulfview Boulevard, Clearwater; (727) 441-4902. Stay at the beach. There are hundreds of motels and hotels to choose from and prices vary between "the seasons."

Gram's Place Bed & Breakfast, 3109 North Ola Avenue (Plymouth Street), Tampa; (813) 221-0596; www.grams-inn-tampa.com. Called alternative/adventure lodging; features dorm-like hostel ($22.50), private rooms ($68 for two), and even camping.

Quorum Hotel, 700 North Westshore Boulevard, Tampa; (813) 289-8200. A touch pricey, but this hotel gets excellent traveler reviews and it is not far from the airport.

Bike Shops

Dud Thames Bike Shop, 2409 South MacDill Avenue, Tampa; (813) 839-0410. A few blocks off the route, but the closest shop to the Interbay Ramble.

Joe Haskins Bicycle Shop, 2310 North Florida Avenue, Tampa; (813) 229-8409. A small one-man shop that has been around forever and still gives personal service. A mile or two north of Davis Island.

Restrooms

There are no public restrooms along this route, but there are thousands of commercial establishments that are accustomed to visitations by itinerants like us!

Maps

DeLorme: Florida Atlas & Gazetteer: Page 91 A-B 1-2.

36 Lake Wales Cruise

An entertaining ride that carries cyclists along the spine of central South Florida's sandy ridge and thus through lake country and orange groves and beside enormous commercial sand pits and phosphate mines.

Start: Offering multiple areas to park your vehicle, Lake Wales City Park is on the shore of the lake by that name in the town of Lake Wales. For this ride, I chose the largest, which is on the northwest side of the lake and closest to downtown.

Length: A 40-mile loop.

Terrain: Much of this ride is flat, but there are long rolling hills and a few short, but surprisingly steep, climbs.

Traffic and hazards: Burns Avenue/County Road 17A is a busy highway as long as it is four-lane, but when it becomes two lanes, its burden of traffic declines to "fairly light" except for morning and evening rush hours. And yes, even small towns such as Lake Wales, population about 13,000, have rush hours as folks drive to work.

Getting there: The town of Lake Wales is east of Tampa and south of Orlando. From Interstate 4, turn south onto U.S. Highway 27. It is about 25 miles to Lake Wales and the start of this cruise. Once you are in Lake Wales, turn left on Central Avenue and it will take you to the lake; it is then a couple of blocks to the parking area.

This is one of the magic areas of Florida that the twenty-first-century world either flies over or drives around. Truly, there is much to see and do and enjoy here in the

Caught in an afternoon rainstorm, bikers gather and commiserate about the weather. ▶

south between the coasts. It isn't Everglades, but it has swamps and rivers that surely hide prehistoric monsters. It isn't the beach, either, or the high-rolling fun of the Orlando attractions, although those are only a few hours north.

This is working Florida, where citrus still grows from horizon to horizon and where one occasionally glimpses phosphate and sand mines next to the highway. It is working Florida, where in small towns like nearby Wimauma (southwest on County Road 674 in Hillsborough County), the Spanish language and Central American culture have become an integral part of the landscape.

Your Lake Wales ride begins next to the little lake of that name and proceeds directly to "Spook Hill." Regarding this locally famous hill, some prankster has invented a legend about an "old Indian chief" and his beautiful daughter, which, like many such tales, is 99 percent silly and 1 percent wishful thinking.

Nevertheless, in "the old days" it was thought that subsurface magnetite would pull your iron-and-steel automobile uphill. It was an illusion then—I was there at 8 years old with a dad excited to show it to me, but even then I somehow knew that it was sleight of hand. Still, even with today's plastic and nonferrous vehicles, there is an odd sense of movement. . . . Regardless, for a couple blocks, this is one steep climb on a bicycle. So ignore the sign about the old Indian chief and his daughter and feel the burn!

Atop the hill, turn right on Burns Avenue, admire the view, and for the next mile, watch for traffic because it can be heavy on this short stretch of four-lane. Fortunately, the traffic bleeds away and you are soon on a long left-hand curve into the sand hills bordering the lakes on the central Florida ridge.

You also pass the entrance to Bok Tower and Gardens, now called the Historic Bok Sanctuary. One thing that has not changed is the other-worldly beauty of this area. The gardens were designed by New York Central Park designer Frederick Law Olmstead Jr. for his friend Edward Bok. Bok, an immigrant from the Netherlands, became wealthy in the American publishing trade. If you fail to spend a day at the tower and gardens, you will have missed one of the lightly visited jewels of central Florida. Meandering sculptured gardens (www.boksanctuary.org) and delightful live concerts from the carillon tower are truly underappreciated. The beautiful tower is also visible from numerous points on the ride. Thank you, Mr. Bok!

During the first half of this pedal, you will swing by lakes and through scrub oak thickets where contractors have not even dreamed of sinking a backhoe. That makes this ride special.

Note that some of the roughest riding sections of road are on "Masterpiece Road," named after the bygone attraction Masterpiece Gardens, whose principal feature was a large mosaic of Leonardo da Vinci's famous *Last Supper*. More than 300,000 tiles were glued to an outdoor wall in the 1950s, and when a curtain was pulled, the faithful could enjoy the representation. The owners coupled the Masterpiece with an outdoor exhibit called Monkey Island, a pink bridge over a pond seeded with alligators, and a small choo-choo train named the *Phantom Express*.

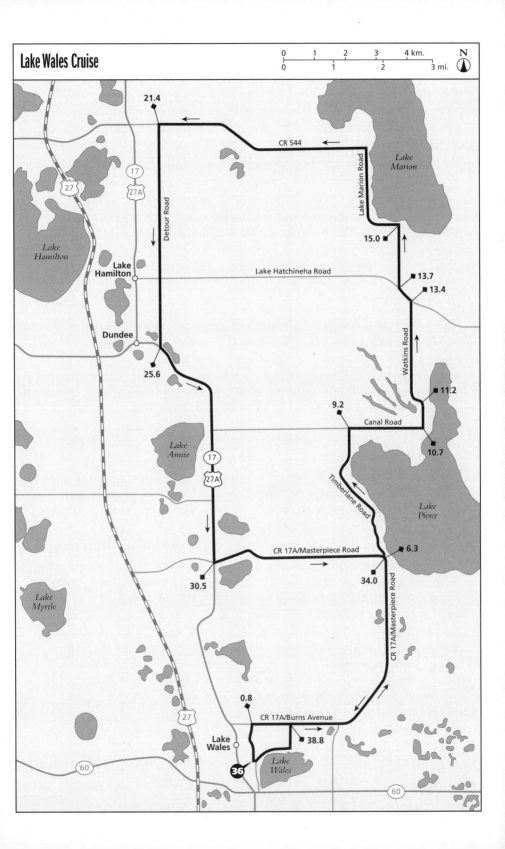

Lake Wales Cruise

21.4

CR 544

Lake Marion Road

Lake Marion

17

27

27A

Detour Road

15.0

Lake Hamilton

Lake Hamilton

Lake Hatchineha Road

13.7

13.4

Dundee

Watkins Road

25.6

11.2

9.2

Canal Road

10.7

Lake Annie

17

27A

Timberlane Road

Lake Pierce

CR 17A/Masterpiece Road

6.3

30.5

34.0

CR 17A/Masterpiece Road

Lake Myrtle

0.8

27

CR 17A/Burns Avenue

Lake Wales

38.8

36

Lake Wales

60

60

Unfortunately, the Masterpiece is gone now, as are most of the great little mom-and-pop attractions from the mid-twentieth century, done in perhaps by an increasingly sophisticated public.

The real highlight of the ride today, however, is not even the older spectacle, Cypress Gardens, which thrives nearby, but a small two-lane street that runs straight as an arrow back toward Lake Wales from the north, a road that carries the improbably permanent name Detour Road. For a little over 4 miles, orange trees are so lush, so thick, and so close to the road that anyone with claustrophobia may want to avoid this road. Here is the heart blood of the Florida citrus industry and the way citrus ought to grow in the Sunshine State. After the trees are picked—navel oranges ripen in winter and spring—the road is a bit olive-drab, but prior to the plucking, expect brilliant orange and yellow and green . . . and beautiful.

The ride culminates at Lake Wales—the lake and the town.

Miles and Directions

0.0   Turn right (north) from the primary Lake Wales City Park parking lot on Lake Wales in the city of Lake Wales.

0.1   Veer left onto North Wales Drive and follow the signs to Spook Hill.

0.8   Turn right (east) after climbing the short but steep Spook Hill onto Burns Avenue/CR 17A, which is a busy four-lane highway at this point, although it soon empties its traffic and narrows to two lanes. As 17A begins a long sweeping turn to the north, it changes names to Masterpiece Road.

6.3   Masterpiece Road makes a 90-degree turn left (west) here at Lake Pierce; in the middle of the turn, turn right (north) onto Timberlane Road.

9.2   Turn right (east) onto Canal Road.

10.7   Canal Road turns 90 degrees left (north).

11.2   Turn left (northwest) onto Watkins Road.

13.4   Turn left (northwest) onto Lake Hatchineha Road.

13.7   Turn right (north) onto Jim Edwards Road.

15.0   Turn left (west) onto Lake Marion Road. (The road simply turns 90 degrees and changes names as it runs around Lake Marion. In the same manner, after about a mile, Lake Marion Road takes a 90-degree left and you begin to see signs for County Road 544.)

21.4   Turn left (south) onto Detour Road. "Detour" is its permanent name, not a temporary designation.

25.6   At the stop sign, Detour Road—which has become North 8th Street in the community of Dundee—ends. Angle very slightly right to the stop sign, which you can see from a hundred feet away, and turn left (roughly southeast) onto State Road 17/US 27A, which is a two-lane road with shoulders at this point.

30.5   Turn left (east) on Masterpiece Road/CR 17A.

34.0   Masterpiece Road turns 90 degrees south at Lake Pierce and after a mile or so becomes Burns Avenue once again, eventually curving due west.

38.8 Turn left (south) on North 9th Street and, with Lake Wales directly ahead, cruise downhill to North Lakeshore Boulevard.

39.3 Turn right (west) on North Lakeshore Boulevard and, with the lake on your immediate left, follow the road to your parking area.

40.0 Turn left into the parking lot and the end of the ride.

Local Information

Central Florida Visitors & Convention Bureau, 600 North Broadway, Suite 300, Bartow; (800) 828-7655; www.visitcentralflorida.org. **Polk County Sheriff's Office,** 455 North Broadway Avenue, Bartow; (863) 534-6200; www.polksheriff.org.

Local Events/Attractions

Bok Sanctuary, 1151 Tower Boulevard, Lake Wales; (863) 686-1408; www.boksanctuary .org. Open every day from 8:00 a.m. to 6:00 p.m. The tower has sixty cast bronze bells in a carillon for daily concerts. Magnificent gardens sprawl over the sanctuary's 245 acres. Definitely worth a long and pleasant visit.
Cypress Gardens Adventure Park, 6000 Cypress Gardens Boulevard, Winter Haven; (800) 808-0872; www.cypressgardens.com. Florida's first theme park. Cypress Gardens offers historic gardens, beautiful belles, and famed waterskiing shows, plus thirty-nine exciting rides, spectacular concerts and shows, and a craftsmen's village.

Restaurants

Harbor Side Steakhouse and Oyster Bar, 2435 7th Street SW, Winter Haven; (863) 293-7070. On Lake Shipp, beside U.S. Highway 17 in Winter Haven, half an hour northwest of Lake Wales.
La Bella Torre, 253 East Stuart Avenue, Lake Wales; (863) 678-9696. Small and almost unnoticed in the shadow of Chalet Suzanne, but uniformly excellent reviews.
Mike's Fine Food, 1590 North Broadway Avenue, Bartow; (863) 533-2060. Steaks, seafood, and an old-fashioned salad bar.

Accommodations

Chalet Suzanne Country Inn & Restaurant, 3800 Chalet Suzanne Drive, Lake Wales; (800) 433-6011; www.chaletsuzanne.com. This Bavarian-themed establishment has become quite famous with a noted restaurant, lounge, wine cellar, vineyard, and its own airstrip. Thirty sumptuous rooms from $169 to $229 per night.
A Prince of Wales Motel, 513 South Scenic Highway, Lake Wales; (863) 676-1249; www.princeofwalesmotel.com. A refurbished, somewhat old-fashioned twenty-two-room motel that, its owners point out, is "clean and good value" (they also take pains to point out that they are British).
Terrace Hotel, 329 East Main Street, Lakeland; (863) 688-0800; www.terracehotel.com. Called the ". . . newest historical treasure and finest new hotel." Not "room rates" but a "tariff schedule" at $169 to $189 per night.

Bike Shops

At this time there is no bike shop in Lake Wales, but the **Bike Shop of Winter Haven** is only 10 miles away at 509 Cypress Gardens Boulevard, (863) 299-9907.

Restrooms

Mile 0.0: Several restroom facilities are located along Lake Wales at the start/end of this ride. Otherwise you will have to slip into a convenience store . . . or an orange grove.

Maps

DeLorme: Florida Atlas & Gazetteer: Pages 93 A 3, 85 D 3.

37 Phosphate Cruise

This ride is all about you and Florida's famous phosphate country. The now-abandoned phosphate pits are often seeded with bass and crappie, osprey nest on high perches by the hundreds, and the scrub that is slowly reclaiming the strip-mined land is filled with turkeys. There are plenty of railroad crossings, so hang on as you pedal through miles that you never knew existed.

Start: Begin this ride at the town hall of Bradley Junction in Polk County. This is a tiny community, so look carefully for it on your map.
Length: A 42.2-mile loop.

Terrain: Flat to gently rolling.
Traffic and hazards: Light to busy. Give the big trucks plenty of room.

Getting there: Drive east from Tampa (or west from Orlando) on Interstate 4 to the exit at U.S. Highway 98, which is about equidistant from either city. Drive south to Bartow, where you will turn right (west) on State Road 60 to Mulberry and then left (south) on State Road 37 to the hamlet of Bradley Junction. Turn left (east) on Main Avenue (it may or may not be marked) and look for the town hall (it may or may not be marked) a few blocks down the street on your left.

To truly enjoy a ride in Florida—or perhaps any location—to the maximum, it helps to understand the area. Not surprisingly, there is a whole lot more to the physical, social, and political peninsula that is America's twenty-seventh state than is generally covered in guidebooks or press releases. News about Florida commonly focuses on citrus, sunshine, and tourism; perhaps its professional sports teams or the weather. Its hardworking, blue-collar underbelly—sugar cane, forestry, and phosphate mining— are rarely newsworthy. This route will help you bring the Sunshine State's lunch bucket into perspective with its glamorous side.

One of the marvelous things about this ride is its sparse traffic, except on County Road 630—which is heavy at times—but there is plenty to see. Long stretches of open road, albeit two-lane from start to finish, and only a few pockets of small-town suburbia.

Speaking of roads, you may not locate all of these, even in your latest *DeLorme Florida Atlas & Gazetteer,* and my Magellan RoadMate 860T Global Positioning Unit, ordinarily very reliable, went blank in several areas. (Trust the force!) The countryside of southwest Florida is curiously managed and small roads are some-times left unnamed and unnumbered.

The striking characteristics of this landscape are the man-made mountains rising next to the roads. Immense sloping walls, towering pyramidal cliffs rising to a height and extent that make the Egyptian or Aztec pyramids seem pathetically unimpres-sive, child's play. I guarantee that you will be astonished by their size.

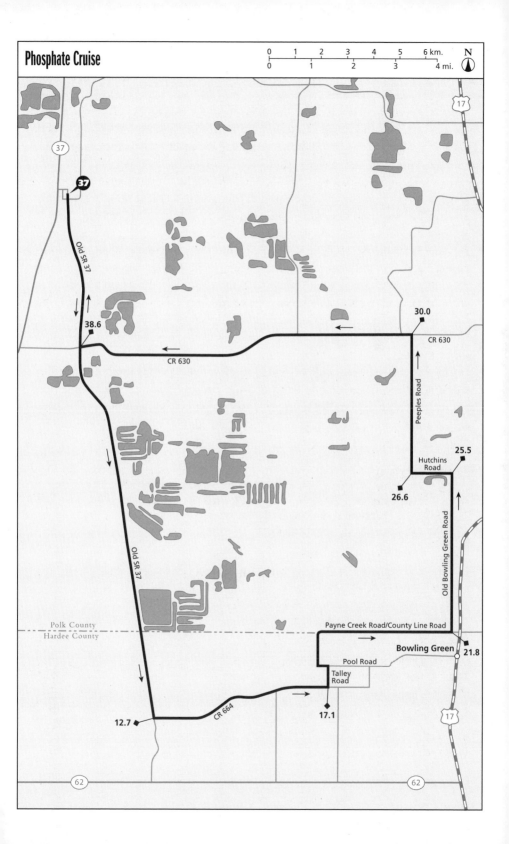

Phosphate Cruise

0   1   2   3   4   5   6 km.
0   1   2   3   4 mi.

N

37

37

Old SR 37

38.6

CR 630

30.0

CR 630

Peeples Road

25.5

Hutchins
Road

26.6

Old Bowling Green Road

Old SR 37

Polk County
Hardee County

Payne Creek Road/County Line Road

Bowling Green

21.8

Pool Road

Talley
Road

17.1

CR 664

12.7

62

62

17

17

This is Florida phosphate country, so let nothing that you see here surprise you. (Check your *DeLorme* for rows of unusually shaped mine pits that have been turned into freshwater lakes.)

Osprey have built nests atop hundreds, perhaps thousands, of antennas and power lines along the route. These beautiful black-and-white fish-eating raptors owe a debt of thanks to the phosphate industry for making their fishing so good. It is often said of these big eagles that once they lock their claws into a fish (or a snake or frog, perhaps) that they cannot release until they are on firm ground. That may explain the immensity of their nests. That and the fact that these are not only beautiful, but are truly impressively sized birds . . . and they live in South Florida year-round.

Other birds that you might notice along the route are in the open and in the brush. Elegant sandhill cranes, which migrate through Florida, flock to open fields where they have a better opportunity to elude natural predators such as coyotes and bobcats. And the Osceola subspecies of America's native wild turkey, found only in south and central Florida, is a relatively secretive bird, but as with most regulated game animals in America, it is more abundant now than it has been for a hundred years.

The Phosphate Cruise does not cycle you through Florida's most lovely pridelands. This is an important ride because, aside from the fun and frolic we anticipate with a trip to the beach or to one of Florida's great family attractions, Florida still has a job to do providing resources for the nation's commerce. Some of that begins right here.

Miles and Directions

0.0   Begin pedaling south on Old SR 37 from the town hall for Bradley Junction. It is disguised as an old and semi-renovated 7-Eleven store.

12.7   Turn left (east) on County Road 664.

17.1   Turn left (north) on Talley Road.

17.6   Turn left (west) on Pool Road. (There may not be a sign here, but Talley Road ends and you can only go left or right.)

17.8   Turn right (north) on Payne Creek Road/County Line Road West. It curves east.

21.8   Turn left (north) on Old Bowling Green Road.

25.5   Turn left (west) on Hutchins Road.

26.6   Turn right (north) on Peeples Road.

30.0   Turn left (west) on CR 630.

38.6   Turn right (north) on Old SR 37.

42.2   Arrive at the beginning and end of the ride.

Local Information

Central Florida Visitors & Convention Bureau, 600 North Broadway, Suite 300, Bartow; (800) 828-7655; www.visitcentralflorida.org. **Polk County Sheriff's Department,** 455 North Broadway Avenue, Bartow; (863) 534-6200; www.polksheriff.org.

Local Events/Attractions

Cypress Gardens Adventure Park, 6000 Cypress Gardens Boulevard, Winter Haven; (800) 808-0872; www.cypressgardens.com. Florida's first theme park. Cypress Gardens offers historic gardens and famed waterskiing shows, plus thirty-nine exciting rides, concerts, and a craftsmen's village.

Fantasy of Flight, 1400 Broadway Boulevard SE, Polk City; (863) 984-3500; www.fantasy offlight.com. More than forty vintage aircraft on display. Daily tours of restoration and wood shops. "Fun with Flight Center" and hang-gliding simulator. New multipassenger Virtual FX. Daily flights. Hot-air-balloon rides. Cafe and gift shop.

Restaurants

There are no restaurants along this route and the only convenience store is at the very beginning of the ride. Here are a few regional eateries:

Broadway Cafe, 119 West Broadway Street, Fort Meade; (863) 285-7077.

Curly Tails Barbecue, 330 Old Winter Haven Road, Bartow; (863) 533-5685; www.wwbf .com/radiostore/curlytailsbarbeque.htm.

Harbor Side, 2435 7th Street SW, Winter Haven; (863) 293-7070.

Wauchula Family Restaurants:
—**Nicholas',** 615 North 6th Avenue, Wauchula; (863) 773-2333.
—**Wilson's,** 1341 US Highway 17 South, Wauchula; (863) 767-0771.

Accommodations

Lake Morgan Bed & Breakfast, 817 South Boulevard, Lakeland; (863) 688-6788.

The Quilter's Inn, 106 South 4th Avenue, Wauchula; (863) 767-8989; www.thequilters inn.com.

Stanford Inn, 555 East Stanford Street, Bartow; (863) 555-2393; www.thestanford inn.com.

Bike Shops

There are no bike shops in the immediate area of this ride, but these are the closest: East: **Bike Shop,** 213 US 27 South, Sebring; (863) 402-2453.

North: **Bike Shop of Winter Haven,** 509 Cypress Gardens Boulevard, Winter Haven; (863) 299-9907.

Trek Bicycle Store, 5183 US 98 North, Lakeland; (863) 858-2000; www.lakelandtrek.com.

Northwest: **Power On Cycling,** 6053 SR 60 East, Plant City; http://store.valueweb.com /servlet/poweron/StoreFront.

Restrooms

There are no public facilities along this route.

Maps

DeLorme Florida Atlas & Gazetteer: Pages 92 B-C 3, 93 B-C 1.

38 Bradenton Country Challenge

A mix of old and new, traffic and country, bike lanes and construction zones, there may be more digging, paving, and building along this ride than in the entire states of Alabama or Kansas or Ohio!

Start: Parking lot of the College of Osteo-pathic Medicine—School of Pharmacy (Lecom Building), 5000 Lakewood Ranch Boulevard, Bradenton, Florida.
Length: A 63.4-mile loop.
Terrain: Lordy, it's flat!

Traffic and hazards: Traffic on some of these roads is heavy and on others it is very light. The place is undergoing a construction boom. So ride this route early in the morning or with a group.

Getting there: From Interstate 75 south of Tampa, take exit 220. Exit to the east on State Road 64. It is about 2 miles to Lakewood Ranch Boulevard, where you will turn right (south) and proceed to the parking lot of the College of Osteopathic Medicine—School of Pharmacy (Lecom Building) on your right, the west side of the road.

The idea of burying a time capsule is fascinating and delightful. Imagine putting together a picture of yourself and your life so that future generations—maybe 100 or 500 years in the future—would know who you were, what you did for a living, how you managed your time on Mother Earth. And not just a photograph, but also a collection of the meaningful things in your life. They might learn something about who you were inside, your dreams, perhaps how you felt about the great events of our time, which, as we know, will recede in importance as we diminish into the tapestry of history.

This is a marvelous area of Florida: hot, humid, and flat. New residents have trickled into the region south of Tampa for 150 years, and during the last quarter century, that trickle has become a tidal surge. Consequently, taking this ride is something like opening a time capsule. There is a little slice of life from all of the eras of Florida's history, and a touch of its prehistory as well.

Beginning on Lakewood Ranch Boulevard, the ride takes off to the north. This area west of Bradenton and I-75 is enthusiastic with sunburned skin, subdivisions, smooth new roads, and small businesses. Gleaming cement sidewalks begin and end abruptly, running the length of developed properties, but absent when lot lines end in scrub and palmetto. The sides of new roads are heavily landscaped with royal palm, bougainvillea, cushy sod, and sparkling new buildings.

The lovely pastel stucco look with white block cornering is much in vogue, although we must suspect that twenty-five years from now people will look at one of these buildings and go, "Oh my. That is so post 9-11 faux modernism."

The north and south ends of the ride boast numerous golf courses. Riders should take special care when in the vicinity of these broad swatches of green, not

Many bike-friendly roads in the southwest Florida region take you beside lagoons, estuaries, and bays so scenic that you will not want the ride to end.

because they may be hit by an errant drive, but because golfers rise early for tee times in the cool of morning, the same time we like to be on the road.

Golf courses use a huge amount of water, although paradoxically, this could be a thirsty ride since there are no public fountains or facilities. Thus, you will want to take plenty of water with you. There are several convenience stores where you can drop in for bottled water or an energy drink, but only at intersections along the western half.

A map shows that the area is abundant in water in the form of bays, estuaries, and rivers. This physical landscape is, by and large, a result of eons of earthmoving by Momma Nature. Man is building for a smaller, perhaps more economic vision of the world. In so doing, development puts pressure on the area's freshwater resources and there is much political discussion about pumping water to the southern end of the state from as far away as the Suwannee or St. Mary's or St. Johns Rivers. Meanwhile, Key West has a facility to turn salt water into drinkable freshwater; Tampa is building one now; and other cities are contemplating purchasing this engineering salt-to-fresh magic.

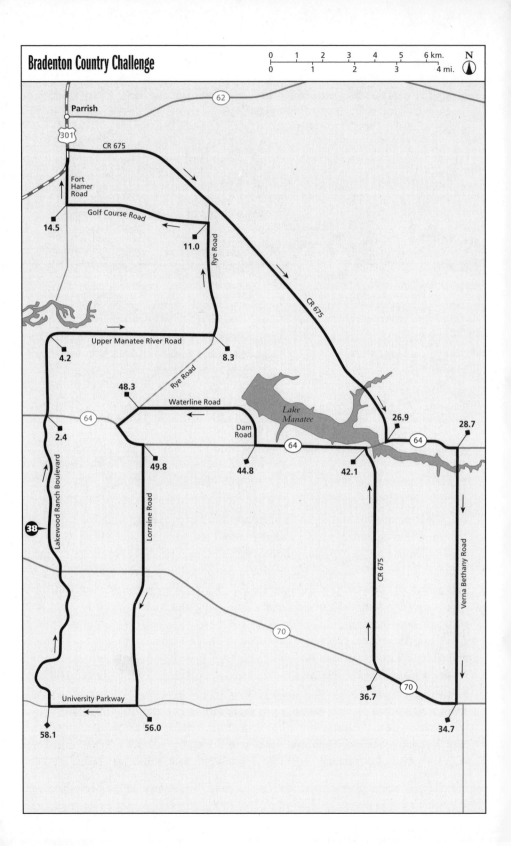

Bradenton Country Challenge

Parrish

301

CR 675

Fort
Hamer
Road

Golf Course Road

14.5

11.0

Rye Road

62

Upper Manatee River Road

4.2

8.3

Rye Road

48.3

Waterline Road

Lake
Manatee

26.9

28.7

64

2.4

64

Dam
Road

49.8

44.8

64

42.1

38

Lakewood Ranch Boulevard

Lorraine Road

CR 675

Verna Bethany Road

70

36.7

70

34.7

University Parkway

58.1

56.0

0 1 2 3 4 5 6 km.
0   1   2   3   4 mi.

N

It is a concern that as the Florida aquifer draws, the balance of pressures that keeps salt water from the Gulf of Mexico and the Atlantic Ocean from seeping in to replace the missing millions of tons of freshwater goes awry. Salt water could infiltrate well water, rendering it undrinkable. Our struggle with this and related definitive and delimiting issues should probably go into our time capsule.

Once you pedal southeast along County Road 675, you find other elements of Florida history for a time capsule: the remnants of citrus groves, for example. There is a dirt racetrack, the DeSoto Speedway, named after a rapacious Spanish explorer. And there are older commercial nurseries shaded beneath black shade cloth. The newest elements for the time capsule are the scores of miniature horses and the winery. Breeding for ever-smaller stature has become something of a curiosity, for no one knows exactly how small a horse could become and stay viable as a horse.

Obviously, the problem with time capsules is that we will not be around to dig them up. We will not be able to see if people half a millennium from now are still cycling; how they solved our water crisis; how they may have balanced increased longevity with declining birth rates. And so the future remains a mystery, just as our time will ultimately be a mystery to those who study our journals and our odd photos and wonder how much we resembled them.

Miles and Directions

0.0 Turn left (north) out of the parking lot of the College of Osteopathic Medicine–School of Pharmacy (Lecom Building) onto Lakewood Ranch Boulevard.

2.4 Cross SR 64. The bike lane ends and the road name changes to Upper Manatee River Road.

4.2 Upper Manatee River Road makes a sweeping 90-degree turn to the right (east).

8.3 Turn left (north) on Rye Road. (There was construction here when I traveled this route so I cannot say what the finished intersection will look like.)

11.0 Turn left (west) on Golf Course Road.

14.5 Turn right (north) at the stop sign on Fort Hamer Road.

15.4 Turn right (north) on U.S. Highway 301.

15.8 Turn right (east) at the flashing lights onto CR 675. This two-lane road will make a couple half turns and end up pointing due south.

26.9 Turn left (east) on SR 64.

28.7 Turn right (south) on Verna Bethany Road.

34.7 Turn right (east) on State Route 70.

36.7 Turn right (north) on CR 675.

42.1 Turn left (west) on SR 64.

44.8 Turn right (north) on Dam Road, which makes a sweeping turn to the left (west) and becomes Waterline Road.

48.3 Turn left (south) on Rye Road.

49.0 Turn left (east) on SR 64.

49.8 Turn right (south) on Lorraine Road.

56.0 Turn right (west) on University Parkway.

58.1 Turn right (north) on Lakewood Ranch Boulevard.

63.4 Turn left (west) into the parking lot of the College of Osteopathic Medicine— School of Pharmacy (Lecom Building) for the end of the ride.

Local Information

Bradenton Area Convention and Visitors Bureau, PO Box 1000, Bradenton; (941) 729-9177; www.flagulfislands.com.

Gulf Coast Latin Chamber of Commerce, 8051 North Tamiami Trail, Sarasota; (941) 358-7065; www.latinchamber.org.

Manatee Chamber of Commerce, 222 10th Street West, Bradenton; (941) 748-3411; www.manateechamber.com.

Manatee County Sheriff's Department, 600 US 301 Boulevard West, Bradenton; (941) 747-3011; http://manateeso.com.

Sarasota-Manatee Bicycle Club, PO Box 15053, Sarasota, FL 34277; www.smbc.us.

Local Events/Attractions

Jungle Gardens, 3701 Bayshore Road, Sarasota; (941) 355-1112; www.sarasotajungle gardens.com. After all these years, this is still fun.

Mote Marine Aquarium, 1600 Ken Thompson Parkway, Sarasota; (941) 388-2451; www .mote.org. Located on Longboat Key, west of downtown Sarasota.

Tampa Bay Devil Rays—Major League Baseball, playing at Tropicana Field, 1 Tropicana Drive, St. Petersburg; (888) 326-7297; www.devil rays.com.

Restaurants

Cracker Barrel, 636 67th Circle East, Bradenton; (941) 706-7886; www.crackerbarrel.com. About the closest restaurant to the ride, although they are building very quickly.

Lost Kangaroo Pub, 427 12th Street West, Bradenton; (941) 747-8114. Haven't been there, but with a name this good. . . .

Smitty's Pub & Grille, 3812 Manatee Avenue West #B, Bradenton; (941) 746-1027; www.smittyspub.com. Relaxed setting, plenty of beer, burgers, and tacos . . . just right.

Zio's Pizzeria & Martini Bar, 533 14th Street West, Bradenton; (941) 708-9001; www.zios flausa.com. A pizzeria with cheap martinis and free wireless Internet—sounds like the perfect date after a long ride.

Accommodations

Econo Lodge Airport, 6727 14th Street/West US Highway 41, Bradenton; (941) 758-7199; www.choicehotels.com.

Harrington House Beachfront Bed & Breakfast Inn, 5626 Gulf Drive, Holmes Beach; (888) 828-5566; www.harringtonhouse.com. Describes itself as having "intimate charm and casual elegance."

Inn at the Bay Bed & Breakfast, 126 4th Avenue NE, St. Petersburg; (727) 822-1700 or (888) 873-2122; www.innatthebay.com. Not cheap and it shouldn't be. Fun for couples or families.

The Ritz-Carlton, 1111 Ritz-Carlton Drive, Sarasota; (941) 309-2000; www.ritzcarlton .com. A minimum of $325 a night—$2,000 a night for the Ritz-Carlton Suite—but this is how the other half lives.

Bike Shops

Ryder Bikes, 1905 Cortez Road West, Bradenton; (941) 756-5480; http://ryderbikes.com.

Village Bikes, 6279 Lake Osprey Drive, Sarasota; http://villagebikes.com.

Restrooms

There are no public restrooms on this route, but there are many private establishments with restrooms available.

Maps

DeLorme: Florida Atlas & Gazetteer: Pages 97 2-3 A, 91 2-3 D.

39 Sanibel Island Cruise

This ride around Sanibel Island is just wonderful. Period. Oh, and it gives you absolutely stunning and unforgettable views of the Gulf of Mexico, San Carlos Bay and Pine Island Sound, too.

Start: Begin from the parking lot of the Sanibel-Captiva Chamber of Commerce, 1159 Causeway Road, Sanibel. It is just across Causeway Boulevard on the right on Sanibel Island.
Length: A 35.4-mile loop.

Terrain: Flat.
Traffic and hazards: Traffic on Periwinkle Way, which is a narrow road, can be very tight, but the speed limit on the island is a maximum of 35 miles per hour. Otherwise, traffic is of suburban quality.

Getting There: From Interstate 75 south of Fort Myers, take exit 131 and drive west to Daniels Parkway. It is about 7.5 miles to McGregor Boulevard, which in about 7 miles becomes Causeway Boulevard.

Sanibel Island is exactly the ticket for everyone in North America's snow zones who, in thinking about "getting away from it all," imagines warm, scenic Florida:

- The good news: Hot in the summer and warm in the winter. Wide, white-sand beaches and surprisingly beautiful seashells available for those who rise early enough, especially after a storm has roiled the surf. Sunsets to die for. Palm trees. Sailboats. Streets lined with condominiums, motels, and quaint, 1950s-style homes for rent. Restaurants by the hundreds; souvenir shops by the thousands; a gazillion tourists; older citizens puttering around on four-wheel bicycles . . . and not a single snowflake!
- The other good news: One great big, beautiful swamp.

The Sanibel Island ride gives you both sides of the Florida coin in abundance. The side that most people come here to enjoy is the "good news" or west side of the island that looks out on the Gulf of Mexico. The surprise that greets vacationers is the "other good news" or east side stretching along San Carlos Bay and Pine Island Sound with a view to the mainland.

Sanibel is not designed for speed. Neither the island nor this ride are for the fast peloton or those who must put their head down and sprint, feel the surge of muscle and body chemistry that makes for a big caloric surge to energy. Instead, this ride is designed for slow, quiet pleasure. If you took an entire day to cruise the 35-odd miles, stopping here and there to take pictures, suck down an oyster, or just sit and enjoy the sights, you would sink into bed in the evening feeling that you had a great day. A successful day.

A number of the side roads that this ride recommends lead to no named place and force you to turn around at the end—or in some cases, just beyond the end—and return the way you came. Always, their purpose is to surprise you with a charismatic view or a road that is less traveled. Even here, at one of the top tourist destinations in Florida, there are numerous pockets that are rarely visited, rarely viewed. The Dixie Beach–Woodring segment is the best example as it gives you a view of the broad and sunny San Carlos Bay and the confined inner estuary of Tarpon Bay, which is almost entirely surrounded by a national wildlife refuge.

J. N. "Ding" Darling National Wildlife Refuge, the refuge with the funny name, was created to "safeguard and enhance the pristine wildlife habitat of Sanibel Island, to protect endangered and threatened species, and to provide feeding, nesting, and roosting areas for migratory birds. Today, the refuge provides important habitat to over 220 species of birds." So says the U.S. Fish and Wildlife Service, which administers America's wonderful 540-refuge system of which this is a part.

A political cartoonist with a passion for conservation, Jay "Ding" Darling was instrumental in the effort to block the sale of a parcel of environmentally valuable land to developers on Sanibel Island. At Darling's urging, President Harry Truman signed an executive order creating the Sanibel National Wildlife Refuge in 1945. The refuge was renamed in 1967 in honor of the conservationist.

Today the Sanibel refuge consists of 6,400 acres of mangrove forest, submerged sea-grass beds, cord-grass marshes, and West Indian hardwood hammocks. About 2,800 acres are a congressionally mandated wilderness area. This refuge is part of a larger complex that encompasses the Caloosahatchee River, Matlacha Pass, Pine Island, and Island Bay refuge system. The majority of the Sanibel system's 8,000 acres are nesting and roosting islands for birds.

Darling was influential because he spoke out and used his editorial cartoon leverage (those were days before television or the Internet) for the public good. He came up with the idea of a federal "Duck Stamp," which hunters of migratory species—ducks and geese—must buy in addition to their licenses. Now in its seventy-fifth year, sales of Duck Stamps have raised more than $700 million to purchase and enhance habitat for waterfowl.

By turning into the entrance to the refuge at mile 12.6, you will be able to cruise through the back of the mangrove and waterfowl habitat. You will probably see alligators as well as roseate spoonbills, raccoons, and a multitude of herons. If you are extremely lucky, you will see a family of otters. Money from the sale of Duck Stamps—and many states have followed suit with their own Duck Stamps—preserved this "swamp" and is collected by and from hunters. An apparent, but not a real, contradiction.

Although we focus on those that are visible and "pretty," such as the roseate spoonbill, this saltwater estuary is home to literally thousands of species—most of

Much of the riding you see on Sanibel will be by tourists or even older folks on three-wheelers. Relax. Enjoy!

Sanibel Island Cruise

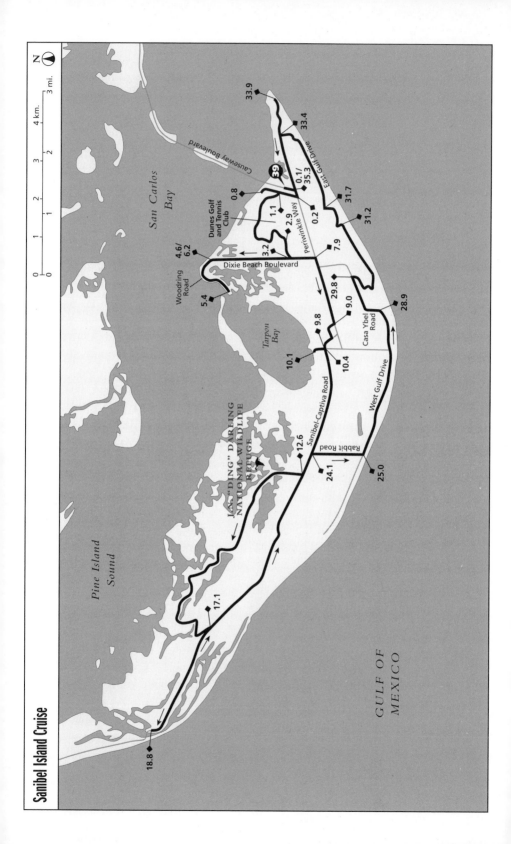

which are absolutely essential to life as we know it on the planet, but are microscopic in size—and by preserving them we help preserve the biodiversity of our planet. The gaudy spoonbill is no more important to our life and well-being than are the hundreds of tiny animals that we cannot see, but which have a role in filtering toxins from the water and air, tiny algae and fungi that exist—not for our human sake, although that is a by-product—but for the preservation of an ecosystem and ultimately life and that fragile dream of "hope" on Planet Earth.

Miles and Directions

0.0 Turn right (south) out of the parking lot of the chamber of commerce and visitor center on Causeway Boulevard.

0.1 Turn right (southwest) on Periwinkle Way.

0.2 Turn right (north) on Bailey Road. It twists left to become Bay Shore Drive.

0.8 Turn around and return on Bay Shore and then on Bailey.

1.1 Turn right (west) on Sand Castle Road and swing right around the Dunes Golf and Tennis Club.

2.9 Turn right (west) on Albatross Road.

3.2 Turn right (north) on Dixie Beach Boulevard.

4.6 Turn left (west) on Woodring Road. Your bike can take this crushed-shell-and-limestone road as long as you dodge the potholes.

5.4 Turn around and return on Woodring Road.

6.2 Turn right (south) on Dixie Beach Boulevard.

7.9 Turn right (southwest) on Periwinkle Way.

9.0 Turn right (north) on Dunlop Road and bear left past City Hall and the library.

9.4 Bear to the left on Wooster Lane.

9.6 Turn right (north) on Palm Ridge Road.

9.8 Turn right (north) on Tarpon Bay Road.

10.1 Turn around and return on Tarpon Bay Road.

10.4 Turn right on Palm Ridge Road, which has become Sanibel-Captiva Road.

12.6 Turn right (north) into the J. N. "Ding" Darling National Wildlife Refuge and follow Memorial Wildlife Drive through the refuge. (At its entrance tollbooth on this drive, the refuge collects $5 for a vehicle and $1 for a cyclist.)

17.1 Turn right (northwest) on Sanibel-Captiva Road.

18.8 The bike lane ends—there is a sign—at the Sunset Grill. This is the official recommended turnaround for bike riders. The roads on Captiva are very narrow.

24.1 Turn right (south) on Rabbit Road.

25.0 Turn left (east) on West Gulf Drive.

28.9 West Gulf Drive becomes Casa Ybel Road.

29.8 Turn right (south) on Middle Gulf Drive.

31.2 Turn left (north) on Fulgur Street.

31.3 Turn right (east) on Middle Gulf Drive.

31.6 Turn left (north) on Nerita Street.

31.7 Turn right (east) on East Gulf Drive.

33.4 Turn right (east) on Periwinkle Way.

33.9 Turn around at Lighthouse Point and return on Periwinkle Way.

35.3 Turn right (north) on Causeway Boulevard.

35.4 Turn left into the visitor center parking lot.

Local Information

City of Sanibel, 800 Dunlop Road, Sanibel; (239) 472-4135; www.mysanibel.com.

Lee County Sheriff's Department, 14750 6 Mile Cypress Parkway, Fort Myers; (239) 477-1000; www.sheriffleefl.org.

Sanibel-Captiva Chamber of Commerce, 1159 Causeway Road, Sanibel; (239) 472-1080; www.sanibel-captiva.org.

Local Events/Attractions

Sanibel Island is the attraction. Its beach is snow white, there is never any snow—although a hurricane or two has been known to land in the vicinity—and its hotels, curio shops, boutiques, and restaurants are legion.

J. N. "Ding" Darling National Wildlife Refuge, 1 Wildlife Drive, Sanibel; (239) 472-1100; www.fws.gov/dingdarling. Part of the largest undeveloped mangrove system in the United States and renowned for its bird life. The Wildlife Drive is closed Fridays.

Restaurants

Chip's Sanibel Steakhouse, 1473 Periwinkle Way, Sanibel; (239) 472-5700; www.the sanibelsteakhouse.com.

Dairy Queen of Sanibel, 1048 Periwinkle Way, Sanibel; (239) 472-1170.

Doc Ford's Sanibel Rum Bar & Grille, 975 Rabbit Road, Sanibel; (239) 472-8311; www.docfordssanibel.com. Open daily at 11:00 a.m.

Ellington's Jazz Bar and Restaurant, 937 East Gulf Drive, Sanibel; (239) 472-0494; www.ellingtonsjazz.com.

Gramma Dot's Restaurant, 634 North Yachtsman Drive, Sanibel; (239) 472-8138.

Accommodations

Holiday Inn Sanibel Island, 1231 Middle Gulf Drive, Sanibel; (239) 472-4123; www.sanibel beachresort.com.

Sanibel Harbour Resort and Spa, 17260 Harbour Pointe Drive, Fort Myers; (239) 466-4000 or (866) 283-3273; www.sanibel-resort.com.

Sanibel Inn, 937 East Gulf Drive, Sanibel; (239) 472-3181; www.sanibelinn.com.

Bike Shops

A. J. Barnes Bicycle Emporium, 15248 South Tamiami Trail #150, Fort Myers; (239) 437-0373.

Bike Route, 14530 South Tamiami Trail, Fort Myers; (239) 481-3376.

Finnimore's Cycle Shop, 2353 Periwinkle Way #101, Sanibel; (239) 472-5577; www.finnimores.com.

Restrooms

0.0 Sanibel-Captiva Chamber of Commerce, 1159 Causeway Road.

9.0 City Hall and library on Dunlop Road.

12.6 Turn right to the J. N. "Ding" Darling National Wildlife Refuge.

20.8 Turn right on Bowman's Beach Road and find the public facilities there.

Maps

DeLorme: Florida Atlas & Gazetteer: Page 110 A 1-2.

40 Wellington Cruise

Here is a busy ride that will acquaint you with south Florida, its way-of-life, its people, and its traffic. This road slips off the busy highways of commerce and winds through horse country. Giddyap!

Begin in the parking lot of Pinewood Park on the west side of U.S. Highway 441 in Palm Beach County and ride that busy highway north to Lake Worth Road, where you will turn toward horse country.

Start: Pinewood Park parking lot on the west side of US 441 at the intersection of Clint Moore Road in Palm Beach County.
Length: A 42.9-mile out-and-back.
Terrain: Flat.

Traffic and hazards: Expect heavy traffic on US 441 at almost any time of the day or night. The best time to tackle this ride is probably early on a holiday or a Saturday or Sunday morning.

Getting there: Take exit 48 on Interstate 95 in South Florida and proceed west for about 7.5 miles on Yamato Road/County Road 794/NW 51st Street in Boca Raton. Continue west past the Florida/Ronald Reagan Turnpike to US 441/State Road 7 and turn right (north). Pinewoods Park is about 1 mile north on the west side of 441.

Almost two-thirds of this Palm Beach cruise of 42.9 miles is ridden on "the open road." That road is the überbusy US 441, which in a now–you-see-it, now-you-don't game of tag with cyclists varies between four and six lanes, seemingly at random. The saving grace is that both the northbound and the southbound lanes have well-marked bike lanes. This is good, because traffic is heavy and fast. Consequently, I was surprised to encounter a number of riders on a weekday morning.

When you turn west from 441 into Wellington, it is only a few miles to the heart or focus of this ride. It will be little relief to discover, though, that you are still on a busy four-lane road. Though it is not in the same traffic league as US 441, Lake Worth Road lasts another 3 miles until you turn left at the flashing light. (Expect, however, that within a year of my ride in the summer of 2007, the large tract of wooded property directly to the west of the flashing light will be developed into subdivisions and that traffic patterns will change.)

Wellington is horse country and it has an affluent side, with polo grounds, private clubs, and numerous private stables that rival the houses in size. Thus, it is a surprise to discover enclaves of smaller properties without horses and barns. These tight middle-class neighborhoods offer quite the opposite in appearance from the broad expanses of pasture and wealthy homes on enormous lots, as they are enclosed with cement block walls and offer limited access.

Once in Wellington, it will not take long to ride to the Barrier on Palm Beach Point Boulevard. The Barrier is a heavy metal bar firmly affixed across the public

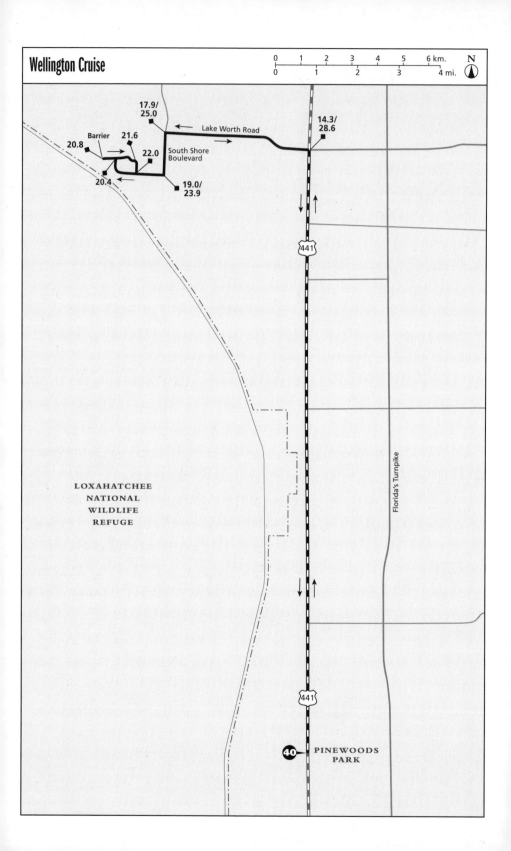

road in the very middle of this ride. The sign clearly states that cyclists are not welcome beyond the Barrier. No biking is allowed.

So amid the broad lawns of well-watered and fertilized green, the red hibiscus and stunning royal poinciana, even the clusters of white-flowering Spanish bayonet—a variety of yucca, by the way—there appears to be an element of inhospitality. It would be easy to take offense and I admit that I fell immediately into that snare. My first thought was to call the city or perhaps a state senator and find out "What the hell is going on here?" After all, someone has closed a public road to a category of conveyance that the state has clearly designated as a vehicle.

With time and upon thinking the issue through, however, it occurred to me that there might be another point of view. Bicycles and horses do not mix. Cyclists know that when horses appear in front of them on a multiuse path, they must be extra-cautious or risk spooking them. At a minimum this involves slowing down and moving to the opposite side of the path. Letting the riders know that you are coming if you are overtaking them from the rear. And if there is the least apparent problem with the horse or if the rider requests it, the cyclist should dismount and wait for the horse to pass, even taking off one's helmet and speaking softly to the horse and rider. I think of this as "going the extra mile," but perhaps, in truth, it is only simple courtesy. It may be this very thing, this inability of oil and water to conform to the same standard of social viscosity that has caused a horse community to bar cyclists from their roadways.

Cyclists, like equestrians, have a unique opportunity to see the world in detail, to live "in the conscious moment." These means of transportation are so slow and so intimate, relatively speaking, that they allow riders to absorb the sociological landscape without the speed and that intervening pane of glass. From a bicycle, one's eyes move slowly beyond the expensive red tile roofs to the encompassing landscape of workers and horses, family compound and side entrances, cement walls and occasional flowering hedges. So, as is often the case, there is more to a simple sign than at first meets the eye. . . .

Miles and Directions

0.0 Turn left (north) from the parking lot of Pinewoods Park onto US 441, a four-lane and sometimes six-lane divided highway. There is a bike lane along 441, but it is narrow and traffic is often heavy.

14.3 Turn left (west) at the traffic signal on Lake Worth Road, which begins as a four-lane divided highway with a bike lane and after 2 miles narrows to two lanes with a bike lane.

17.9 At the flashing light, turn left (south) onto South Shore Boulevard, a two-lane road with no bike lanes.

19.0 Turn right (west) onto 50th Street South.

20.1 The road veers 90 degrees right (north) and becomes South Road.

20.4 At the stop sign, turn left (west) onto Palm Beach Point Boulevard.

20.8 At the barrier you may take a picture, spit, or urinate (though it would be best not to get caught, urinating especially), before you turn around and return east on Palm Beach Point Boulevard past South Road.

21.6 At the fork in the road, turn right (south) on Stable Way.

22.0 Turn left (east) on 50th Street South.

23.9 Turn left (north) on South Shore Boulevard.

25.0 Turn right (east) on Lake Worth Road.

28.6 Turn right (south) on US 441.

42.9 Turn into the parking lot of Pinewoods Park and the end of the ride.

Local Information

Palm Beach Chamber of Commerce, 400 Royal Palm Way, Palm Beach; (561) 655-3282; www.palmbeachchamber.com.

Palm Beach County Convention and Visitors Bureau, 1555 Palm Beach Lakes Boulevard, Suite 800, West Palm Beach; (800) 833-5733 or (561) 233-3000; www.palmbeachfl.com.

Palm Beach County Sheriff's Department, 3228 Gun Club Road, West Palm Beach; (561) 688-3000; www.pbso.org.

State of Florida Official Travel Planning Web site: www.visitflorida.com.

Local Events/Attractions

Lion Country Safari, 2003 Lion Country Safari Road, Loxahatchee; (561) 793-1084; www.lioncountrysafari.com. Since 1967, "America's first drive-through cage-less zoo." A few miles north of your ride.

Palm Beach Kennel Club, 1111 North Congress Avenue, West Palm Beach; (561) 683-2222; www.pbkennelclub.com. Greyhound racing and betting on the dogs.

Stadium Jumping, 14440 Pierson Road, Wellington; (561) 753-6431; www.stadium jumping.com. You have to appreciate 165-pound riders who can make thousand-pound horses jump over logs and walls.

Restaurants

Cheesecake Factory, 5530 Glades Road, Boca Raton; (561) 393-0344; www.thecheesecake factory.com. A chain, but pretty good lunches and dinners for a moderate price.

Fire of Brazil, 10300 West Forest Hill Boulevard, Wellington; (561) 333-1309; www.fireof brazil.com. "Authentic" Brazilian steakhouse.

All-you-can-eat meat and salad bar for about $40; drinks and tips extra. Dinner only.

Johannes, 47 East Palmetto Park Road, Boca Raton; (561) 394-0007. Small seating. Open for dinner only. Expect to pay $100 per.

Pete's of Boca Raton, 7940 Glades Road, Boca Raton; (561) 487-1600 or (954) 763-1600. "Casual, elegant waterfront dining featuring continental and traditional cuisine with a contemporary flair."

Accommodations

Breakers on the Ocean, 1875 South Ocean Boulevard, Delray Beach; (561) 278-4501; www.breakersontheocean.com. At one time this was *the* place on the beach. Now showing a touch of age.

Hilton Hotel & Resorts, 7920 Glades Road, Boca Raton; (561) 483-3600; www.hilton.com. The closest hotel to the ride.

Sundy House Bed & Breakfast Inn, 106 South Swinton Avenue, Delray Beach; (561) 272-5678 or (877) 439-9601; www.sundyhouse .com. A "boutique inn" and restaurant centered around an acre garden.

Bike Shops

Bicyclery, 1649 North Military Trail, West Palm Beach; (561) 684-8444; www.thebicyclery.com.

Bike America, 21643 State Road 7, Boca Raton; (561) 451-4448; www.bikeam.com. Multiple area stores. About 4 miles south of Pinewoods Park.

Boca Raton Bicycle Club, PO Box 810744, Boca Raton, FL 33432; www.bocaraton bicycleclub.com.

Wheels of Wellington, 12794 West Forest Hill Boulevard #36, Wellington; (561) 795-3038.

Mile 0.0: Public facilities are available in Pinewoods Park at the beginning and end of the ride.

DeLorme: Florida Atlas & Gazetteer: Pages 115 A 2, 109 D 2.

41 Lake Okeechobee Classic

This is the longest ride in the book, more than 100 miles. If you take it between the middle of May and the middle of October, you will feel that it is the longest ride of your life; it is very flat, and will be hot and windy. I recommend that you alternate riding the roads with the trail on top of the dike around the lake. Each has strong points. This is indeed a challenging ride, so keep your eyes open and let it all hang out.

Start: The parking lot of the Clewiston Civic Center Park on the west side of the great lake.
Length: A 116.6-mile loop.
Terrain: Flat.
Traffic and hazards: On the roads, the traffic will be light. Fast but light, with the occasional big truck. On the trail, there will be no traffic except for an occasional slow-moving maintenance vehicle. At the periodic nodes with boat ramps, facilities, and shelters, you must watch for traffic crossing the trail, but these points are easily identified in advance because the terrain is incredibly flat.

Getting there: From Interstate 75 on the west side of Florida, take exit 141 onto State Road 80 east to Clewiston. From Interstate 95 on the east side of Florida, take exit 129 onto State Road 70 west to the town of Okeechobee; turn left (south) onto U.S. Highway 441/98; turn right (west) after 4 miles onto State Road 78 and follow it around the lake to U.S. Highway 27, where you will turn left (east) and take this highway into Clewiston . . . or just begin the ride from Okeechobee!

God created Lake Okeechobee, but man manages it for him. For better or worse.

Okeechobee is the second-largest freshwater lake in the lower forty-eight states. It measures 451,000 acres of water surface, or 705 square miles, and on average is only 9.5 feet deep. Then there are the locks and dams, the canals, and especially the 34-foot-high dike around it, which is named for U.S. president Herbert Hoover. You can travel from the Atlantic Ocean to the Gulf of Mexico, Stuart to Fort Myers, via the St. Lucie Canal, the Caloosahatchee River, and the unusual dredged ditch through the south-central portion of the lake.

Atop the dike is the Lake Okeechobee Scenic Trail (LOST). In some places the trail is paved and in some places it is not; there is unannounced construction and there are bypasses, not all of which are especially well marked. So when you plan for this 100-plus-mile classic ride, you may want to take your hybrid or even a

smooth-cruising fat tire. A thin-tire bike will operate at less than peak efficiency on some of the unpaved sections or construction zones, but should be fine until you hit a patch of sand.

Now, 100 miles is a long way on a bicycle, especially in an underdeveloped area like this one, so there are some special precautions that will make your ride easier/better/more fun.

- Have plenty of liquid refreshment and be in shape. Whether you are riding the trail or the nearby roadways, there is access to convenience stores, but you don't want to halt your ride to clunk into a gas station for water or Gatorade every time you get thirsty.

- Your preride regimen should include a liberal dosing of sunscreen. There is little shade on the roads and none at all on top of the dike. In this flat country the sun can be intense, whether it is direct or reflected, so wear sunglasses and a helmet with a brim. You should stop and reapply sunscreen about halfway through the ride, too.

- Mosquitoes come out at sunset, so take repellent in your fanny or seat pack. For those who pooh-pooh the occasional biting bug, think: This isn't just any old mosquito country. Okeechobee is on the north side of the Everglades, the largest swamp in North America. People actually die from West Nile virus and encephalitis in Florida. And these mosquitoes may also carry dengue fever, malaria, and yellow fever. Please be prepared.

This is not a book about trail riding, but on this terrific trip, one should sample both the surrounding roads and the trail atop the dike. The difficulties with the trail are noted—no shade, intermittent or no facilities, intermittent paved surfaces, and the wind, which if it is blowing will feel like it is always in your face—while the roads around the lake are not heavy with traffic. These roads take you through some of Florida's most fascinating little towns: Clewiston, Belle Glade, Pahokee, and Okeechobee. And down off the big dike, the wind will not be such an issue, either.

The southwest quarter of the lake is affiliated with "big sugar." Spend a day in Clewiston and you may be able to visit some of the fields and refineries on a chamber-of-commerce tour. It's cheap and well worth it. The federal government regulates the sugar industry in the same manner that tobacco once was regulated and both industries have been supported with tax dollars.

The northern sector of the lake around Okeechobee is heavily invested with cattle ranching while the eastern sector toward Palm Beach is heavily agricultural. Soils are rich and black in South Florida and bountiful rainfall supports intensive

◀ *Big sugar, with generous price support from the federal government, is entirely controlled by no more than three tightly knit families, and hundreds of thousands of acres of flat, fertile land around the Everglades are planted in . . . sugar cane!*

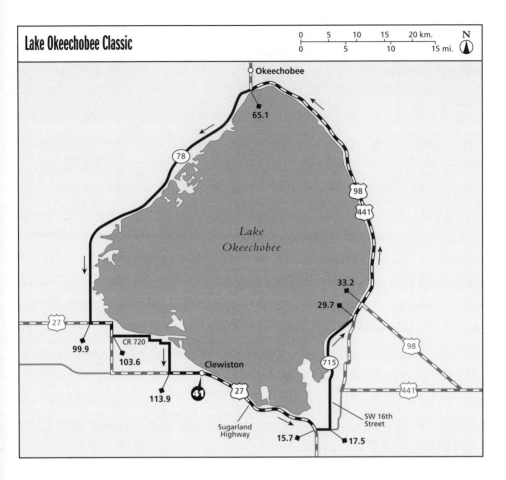

Lake Okeechobee Classic

0   5   10   15   20 km.

0   5   10   15 mi.

N

Okeechobee

65.1

78

98

441

*Lake
Okeechobee*

33.2

29.7

98

27

99.9

CR 720

103.6

Clewiston

715

113.9

41

27

441

SW 16th
Street

Sugarland
Highway

15.7

17.5

farming. Thus, many workers from Central and South America are employed in agriculture here. So if you like food with a Latin flair, there are plenty of small restaurants.

In the middle of the nineteenth century, commercial interests lured settlers to South Florida. Indeed, the environment was rich in potential, but the natural ecological system (and the seasonal hurricanes) often caused extensive flooding. The system was very dynamic; it was as if the land was breathing and the flow of nutrient-rich water was its lifeblood. Unfortunately, the government has attempted to control that breathing—hence the dike around the dam and the various drainage canals. The restriction of natural water flow has led to immense problems with water quality and water delivery to the coastal municipalities, and with the area's rich biodiversity. There is an ongoing clash of ideas playing out in the area that has national implications.

There is much to see around this lake. The land is so flat that the dome of sky seems to arc overhead as if it were a bowl, as if you were cycling in central Texas.

And the freshwater system, threatened and channeled everywhere, seems much bigger and more complex than the men and women who are attempting to control it. Nature's systems will probably outlive us, and because of that we believe that the Power that created the lake would enjoy this ride. After all, he or she or it is probably going to get the last laugh here.

Miles and Directions

I give the street-by-street routing, but at dozens of points around the lake, often points with boat ramps and facilities, you will be able to leave the roads and bike onto the trail on top of the dike, or come down from the trail to the roads.

0.0 Turn left (east) out of the Civic Center Park parking lot in downtown Clewiston onto US 27/Sugarland Highway.

15.5 Cross the railroad tracks.

15.7 Turn left (east) on SR 80/East Palm Beach Road.

17.5 Turn left (north) on State Road 715/SW 16th Street in Belle Glade.

19.9 Cross the railroad tracks.

26.9 Ride into Pahokee on SR 715, which becomes Bacom Point Road.

29.7 Turn left (northwest) on US 441/Lake Avenue.

29.8 Turn right (northeast) after 1 block on US 441/East Main Street.

31.7 Cross multiple railroad tracks.

33.2 Turn left (west) at the flashing light where US 441 joins US 98.

33.3 Turn right as US 441/98 takes a 90-degree right turn.

39.5 Cross the railroad tracks.

65.1 Go straight on SR 78. US 441/98 will turn right here into the town of Okeechobee.

98.7 Cross the railroad tracks.

99.9 Turn left (east) on US 27.

103.6 Turn left (east) on County Road 720.

104.1 Cross the railroad tracks.

104.9 Cross another set of railroad tracks.

113.1 Cross railroad tracks again.

113.9 Turn left (east) on US 27.

115.0 Cross the railroad tracks.

116.6 Arrive at the park in Clewiston, the end of the ride.

Local Information

Clewiston Chamber of Commerce, 109 Central Avenue, Clewiston; (863) 983-7979; www .clewiston.org.

County Sheriff's Departments: The Okee-chobee Classic takes you through the follow-ing counties: Glades (863-946-0100), Hendry (863-674-4060), Martin (772-220-7000), Okeechobee (863-763-3117), and Palm Beach (561-996-1670).

The LOST Bicycle Club, www.lostcyclist.net/ lostcyclists/index.html.

Local Events/Attractions

Billie Swamp Safari, Everglades Eco-Tours, 40 miles south of Clewiston on County Road 833; (800) 949-6101; www.seminoletribe.com /safari. Seminole-led Big Cypress Swamp tours on giant swamp buggies.

Sugar Festival, around the City Library, Clewiston; (863) 983-7979; www.clewiston.org /festival.htm. Arts and crafts, music, games, exhibits, food, and a rodeo. It is held each year in April.

Sugarland Tours, 109 Central Avenue, Clewiston; (863) 983-7979; www.clewiston.org /sugarlandtours.htm. Offers heritage, agriculture, and Lake Okeechobee tours.

Restaurants

Clewiston Inn, 108 North Royal Palm Avenue, Clewiston; (863) 983-8151; www.clewiston inn.com. Breakfast, lunch, and dinner in this striking old establishment.

Florida Cafeteria, 446 East Sugarland Highway, Clewiston; (863) 983-6460. It isn't every day you get to go to a cafeteria.

Mr. Shrimp, 880 West Sugarland Highway, Clewiston; (863) 983-9993; www.mrshrimp seafood.com. That's Mister Shrimp to you!

Tico's Spanish Cuisine, 442 South US 27, Moore Haven; (863) 946-3500.

Accommodations

Clewiston Inn, 108 North Royal Palm Avenue, Clewiston; (863) 983-8151; www.clewiston inn.com. The inn is 60 miles east of Fort Myers and 60 miles west of Palm Beach. Not yet fully restored, but it is a great old-fashioned place to stay and adjacent to the park that is the start of the ride.

Holiday Inn Express, 1024 West Sugarland Highway, Clewiston; (863) 983-5101; www.hiexpress.com. Okay, the commercials are great: "No I'm not a jet pilot but I stayed at a Holiday Inn Express last night!"

Seminole Inn, 15885 SW Warfield Boulevard, Indiantown; (772) 597-3747; www.seminole inn.com. About 10 miles east of the lake. Dining room, too. Pretty sophisticated for Indiantown. Web site has music. . . .

Southern Palm Bed & Breakfast, 15130 Southern Palm Way, Loxahatchee; (561) 790-1413; www.southernpalmbandb.com. About 40 miles east of Clewiston in Loxahatchee on US 441/98. Pricey. Alternatively, you could stay in the Angler's Motel in Clewiston (www.anglersmarina.com).

Bike Shops

There are no bike shops in the immediate vicinity of this lake.

Restrooms

Facilities are not a problem on this ride as small parks and boat ramps are liberally sprinkled around the lake.

Maps

DeLorme: Florida Atlas & Gazetteer: Pages 107 B 2, C 3; 108 C 1, B 1, A 1; 102 C-D 1; 101 C 3-2, D 1; and 107 A 1, B 1-2.

42 Florida Keys Over-the-Ocean Classic

This is Florida's Royal Ride, with ocean and lagoon views so spectacular that words are simply insufficient to describe them. The ride, though limited to a single highway, has flexible beginning and ending points. There are jillions of places to stay, to eat and drink, picnic and party.

Start: I began this ride in Key West, but if you were to pedal from Islamorada, Marathon, Tavernier, Florida City, or from any bar stool or campsite along the way, you could hardly go wrong.

Length: 105 miles, but consider this a flexible ride with many options.

Terrain: Flat.

Traffic and hazards: Choose your time carefully as traffic on U.S. Highway 1 can be heavy and the road is very open for vehicles to pull on and off at almost any moment. In addition, many drivers will be sightseeing as they plod along the highway in bumper-to-bumper traffic, so enjoy, but exercise caution.

Getting there: You can fly, or drive directly to Key West on US 1 from Miami. It is the only road. Miss it and we take away your driver's license and passport.

This is *the* classic Florida ride. The scenery is phenomenal. Luminous vistas of water the color of emeralds as far as the eye can see. Lagoons slashed with brilliant aquamarine. The deeper ocean reflecting a hard blue. And white puffy clouds floating, drifting over the land-and-sea-scape as if their only purpose is to add texture, to highlight a depth of vision in limitless beauty. If this ride doesn't lift your spirit, nothing will.

On a bicycle, you can ride the Keys for miles and, every now and then, imagine that you are dreaming. There are numerous high spans where you can look far over this ultra-flat landscape: the Niles Channel Bridge by Ramrod Key (about mile 24), the Seven-Mile Bridge span over Moser Channel (about mile 40), the bridge over Channel 5 between Long Key and Craig Key (about mile 66), and elsewhere. If you only rode the high span of the Seven-Mile Bridge, with water and seabirds far below and nothing but water around you, the ride would be unforgettable.

What may surprise you—and make you a bit jealous—is the party atmosphere on the water. Depending on water conditions, you may look out and see a gaggle of boats and personal watercraft, swimmers, and picnickers all having a great time splashing and swimming far from land. Of course, they are all anchored on a sandbar and these sometimes come and go at the whim of Mother Nature and her wind and water elements, for the Keys are subject to them first and to man second.

What else may surprise you are the numerous "bike lanes" along the road. A few of them are well marked, indeed are true bike lanes, as we would understand them. Other sections marked as bike lanes are only sidewalks and several either are falling

Everyone gets into the act in the Keys. Perhaps it is the abundance of sunlight, clear water, and beer.

or have long ago fallen into disrepair. So beware of the signs and use your best judgment about where to ride. I have included several bike lane notations in the "Miles and Directions" section, but you will notice numerous others of various lengths and construction circumstances (several are crushed oyster or lime rock) as you ride.

The Overseas Highway, known as US 1, in the Keys is an old road, and bike lanes were not dreamed of when it was engineered. US 1 was built on the former right-of-way of the Overseas Railroad, an extension of the Florida East Coast Railway to Key West. Completed in 1912, the Overseas Railroad was heavily damaged and partially destroyed by the disastrous Category 5 Labor Day hurricane of 1935. The storm drowned 400 World War I veterans working on the railroad when their relief train was overwhelmed. Sustained winds measured an incredible 185 miles per hour. The Florida East Coast Railway was financially unable to rebuild, so the roadbed and remaining bridges were eventually sold to the state of Florida for $640,000; quite a sum in those days.

Today most but not all of the Overseas Highway has been rebuilt for modern vehicles and heavier loads. Still, you can occasionally see portions of the original rail system and its highway overlay in the side bridges that are now used by anglers. On the west side of the Seven-Mile Bridge, look for Pigeon Key (Google Maps incorrectly indicates a smaller and more isolated key) and the old road that crosses to this unusual island from the western end of the group of Keys that make up the Marathon group.

Not only are the Keys steeped in history—and they are, from wrecks of Spanish treasure ships to the homes of writers such as Ernest Hemingway and Tennessee Williams—but as true subtropical islands they have a diversity of wildlife that you will not see anywhere else in the continental United States. Watch for the CROCODILE CROSSING sign in the Key Largo area, which is not a misprint, for Florida has a small, native population of crocodiles. Watch for dolphins and the tiny, endangered Key deer, as well. If, as you cross the Big Pine Key area, you notice the high fences that appear to uglify an otherwise lush and lovely landscape, realize that these have been erected to help preserve these deer. No larger than a German shepherd, the deer have been decimated by loss of habitat and from collisions with vehicles. These little ungulates are so small that hitting one with your SUV at night might feel like nothing more than a bump in the road.

You never know what you might see in Florida. Sitting on the side of the road drinking water in the vicinity of the Saddlebunch Keys—around mile marker 12 or so—a very green iguana plodded across the road within 10 yards. It was wary but unconcerned until I began fumbling for my camera, at which point it waddled into the brush and disappeared. These creatures are not native to Florida but, released by collectors, have established breeding colonies in numerous places. So have boa constrictors, tarantulas, Nile monitor lizards, several species of parrots, and a host of other nonindigenous and ecologically out-of-place (and generally harmful) critters.

Who knows, though? The special theme of living in the Keys is to promote a relaxed and welcoming atmosphere. So perhaps the new exotic, invasive species just go with the territory. It is, after all, one of the most remarkable and scenic areas in America . . . maybe in the world.

Miles and Directions

This ride takes place entirely on US 1. So instead of giving conventional information for turns—which would be very short in this case, one line for beginning and one line for ending—I give casual waypoint information. On the mainland end of the ride, I recommend deviating from US 1 and note that for cyclists who wish to complete the entire journey from Key West to Florida City.

Begin at any parking area in Key West and ride northeast on Truman Avenue. NOTE: Because this is not our usual loop ride and rides may be for any length or duration, you may want to pre-position a vehicle at the end.

0.0 At Bayview Park, Truman Avenue becomes North Roosevelt Boulevard on Google Maps, but on the ground in Key West, roads may be marked either way . . . or both ways. There

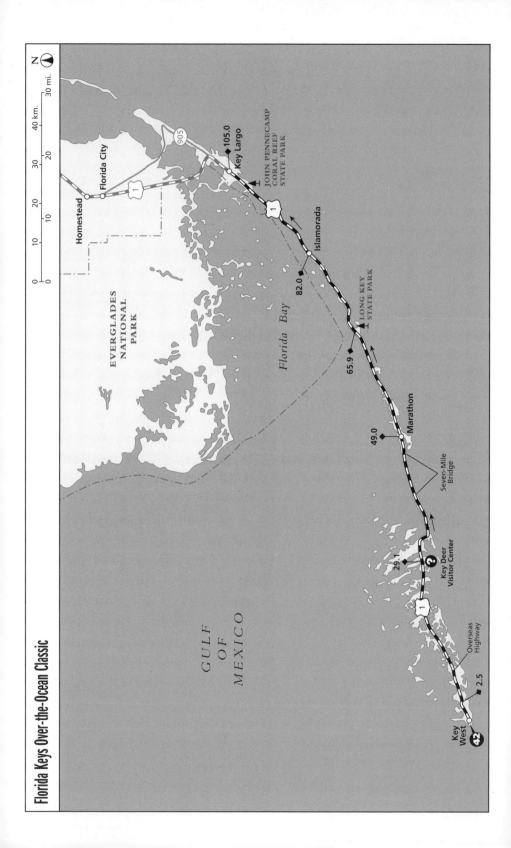

Florida Keys Over-the-Ocean Classic

is a bike path off the road to the west. If there is much traffic, you may want to consider using the path when you can, especially here where the road narrows.

2.5 Turn left (northeast) onto the Overseas Highway and ride past the Key West Golf Club on the west and Raccoon Key.

3.8 The bike lane ends here on Boca Chica Key, but four-lane US 1 now has paved shoulders. You pass west of the Key West Naval Air Station, and on East Rockland Key the road narrows to two lanes.

8.4 The bike lane runs for 0.8 mile from Big Coppit Key.

9.6 The bike lane resumes on the right over Shark Channel and continues over the Saddle Bunch Keys and sounds.

13.5 The bike lane ends.

28.4 The bike lane begins again.

29.1 Arrive at the Key Deer Visitor Center.

29.4 The bike lane ends.

35.3 Entrance to Bahia Honda State Park and then, after the small Ohio and Little Duck Keys, comes the famous Seven-Mile Bridge.

46.3 The bike lane resumes.

49.0 Arrive in Marathon.

54.7 This is the entrance to Curry Hammock State Park on Little Crawl Key.

56.7 The bike lane ends.

65.9 Arrive at the entrance to Long Key State Park.

72.5 Arrive at Safety Harbor.

82.0 This is Founder's Park in Islamorada.

101.3 Arrive at the entrance to John Pennekamp Coral Reef State Park.

105.0 This is the end of the Florida Keys Classic. **Option:** US 1 veers left here in Key Largo while County Road 905 veers right. It is about 25 miles from this point to Florida City on US 1; about 30 miles on 905. Whereas US 1 is crowded with traffic, CR 905 is—at this writing—undeveloped and traffic-free.

Local Information

Informative Key West Web sites:
www.keywest.com, www.keywestchamber.org, www.sunshinekeywest.com, www.visitkeywest online.com, and www.fla-keys.com.

Monroe County Sheriff, 5525 College Road, Key West; (305) 292-7000; www.keysso.net; (Lower Keys, 305-745-3184; Middle Keys, 305-289-2430; Upper Keys, 305-853-3211).

Local Events/Attractions

Dry Tortugas National Park, seven remote islands and Fort Jefferson, 70 miles west of Key West; www.nps.gov/drto. Can only be reached by boat or seaplane. Camping, fishing, bird watching, and historical fun. $5 per person park admission. Also check these sites for travel to Dry Tortugas: www.seaplanesof keywest.com (seaplane flight—full day on the island for $345 adults), www.yankeefreedom .com (high-speed ferry—full day for $139 adults), or www.sunnydayskeywest.com /fastcat.htm (high-speed catamaran hull—full day for $120).

Ernest Hemingway Home & Museum, 907 Whitehead Street, Key West; (305) 295-9112; www.hemingwayhome.com. Open 365 days a year from 9:00 a.m. to 5:00 p.m. Hemingway's home and his polydactyl cats!

Fantasy Fest, www.fantasyfest.net. Gnomes, toads, and white-rabbit tea parties! Tens of thousands of exotic revelers in costume in late October.

Key West Lighthouse and Keeper's Quarters Museum, 938 Whitehead Street, Key West; (305) 294-0012. Once essential to ships navigating dangerous reefs. Now houses collection of lighthouse artifacts and the maritime history of the Florida Keys.

Restaurants

Alonzo's Oyster House, 700 Front Street, Key West; (305) 294-5880; www.alonzosoysterbar.com. Did you know that an oyster might grow for six years?

Island House, 1129 Fleming Street, Key West; (305) 294-6284; www.islandhousekeywest.com. If you are gay and male, this is the ticket.

Roof Top Cafe, 308 Front Street, Key West; (305) 294-2042; http://rooftopcafekeywest.com. Breakfast, lunch, and dinner in the treetops.

Sloppy Joe's Bar, 201 Duval Street, Key West; (305) 294-8759; www.sloppyjoes.com. A Conch Republic institution since 1933. Features annual Ernest Hemingway Look-Alike Contest each July.

Square One Restaurant, 1075 Duval Street, Key West; (305) 296-4300; www.squareonerestaurant.com. Considered tropical fine dining.

Accommodations

Author's Guest House, 725 White Street, Key West; (305) 294-7381 or (800) 898-8909; www.authorskeywest.com. "Conceived to honor the literary masters who lived and worked in quaint, colorful Key West." $100 to $170 per night depending on room and season.

Key Lime Inn, 725 Truman Avenue, Key West; (305) 294-5229 or (800) 549-4430; www.keylimeinn.com. A thirty-seven-room historic hotel located in the center of Key West's old town district. Expect to pay $175 per night.

Simonton Court Historic Inn and Cottages, 320 Simonton Street, Key West; (305) 294-6386 or (800) 944-2687; www.simontoncourt.com. $145 to $425 depending on room and season.

Wicker Guesthouse an Island Bed & Breakfast, 913 Duval Street, Key West; (305) 296-4275 or (800) 880-4275; www.wickerhousekw.com. Downtown with a pool. Covers a city block. Expect to pay $125 to $300 per night depending on room and season.

Bike Shops

Big Pine Bicycle Center, 31 County Road, Big Pine Key; (305) 872-0130.

Island Bicycles and Skateboards, 929 Truman Avenue, Key West; (305) 292-9707.

Restrooms

Some public facilities are scattered along this ride at state parks and various public buildings. The bar and restaurant scene is so casual, however, that few would notice or care that—unless you trash the joint—you use their facilities.

Maps

DeLorme: Florida Atlas & Gazetteer: Pages 127 D-C 1-2-3, 124 C 1-2-3, 125 C-B 1-2-3, 122 D-C 2-3, 123 B-C 1.

Index

About the Author

Rick Sapp grew up biking the steepest hill in Florida and decorating his J. C. Higgins one-speed with crepe-paper streamers for elementary school bike races. Since then, he has ridden throughout the state, from Pensacola to Key West, and broadened his enthusiasm for all-things-outdoors to kayaks and canoes, fishing, hunting, hiking, sailing, and birdwatching. An accomplished writer for thirty years, Sapp has authored a dozen books and hundreds of articles for newspapers, magazines, and the Internet. He lives in Gainesville, Florida.